Too Small to Be Big

THE **AllStride** SOLUTION

Medical Disclaimer: Before you begin this or any other diet or exercise program, consult with your doctor or other health-care provider to discuss any risks.

Published and distributed in the United States by:
JKRLHB, L.L.C., DBA AllStride
Los Angeles, CA
855-478-7433
www.allstride.com

Printed and distributed in the United States by:
Thomson Shore
7300 West Joy Road
Dexter, MI 48130
www.thomsonshore.com

Editorial services by:
Olivia Bell Buehl
Editorial Strategies, L.L.C.
914-243-9751
www.editorialstrategies.com

Jacket and interior design by:
Daniel Rembert
www.danielrembert.com

ISBN 978-0-615-41218-4

Too Small to Be Big

THE **AllStride** SOLUTION

Ricki Lake
AND JOHN MONACO, M.D.

Dedication

We dedicate this book to our children,
Milo, Owen, Alexandra, and John, Jr.
We wish them, as we do all children everywhere,
the blessings of total wellness,
self-esteem, and joy.

Table of Contents

Part 4: **Become Part of the Solution**

A Crisis and a Solution

You might assume I coauthored this book because I was a famously obese teen-ager who later shed excess pounds and is now ready to reveal her secrets for fast, effortless weight loss so you can help your kids do the same. No way! Yes, losing more than 125 pounds was a major achievement, but it pales next to some of the other things I've done, such as becoming a mother to my two exceptional sons, Milo and Owen. That's been the most challenging and wonderful experience of my life.

Birthing Owen at home with a midwife led to another reinvention of myself—producing the documentary film "The Business of Being Born," which advocates natural home birth. Losing weight is dwarfed by the experience of having strangers come up to me or write me from around the world to say that the film allowed them to have an amazing birth experience. To be able to offer them such a gift is powerful. Until now, it's the most important work I've ever done in a life that seems to be one of continual reinvention.

The Crisis

Now I'm tackling a huge issue that's also dear to my heart and is a natural outgrowth of my advocacy work for mothers and infants: the epidemic of overweight children. After all, making birth as easy and natural as possible for both mother and infant is only the beginning of giving a child a happy, healthy life. Then the real work starts! Integral to a child's physical and emotional health is eating well, being physically active, having friends, and maintaining a suitable weight. It's part of our job as parents to give our kids every opportunity to experience these four things. The first part of this book addresses the growing crisis of overweight kids. The rest is about an amazing program that will enable your child to achieve a healthy weight. I've always been reluctant to endorse any diet product or program—until I became a part of AllStride.

I don't like to tell people what to do. I don't have the answers. But I can tell you this: a quick weight-loss diet isn't a permanent solution to being heavy. But reduce the amount of food you eat and improve its quality—and move your body—and you'll lose weight and keep it off. Which is not to say that slimming down is easy. It's hard, especially for children, and it's especially hard in today's culture of fast food and electronic games. Losing excess pounds and getting healthy are inextricably linked, and you need to have the right resources and supportive people around you.

I'm great at providing resources. It's a lot of what I did for eleven years on "The Ricki Lake Show." AllStride brings resources to kids and parents in a friendly, supportive environment. Again, this book is not about my weight loss or me. Instead, it's about giving you and your kids the access to an invaluable resource to make your whole family healthier, happier, fitter, more in tune with one another—and yes, slimmer.

My concern isn't just for my own boys. My heart breaks when I look around and see so many overweight kids. And I know all too well that other kids who may *look* fine are also risking their health now and in the future through poor eating habits and inactivity. I'm also aware that an extra 5 or 10 pounds that an adult can carry without much health impact can be much more significant for a 7- or 8-year-old. Many "big" kids also suffer from low self-esteem and are the butt of teasing by their peers. Being heavy as a child is a physical and a psychological burden that can continue into adulthood. Childhood and adolescence are difficult enough without lugging around extra baggage.

The Team

Again, I'm no expert on weight loss or parenting, but my years as a talk show host made me expert at asking the right questions and bringing the right people together. Every day I struggle with how to raise my sons. It's an ongoing process. Each time my kids reach a new milestone, I think it will get easier, but it only gets harder. You don't want them to struggle with the same things you had to struggle with, and you don't want to make the same mistakes your parents made. As you well know, it's not always easy. We parents need all the help we can get.

The more people I talked to about my concerns, the more I realized the scope of the childhood obesity crisis—and that it's not just a matter of overeating. I also knew this was something I couldn't solve alone. I could be the committed mom doing the legwork, but I also needed a team of experts. I also knew that if I could find an existing program that we could grow, we could get traction that much faster.

Where do you begin to research any subject? Online, of course. When I started researching solutions to the childhood obesity crisis, I found *45pounds.com,* a customized meal program for kids. The program was established by Mark and Lisa Daniel (read their story on page 13), with whom I began discussions about how to expand their service. Because being overweight has numerous health implications, and putting kids on a weight-loss program is controversial, I knew we needed to have a physician on board too. I'm delighted to have found John Monaco, M.D., a brilliant pediatrician and authority on childhood obesity who has already written one book on the subject. He is my coauthor. We both want to share this body of knowledge with other families so that together we can make this a better world for all children.

Dr. John, as his patients call him, is literally on the front lines in this battle for our children's lives. He runs a critical-care clinic attached to a hospital and has the opportunity to see firsthand the role of obesity in many pediatric health crises. He's also a wonderfully compassionate person—and the loving father of two—who shares my emotional commitment to the issues.

I still needed to fill three more key roles: a certified nutritionist to expand our meal-planning program and firmly ground it in accepted nutritional wisdom, a fitness expert to direct the activity program, and someone trained in psychology to deal with the emotional issues attached to overeating. In each case, I was looking for individuals who not only had the right credentials but who also possess a special sensitivity to what it's like to be a child who's labeled as different by his peers—and often by his parents.

A dear friend who has trained with him led me to Isaiah Truyman, a fitness trainer and coach. Not only is Isaiah certified in numerous fitness fields, he has had extensive experience working with kids and families through his company, EZIA Human Performance, a one-on-one program committed to personal change. He also developed a pilot program for the New York City school system that used videos to take kids through a 20-minute workout comprising jumping jacks, cats and dogs, inchworms, and bear crawls, plus other exercises they could do at their desks. Many city schools had dropped their gym classes due to budget cuts, and this program enabled kids to let off some steam and get a bit of healthy activity under a teacher's supervision. Kids, including my own sons, just naturally gravitate to Isaiah. No doubt that's because he's retained a childlike wonder about life and human potential that inspires people of all ages.

Next up were a nutritionist and a family coach. Then I got lucky, finding both these talents in one remarkable person. Robert Ferguson is a certified nutritionist who has developed several weight-loss programs, and is also a family coach who works one-on-one with parents and kids. He's no slouch in the fitness department either. His approach to nutrition is down to earth, focusing on meals that are accessible and affordable. He understands intuitively that to get kids on board, you have to meet them where they are—and that includes eating food they already like. As the father of two young daughters, he, too, displays the compassion toward kids and the youthful optimism that helps to unite our whole team.

Once we had our dream team, we married everyone's expertise to an online social network that enables your kids to share their challenges and successes with others in their age bracket. At the same time, you can "talk" to other parents about common concerns. Customized meal plans incorporate your child's favorite foods—and eliminate those he or she doesn't like. Plus there are more than 40 of Isaiah's online fitness videos to round out the menu. All this means that once you become part of AllStride, you're no longer struggling with your child's weight problem alone.

You'll get to know the AllStride team members soon. For now, I'd like to double-back to my own experiences, which have played such a pivotal role in my involvement in this program. Then I'll return to how *Too Small to Be Big* and the companion online program, *allstride.com,* can change your kids' lives and bring you closer together as a family.

My Childhood and Adolescence

OK, I know I said I don't usually tell people what to do, but I'll make an exception here: don't feel guilty if your kid is over-weight. (Which is not to say that a child with a weight issue isn't often part of a larger family health issue.) Telling you a bit about my childhood and adolescence will hopefully drive home this point.

My father's mother, Sylvia, was my guiding force. Even when I was 3 years old and pretending to be Shirley Temple, my grandmother absolutely believed that I was a great singer and actress and that I was headed for stardom. She loved the arts and every weekend would take my sister and me to the theater, ballet, or opera. I was 6 or 7 when she took us to see "Annie" on Broadway. I remember crying through the whole play and not wanting it to end. Sylvia took us backstage afterward, and that was my defining moment: I decided that performing is what I was born to do.

My mom was also supportive, signing me up for singing les-sons, which I started at about age 9, and driving me to them every Saturday. During my last two years in high school, my parents paid for me to go to the Professional Children's School in Manhattan. But my mother discouraged me from audition-ing for roles because she wanted to protect me from rejection that might result from my excess weight.

My eating habits as a kid were appalling, and I began to put on weight at age 10. We never sat down to dinner as a fam-ily, unless we went out to a restaurant. My main food was Hungry-Man® frozen dinners—and often two at that. I would heat them up myself and eat alone, and then I would sneak snacks and candy. I remember saying good night to my par-ents as I walked by their bedroom with candy hidden under my nightgown. Still, I don't think I was initially conscious of my weight. (Several of the kids profiled in our Success Stories were similarly unaware that they were overweight.) But I remember that at the beginning of the year in elementary school gym class, we'd have to line up by height and get on a scale in front of everyone. Our weight was then called out. It was absolutely traumatizing to be identified as being 5 or 10 pounds heavier than the other kids.

Despite my size, I was in school plays, chorus, and band. I was also pretty athletic. I played volleyball, although I was the shortest kid on the team. Then in high school I joined the track team; this time I was the slowest runner. Like all girls, I had crushes on the cool boys, but I was never the object of their affection. When I was about 11, I saw "The Early Show," a kids' review at an Off-Broadway place called Don't Tell Mama. I wanted to be in the review, so I got subscriptions to *Back Stage* and *Show Business* and went to open auditions until I was accepted. I also did a review show called "Young Stars." When I was 15, I was an extra in "Fame" with Janet Jackson, which got me my SAG union card. Then I played a bully in an episode of "Kate and Ally."

Because there was no athletics program at the Professional Children's School, I wasn't getting any exercise, which was aggravated by my daily commute to school. I used to take the train to Manhattan from the suburbs by myself. I would eat on the way in, and then I would buy two hot dogs on the way home to tide me over until dinner! Eating became my hobby.

My mother didn't know what to do about my weight. It's a very precarious position for a parent to be in. She was obsessed with her own weight—she was always on one diet or another—and would come down on me about mine. She never said the right things to encourage me. On the other hand, I don't know what she could have said that I would have listened to. Nor was my physician any help. I would break out in hives before a checkup, but usually he said nothing about my weight. Part of me wanted to hear it, but I reasoned that if he didn't say there was a problem, there wasn't one. I was in a state of complete denial. Even if I'd gone to my parents for help, there really was no support system available for overweight kids or their families at that time.

Cut to the end of a miserable freshman year in the Performing Arts Program at Ithaca College. My department head tried to quash my dreams by never casting me in a play, telling me I was not going to make it as a performer, and giving me a C. This despite the fact that I went to every class and gave 100 percent. In retrospect, I think she was a "fattist." To make things worse, I had no social life. I didn't like the theater geeks and I didn't fit in with the other kids. I didn't do drugs. I didn't drink. I was fat and getting fatter. In my case, the "freshman 15" (the average weight gain the first year away from home) was more like the "freshman 25."

My Big Break

Then my agent tipped me off to an audition in Manhattan for a fat, pretty girl who could dance. I had a day off between finals, so I drove down and back the same day, wearing a big Ithaca College sweatshirt. I'd never heard of John Waters or Divine. Nor did I understand that the part I was auditioning for was the starring role of Tracy Turnblad in "Hairspray." I had no idea that that audition would change my life, opening every door and introducing me to a circle of people who became like a second family. It was really a Cinderella story to have had this terrible, terrible year at school, to be kind of lost, and then to get this part in which I win the dance contest—and get the cute guy. On top of that, I also become a star in real life, all the while weighing 200 pounds. I can tell you that when it came to my department head at Ithaca, success was definitely the sweetest revenge.

For four years I rode the wave of being this heavy girl who was famous and successful and had money and was working and had all these friends and had guys who liked me. I did other films with John Waters and then a season on the TV series

"China Beach." I would go out to dinner with Jennifer Anniston and these other beautiful actresses who were all on diets. They would order a salad and I would say, "Give me a cheeseburger and a milk shake," because *I* didn't have to be on a diet. I was me and I was thriving.

Taking Control of My Body

So why did I finally decide to lose the weight? Well, at 21, for the first time since "Hairspray," I was out of work—"China Beach" didn't pick up my option for another year. The house I'd bought based on that job was foreclosed and I lost all my money. To top everything off, I'd gained another 60 pounds. I'd hit bottom. I'd been on my own since I was 18, and needed to pay my bills. And suddenly 260 pounds on a 5-foot, 3^1/$_2$-inch girl wasn't cute anymore. Nor was I the new girl any longer; people were used to me. I had to do something to resurrect my career.

I had no control over where the next job was coming from, but I could control what I put in my mouth and how I took care of myself. I bought a bike and a gym membership. I didn't see anyone (I'd moved way, way out to the San Fernando Valley to a rented pool house) and I didn't tell anyone what I was doing because I'd failed so many times before. Basically, I decided not to eat. Starving myself was effective—I lost a lot of weight—and I worked out. But it was a terrible way to do it. I was young, foolish, and desperate. But when people saw me again, I looked dramatically different. I'd reinvented myself and suddenly everyone was talking about me again. The next year I was offered the talk show. At that time, coming to grips with my weight wasn't about health; it was about having a career. Now I realize that it's *all* about health.

There's no question that I was headed down a dangerous road until I came to grips with my situation. And I've been extremely lucky because despite my obesity, I never lost my optimism and strong belief in myself, and I was never the object of bullying by other kids. Lucky also because my weight actually led to my getting the role in "Hairspray," which launched my career. Lucky because when I put my mind to it, I was able to lose my excess pounds and get control of my weight before it caused any health problems. Finally, and perhaps most importantly, lucky because I'm one of the 5 percent of people who have actually been able to keep off the lost weight. Not that I don't have to work at it every day and not that I haven't veered back into an unhealthy zone at least once!

Does my luck mean I was a happy as a fat girl? Of course not. If I had my choice, I would definitely have preferred not being obese as a teen. Still, I wouldn't be where I am today if I hadn't gone through that.

Your child is also lucky, because you've obviously realized you need to give him or her access to resources that will encourage healthy eating habits and fun ways to be active. With the skills offered on the AllStride program, your kid—and perhaps you too—can slim down and gain self-confidence. Plus he or she will learn new skills—from cooking to kickboxing—and get to interface with other kids facing the same challenges.

The AllStride Solution

Remember the old saying that you can lead a horse to water but you can't make him drink? Well, with AllStride, you'll be taking charge of your family's life by offering them healthful foods and by encouraging them to get enough exercise. But for lasting success, they'll have to make these changes of their own volition. By participating in the AllStride program, you can empower your children to make the right choices for the right reasons. Along the way, I bet you'll empower yourself as well. It's a win-win solution. The AllStride team is also committed to ending childhood obesity and the health problems it causes or aggravates. As my coauthor, Dr. John, likes to say, "Our goal is to give children back their childhood."

In Hillary Clinton's 1996 book *It Takes a Village,* the former first lady envisions a society in which all the needs of a child are met. Clinton emphasizes the role of individuals outside the nuclear family, as well as schools, community organizations, and other institutions. Likewise, we're all in the fight against childhood obesity together. Throughout this book, we'll introduce you to individuals who've led by example and explain how you too can become a force for change beyond your own family. In tackling the crisis of overweight children, the AllStride program rests on four pillars:

- **Food: providing nutritious foods that kids love**
- **Fun: engaging in enjoyable fitness activities**
- **Friends: joining a community in which kids help kids, families help families, and experts help everyone**
- **Family: adopting new, healthy habits as a family**

Combating the epidemic of childhood overweight and obesity also requires a multifaceted approach. That's why AllStride is a two-part program—the book and the website, each with a distinct purpose, but simultaneously reinforcing each other.

The Book

Many books have been written about the crisis of overweight children, often explaining clearly and painfully the causes of the epidemic. What makes this book different is that we actually have a solution: the AllStride program. But this is not just a book for parents with heavy kids. Rather, it's for every parent and every person who loves kids. Nor is this a "diet book." Instead, it introduces a lifestyle that ensures good health, happiness, high energy, self-confidence—and long life.

Here we explain the problem, look at the root causes, discuss the ramifications for families, introduce the program, and help parents decide who could benefit from it. And, of course, our team of experts—along with the real "experts," the kids and parents who've succeeded on the program—provide the secrets to successfully follow it. If you're impatient to learn the specific steps you can take to help your child get on the path to health and happiness, feel free to read Chapter 1 and then jump to Parts II and III to learn how AllStride can help your child and your family. Just be sure to circle back later to read about the underlying causes of this crisis. Part IV explains how you can get involved in school and community activities and become part of the larger solution.

The Website

Allstride.com is where you and your child actually learn how to do the program, which includes personalized meal plans and dozens of fun activities. You'll also have access to our nutritionist, fitness expert, and family coach, plus support from a like-minded community of kids and families. We all know that when we do things together, we're far more motivated to stick with them, whether out of sense of obligation to others, to support someone we care about, or because we are buoyed by the spirit of teamwork. Whether it's getting out to walk on a cold winter morning or volunteering at a fund-raiser, you're far more likely to show up if you know others are counting on you to be there. In the same way, *allstride.com* harnesses the power of a virtual community to create successful results.

Now read about the evolution of AllStride and the young girl who was its inspiration. Then move on to Part I, written by Dr. John. I'll be back between chapters to interview kids and families whose lives have been changed by the program, and then in later chapters, assisted by our team of experts, to explain the program.

As the queen of reinvention, I wish you good luck reinventing yourself and empowering your kids to do the same.

Ricki Lake

Meet the Family That Started It All

Every once in a while, you run into amazing parents who, in trying to make life better for their own child, end up making the world a better place for all children. Such is the case with Mark and Lisa Daniel. Concerned about Krystal, their 12-year-old daughter, Lisa came up with a weight-loss plan for her. She had recently helped Mark slim down by adapting a diet prescribed for his father to manage his diabetes. Lisa also sought advice from a nutritionist and a couple of fitness experts. Let's hear how the program began.

Ricki: Your husband, Mark, and his father had weight issues. Was there a family history on your side as well, Lisa?
Lisa: My father's sisters all probably weighed 250 to 300 pounds, and one of my aunts had had gastric bypass surgery. My mother put my younger sister, who was also overweight, on a diet when she was 7 years old. She's fought obesity all her life. I was terrified that if we didn't take control of Krystal's weight at a young age she'd have the same problems as my aunts and sister.
Ricki: Believe me, I understand. I was 10 when I began gaining weight. How about your own weight?

Lisa: I was always careful because my sister was so heavy, but my eating habits when I was younger were terrible. I'd go for three days without eating or have just coffee and a candy bar. At 15 I was anorexic and bulimic, and I'm still paying the price for that today. (Later I lost 18 pounds on the program.) I was terrified to put my daughter on a diet because I'd seen with my sister that it just doesn't work. You never want to say to your child, "You're fat and you need to go on a diet," as my mother did.

Ricki: Were you concerned about hurting Krystal's feelings by bringing up the subject?

Lisa: Absolutely. Mark and I knew that Krystal was always a little on the heavy side, but we didn't want to hurt her self-esteem or provoke a pattern of eating disorders by calling attention to it. Girls from 9 to 14 are extremely fragile and emotional, and we didn't want her to think we loved her any less because of her extra pounds. Fortunately, at around the same time that we knew we had to step in, she came to us for help after a particularly unpleasant experience on the school bus. (Read Krystal's story on page 25.) Within six months on the program, she'd lost 21 pounds.

Mark: The change in Krystal wasn't just a matter of size. She was a whole new girl when she went back to school in the fall.

Lisa: I used to tease her because I'd find her looking in the mirror and I'd say, "Honey, now don't be vain. Remember those girls who used to tease you. This is just the icing on the cake."

Ricki: Mark, what did the program Lisa created for you and later Krystal entail?

Mark: It relies on the simple premise that weight control depends upon establishing a balance between energy in (food) and energy out (activity). A well-designed meal plan allows a person to consume just a few fewer calories each day than are burned for energy. This results in slow weight loss, but enables the development of new habits, which makes it possible to keep the weight off. Equally important is eating healthy foods that taste good. If a child doesn't like the food, no program is going to work. Because kids are eating their favorite foods, emotional issues about being deprived or feeling different don't come up. The first week that Krystal took her lunch to school we had to get on her because she was trading her foods with her friends who wanted all the great foods she had brought!

Lisa: Let me repeat, it's not a diet; it's a healthy lifestyle change. And because the whole family is doing it, the child doesn't feel singled out—that she's eating one thing and we're eating what we want.

Ricki: So what did Krystal eat?

Lisa: Well, first, all food groups are included, including fat and carbs. When I first worked out Mark's meal plans, he said, "I have to be able to eat pizza, spaghetti, and tacos once a week—and he did and still lost 50 pounds. Krystal was eating fruit and vegetables and dishes like baked halibut, Chinese chicken stir-fry, chicken-enchilada casserole, and spicy shrimp fajitas.

Ricki: How did your eating program turn into something more than one family's successful mutual-support system?

Lisa: After Krystal had lost a significant amount of weight, we'd get e-mails from other parents asking what she was doing. That led to my developing meal plans for family, friends, and some of Mark's coworkers. When we realized how much this program had helped Krystal, Mark said, "There must be a way we can help other kids."

Ricki: What was the first thing you did?

Mark: Lisa and I wrote a pamphlet called "Helping Your Child Lose Weight" and sold it online. But soon parents told us they needed help putting together meal plans. I've always been a bit of a computer geek, so I figured out how to turn the meal plans that Lisa developed into a program. She had become certified as a kids' nutrition specialist, and we created 45pounds.com. The name represented the average amount of weight kids on our program had lost. All the meal plans are customized for each child, based on his or her likes and dislikes and tailored to age and size. Pretty soon we were producing recipes and then exercise videos.

Ricki: Thank you, Lisa and Mark, for your simple but brilliant idea.

A New Name, a New Scope, and a New Site

We've renamed the updated website *allstride.com* to symbolize the forward momentum that occurs when children, families, communities, and other forces come together. But that's only one of many changes that makes AllStride such a quantum leap. We've taken the core premise of the Daniels' program and scaled it up so that kids all across the country (and eventually the world) can benefit. We've added dozens of fun activities that kids will love to do. And, most importantly, we've created a community composed of experts, kids, and their families and friends to help ensure success on the program.

Dr. John and I and the rest of the AllStride team recognize that the battle for our children's health needs to be fought on many fronts: we call them food, fun, and friends, supported, of course, by family. We'll look at each one of these four interlocking "F" pieces of the puzzle in the chapters to come.

Part 1

Let's Raise Healthy Kids

By John Monaco, M.D.

Too Small to Be Big

Chapter 1

One Doctor's Dilemma

You've already heard a bit about the AllStride program from Ricki, along with her personal weight struggles and concerns about her own children—as well as millions of other kids. I share those concerns, and as a pediatrician I'm on the front lines battling the epidemic of childhood overweight and obesity and poor health, patient by patient. (There's a clinical distinction between being overweight and obese as defined on page 49, but for the sake of simplicity, when we talk about the crisis children are facing, we'll use the term "obesity.") I practice in a typical American town. Brandon, Florida, a bedroom community of Tampa, is growing fast and the median age of the population is very young. As a result, there are lots of kids, lots of schools, lots of pediatricians, and certainly lots of kids toting around extra pounds.

By the mid-1990s, I'd been practicing critical-care and inpatient pediatrics for a decade and was astonished by the number of overweight kids I was seeing. Even more than the number, I was troubled by the severity of their problems. I saw 7-year-old asthmatics who weighed 120 pounds and many, many teen-agers carrying around more than 250 pounds, often on relatively small frames. Even toddlers and infants seemed to be getting plumper.

Identifying the Problem

I don't see my young patients until they're admitted to the hospital, so I knew that I was probably only witnessing the tip of the iceberg. When I asked my colleagues in primary care if they were seeing the same phenomenon, they echoed my suspicions. Kids did seem to be getting heavier, and there were more truly obese kids than ever before. Despite sensing that obesity was profoundly affecting the health of their young pa-tients and promising to plague them long into adulthood, my pediatrician peers found themselves just as much as at a loss for a solution as I was.

A dozen years ago when I began my research, many scholarly articles on childhood obesity had been published in medical journals, and juvenile obesity clinics were beginning to pop up in major university teaching programs. At that time, the mainstream media had not focused on the issue, but today, of course, it's been discussed ad nauseam on the talk show circuit and has been the subject of countless news specials and health seminars. Throughout this book, we'll showcase some of the programs that are making a difference, such as those in schools that have upgraded their lunch menus and brought the study of nutrition into their classrooms.

Despite some admirable efforts in the last decade, it's only now that we've reached critical mass in terms of awareness. And we've clearly not yet attacked this problem nationally with the aggressiveness that characterized the antismoking campaign, the war on drugs, or the need to wear seatbelts in a moving vehicle. To date there simply hasn't been a holistic solution to childhood obesity. And therein lies the challenge: how do we eliminate this plague by attacking it on all fronts?

The Pain of Personal Experience

I was heavy as a child and have battled to control my weight most of my life. Since my talents weren't physical ones, I wasn't inclined to put myself in situations where I'd be constantly reminded of my inadequacies. If there was a choice between an after-school kickball game or a really good "Superman" rerun on television, I usually picked the latter. During recess, when most kids were tearing through the schoolyard screaming at the top of their lungs, I chose more quiet pursuits. I was usually the last picked for sandlot baseball, basketball, and football games. When other kids were playing sports, I was taking piano lessons.

In late elementary school, the result of my inactivity manifested itself in my size. Anyone who spends much time around kids knows that being different is about the worst thing that any kid can ever feel. It's not as bad as being picked on, however, which also happened to me. I was the butt of jokes—excuse the pun—not only by my friends but also within my family. My younger brother and chief tormentor was the picture of virility, vitality, and physical prowess. Where did I seek comfort from this psychological trauma? That's right, food. I still have lovely memories of sitting in front of the television, chowing down a bag of Wise® Potato Chips to soothe my pain.

I mention my own situation not as a form of public therapy, but to let you know how deeply it hits home when I see a heavy child in my practice and why I originally decided to start researching the childhood obesity epidemic. I knew how badly I felt as an overweight kid, even though I was never as big as many of the kids I see today. What could this possibly mean for the future of this generation?

My objective is not to remind you of what you already know: childhood obesity is one of the most serious health crises facing this country, as we'll discuss in Chapter 3. I'm far more interested in being part of the solution. I joined AllStride because after more than a decade of searching, I'd finally found an approach that I truly believe can work for millions of children and their families.

Like Ricki and millions of other parents, myself included, you want to help your children thrive in every aspect of their lives. Without the blessing of good health—which includes an appropriate weight—no child can achieve his or her potential. But we all know that a number of forces in our society and the lifestyle most of us lead conspire to frustrate those goals. The first thing you should know is that you're not alone. We're all in this dilemma together. With the AllStride virtual community and the exciting initiatives taking place in communities across the nation, I know we can solve it.

Becoming an Authority

About 10 years ago, the late Judy Mazel and I wrote a book that I thought would make a real difference: *Slim & Fit Kids: Raising Healthy Children in a Fast-Food World*. Judy was the originator of the Beverly Hills Diet and the author of the best-selling book of the same name. Knowing that traditional "diets" aren't appropriate for growing children, we instead focused on educating them about eating properly. We also addressed activity and acknowledged that food is not just about providing energy and crucial nutrients; it's also a source of comfort, and there are complex reasons for people eating what they do.

We explained that protein, carbohydrates, and fats are all important and none should be considered "bad." We stressed the avoidance of hydrogenated fats, refined sugars, and preservatives of any kind. We de-emphasized cow's milk and meat and recommended soy and other plants as alternative protein sources. Much of this has become mainstream. If anything, our book was ahead of the curve. I remember that on a promotional book tour, I often had to convince questioners that there even was a problem of childhood obesity, much less how severe it was. My critics suggested that I was creating an issue so I could then offer a solution! Would that it were so.

"Diets" Are Not the Answer

After the publication of *Slim & Fit Kids,* several pediatricians asked me to open a clinic or offered me office space to care for their overweight patients. I was actually told that running an obesity clinic is the perfect practice from a business standpoint, because everyone knows that there is no real solution to this problem. "Get these overweight kids in the system and they'll never leave," advised some entrepreneurial pediatricians. Naturally I couldn't live with that attitude. We must deal with weight issues before they're health and life threatening.

Although I agreed to serve as a resource for addressing childhood obesity, my heart was still with children sick enough to be admitted to the hospital. I continue to meet with parent groups and with families individually to field their questions and offer suggestions. But my efforts were reaching only a relatively small number of kids and families in distress, even as more and more kids were becoming overweight. I also soon realized that although *Slim & Fit Kids* offered some very useful tools, no diet in and of itself is the answer for an individual child. Nor will simply putting millions of heavy youngsters on a weight-loss diet eliminate the problem.

A Family Matter

When I tried to offer solutions to families with heavy kids, I made a shocking discovery: all too often the parents were unwilling to make the changes needed to improve their child's situation. From that I learned a very important lesson: childhood obesity is a family issue. Until parents change their behavior or at the very least create an environment in which their kids can change, it's almost impossible for them to eat better, become more active, and lose weight. After all, why should Sally have to dine on chicken breast and steamed beans for dinner when the rest of the family is tucking into takeout pizza and bread sticks? And why should she take walks while the rest of the gang stays home glued to the flat screen?

If we truly care about our kids' health and welfare, we must encourage healthy habits and enable parents to serve as guides for nutritious eating. Working as a team, we can give our kids back their childhood. You'll understand what I mean by this phrase in the next chapter.

Meet Krystal, Who Inspired the Program

Success Story

When 12-year-old Krystal came home from school one day in tears because she was being teased about her weight, little did she realize that her situation would ultimately allow many other children to change their lives the way she did. Her parents decided they had to do something to help. (See "Meet The Family That Started It All" on page 13.) Krystal's successful experience—she lost 23 pounds—inspired her parents to offer the program to other families. Now a recent high-school graduate, Krystal looks back on that time and how it changed her life forever.

Ricki: I started to gain weight at about age 10. How old were you?

Krystal: I was about the same age when it started, and I was in sixth grade when it hit its peak. At 12 I weighed 136 pounds. I had two best friends. One was big, but not as big as me, and the other one was real thin, and they were fine. But other kids would make subtle comments, and some were really mean.

Ricki: Did you go to your parents or did they say something to you first?

Krystal: I remember being on the school bus and a girl who had been my friend complimented everyone else on something, but when she got to me, she said, "You're fat and ugly." When I got home I shared what had happened with my mom and dad. Around the same time, my parents approached me about doing something about my weight. Mom said they were willing to help, and it made me feel nurtured.

Ricki: What did they suggest?

Krystal: My parents knew that something had to be done, but they didn't want to put me on a diet. So my mother worked out a healthy eating program. A few months earlier my dad had asked her to put together a "non-diet" meal plan. He'd already lost about 50 pounds. Mom had me follow dad's program, but with smaller portions. She kept track of the foods I ate, but I memorized my program pretty quickly and always knew what I had eaten. We weighed in twice a week, and that's become a habit I continue to this day.

Ricki: Let's back up a bit. Were you experiencing any health issues in addition to being heavy?

Krystal: When I was 9, I was the only girl in my class wearing a training bra. Then I started having periods when I was 11, and the doctor said that it was because I was overweight. After I started the program and lost almost all the excess weight, my periods stopped. My mom took me to the doctor in a panic. The doctor looked at mom and said, "You're doing everything right by helping your daughter lose weight because obesity messes with the whole hormone system."

Ricki: Were you into clothes at 12? Was that an issue for you too?

Krystal: I wanted to dress like my mom. We'd trade tops in the summer. Then all of a sudden, her tank tops weren't fitting me. I also wanted to show my belly like all my friends were, but I couldn't pull it off. Then I was wearing pants in a size bigger than mom's, and I was only a little kid. That's when the kids in school started teasing me.

Ricki: How did you feel about starting a "non diet?"

Krystal: At first, I was scared. I didn't know if I would get enough to eat or if I would even get some of the foods I enjoyed. It turned out I did. I had plenty to eat, and at times I couldn't even finish all of my food because I would get full. Plus, I was able to eat the foods I liked.

Ricki: That's cool because on a "diet" most people feel hungry and deprived all the time. What kind of results did you see?

Krystal: By the end of sixth grade, after two weeks on the program, I'd lost 5 pounds. My friends started noticing and that made me happy and gave me motivation. By the time I started seventh grade in the fall, I'd lost 21 pounds and I looked completely different. Some of the kids I'd gone to school with for years didn't recognize me. They thought I was a new kid!

Ricki: What else was different?

Krystal: It was obvious that I looked different, but I also felt different. I was happier and more confident. I liked the way I looked for the first time in a long time. I was no longer sad. I had more friends and no one picked on me anymore. I was so grateful. I thank my parents all the time for putting me on the program. It changed my life.

Ricki: Like how?

Krystal: I never used to cook. Now I love to cook healthy, yummy meals. I'm taking a year off after high school and then I plan to study nutrition in college. I want to do this for the rest of my life.

Chapter 2

Is My Child at Risk?

Being a "big" kid isn't just a matter of appearance, of not being able to wear trendy clothes, being teased, or having a poor self-image. As devastating as all these things may be, carrying around extra pounds can also impact your child's health and longevity. As a pediatric critical-care physician, I regularly see sick kids who wouldn't be in my care if they weren't overweight, in some cases horribly so. In a moment, you'll meet some of them.

We face the tragic prospect that this generation of children won't live as long as their parents, and that during their lives they'll be sicker. Even sadder, this crisis could have been prevented, but, without realizing, it, we chose not to. We were so caught up in our busy lives, so subject to the temptations beamed forth by Madison Avenue that we lost sight of some basics: eat good foods, consume less overall, and stay active. The good news is that if we collectively take the right actions now—and by that I mean AllStride, parents, kids, the health-care community and other organizations—we can restore a carefree childhood to future generations of children.

A Difficult Diagnosis

Kaitlyn, as I'll call her, is rather typical of many of my heavy patients. At 10 years old and 4-feet, 8-inches tall, she weighs 130 pounds, which puts her in the 95th percentile for her age. That means she is considered clinically obese. Kaitlyn's mother brought her to the emergency room after she complained for two days of abdominal pain and was running a slight fever. She'd thrown up a couple of times and her usually voracious appetite, particularly for French fries and chicken fingers, was decidedly down. This fact was the most alarming to mom, because it was such a dramatic change in behavior.

The ER doctor's job in this scenario is to rule out emergency situations or those that require surgical intervention. Kaitlyn didn't have typical appendicitis pain; nor could it be localized to the right lower quadrant, which is where most of the pain is localized if the appendix hasn't ruptured. Her excessive belly fat made it difficult to perform an exam. For the same reason, the ER doctor—and later the surgeon—had a hard time determining whether her belly was distended or even the degree of her pain. Hoping to visualize the appendix, the surgeon ordered a CT scan of her abdomen, but her excess weight made it impossible to get a clear view.

With such an inconclusive diagnosis, the surgeon's strategy was to admit her to the pediatric floor, withhold food, give her IV fluids, and see what evolved. Perhaps another CT scan the following morning would provide meaningful information.

During the night Kaitlyn's temperature suddenly spiked to over 103°F. She was given acetaminophen to bring down her fever, which prompted unrelenting vomiting. Her belly was now distended, confirming the diagnosis of appendicitis, and she screamed in pain whenever it was touched. Despite administration of intravenous antibiotics, by the time the surgeon operated, her appendix had ruptured, leaking contents into her abdominal cavity. This resulted in peritonitis, an infection caused by inflammation of the lining of the abdominal cavity, a much more significant problem than straightforward appendicitis.

Post-Op Distress

In the three or four days after surgery, Kaitlyn's fever persisted and she needed intravenous narcotics for pain. It was 10 days before she could eat regularly, her fever had subsided, and she was able to get up and walk the halls. It's impossible to say for sure, but we wondered if Kaitlyn had gone to the operating room that first night and had her appendix removed, whether she would have avoided rupture and peritonitis. Might she have been able to leave the hospital the next day? Instead, she endured 10 days with the torture of IVs, needle sticks, agonizing pain, and the life-altering effects a prolonged hospitalization at a young age. I hate to even think of the difference in the hospital bill between a one- or two-day stay and a 10-day stay with intensive interventions. I wouldn't be surprised if it is of the order of tens of thousands of dollars.

But here's the rub. I firmly believe, as do all those who cared for Kaitlyn while she was in the hospital, that all of this could have been avoided had she not been so overweight. And please understand me, this is not a judgment in any way against the child or her family. We might just as well blame ourselves for allowing the situation to exist in which an otherwise average child is placed in mortal danger because she's so heavy.

The point is that our children are facing devastating consequences because of their belly rolls and thunder thighs. I'm talking about premature heart disease, hypertension, and a dramatic rise in the incidence of asthma and type 2 diabetes. In fact, being overweight affects every aspect of a kid's health, and makes everything more difficult as far as hospital care is concerned. We saw in Kaitlyn's case how her big tummy made her physical exam difficult and her CT scan hard to interpret. It's also difficult to find veins in a chubby kid in order to hook up IV lines or draw blood.

Pneumonia and Respiratory Distress

Now meet Jeremy, who's asthmatic. At 15, he's 5-feet, 8-inches tall and weighs 250 pounds. He has the lungs of a 70-year-old and the belly of a 50-year-old. He was admitted to our pediatric intensive care unit with pneumonia and respiratory distress, after passing out. In the ER Jeremy required high concentrations of oxygen. He was nearly placed on a ventilator, but his size made this procedure difficult and dangerous. So Jeremy was caught between the proverbial rock and a hard place. His weight meant that the very life-saving procedure he might need could kill him.

The ER staff got Jeremy through this crisis and he was admitted to our pediatric intensive-care unit, where, beside a toddler with bronchiolitis in the next bed, he looked like a giant. It was very difficult to wean Jeremy off his oxygen because his abdomen pushed his diaphragm so high up in his chest that he was simply incapable of taking a deep breath.

Jeremy stayed in the hospital for five days, at least two days longer than the average kid with pneumonia. The only way to successfully wean him off the respirator was to lower the bar of acceptability. We realized, finally, that he probably never had good oxygen levels, even when he was feeling well. Obese guys are also very prone to sleep apnea, congestive heart failure, and even sudden death, so we decided to talk to his mother about home oxygen. She vehemently refused this option, but did say that she would take Jeremy to the pulmonologist as an outpatient. Let me remind you again that he was only 15 years old.

Condemned to a Sedentary Life

Jeremy was a decent student and loved playing on his computer. He didn't engage in sports or go outside much. "It's just too hard," he told the nurses. I looked at Jeremy as he was about to finally be discharged from our unit, and I realized that his childhood had been forfeited. He'll never ride his bike outside or shoot hoops in someone's driveway. He'll never scheme about how to be alone with a girl. Perhaps he'll go to college, if he lives that long, where he'll struggle to fit in. If he makes it to adulthood, he'll experience a vastly accelerated version of the normal aging process.

Old Before Their Time

Children are routinely getting diseases that used to be seen in late middle age. Not only is obesity shortening their lives, it is also stealing their childhood. Teens are increasingly subject to such conditions as asthma, diabetes, or joint problems that their grandparents may have, along with hypertension and the early signs of heart disease. Even fatty livers and other organ dysfunctions are on the rise in teens. We'll review all of these later in this chapter. But first I want to look at this part of the problem from a slightly different perspective. It's the quality of the lives of these children that I'm concerned about. It kind of reminds me of an 80-year-old man who says he has no interest in anything that will help him live to be 120. Why would he want to be old for 40 more years?

The Epidemic of Childhood Diabetes

Let's start with diabetes, one of the clearest examples of how the obesity epidemic is robbing our kids of their youth. The dramatic rise in the incidence of diabetes almost perfectly mirrors that of obesity, a parallel that has led to the coining of the term "diabesity." It's estimated that one-third of the children born in the year 2000 will develop diabetes later in life, some of them before they're even old enough to vote.

There are two major forms of diabetes. Type 1, formerly known as "juvenile" diabetes, is caused by the inability of cells in the pancreas to produce insulin. This hormone drives sugar, or glucose, from the bloodstream to the cells, where it can be stored and accessed for energy. When insulin is absent or deficient, glucose remains in the bloodstream, where it wreaks havoc on almost all organs and tissues. The treatment for this type of diabetes is essentially to replace insulin.

In type 2 diabetes, or so-called adult-onset diabetes, insulin production is normal, but its effects are limited. In obese individuals, the action of insulin is compromised, and the heavier a person is, the more resistant his body is to the effects of insulin, resulting in higher and higher blood sugar levels. Over a prolonged period of time, this condition, known as hyperglycemia, can result in devastating damage to kidneys, eyes, joints, the heart, the central nervous system, and almost all other organs and tissues. Circulatory problems to the arms and legs can result in amputations. The degenerative effect that prolonged hyperglycemia has on the human body causes rapid and premature aging. The most effective treatment for type 2 is diet and exercise—basically the same treatment for obesity.

The Increase in Childhood Asthma

The frequency and severity of this difficult disease are on the rise among people of all ages. We see more kids with asthma each year, and they tend to be progressively sicker. Interestingly, the rise in the incidence of asthma exactly parallels the rise in obesity—just as with diabetes. Are obesity and asthma related? Undoubtedly, and here's why. First is the mechanical process of respiration. The muscles of the chest wall between the ribs, the abdominal wall, and the diaphragm work in concert to create the smooth intake and exhalation of air. Also at work is the thin rim of smooth muscle lining the bronchioles, or breathing tubes. We cannot voluntarily control these muscles, but they're essential for normal respiration. In asthma these muscles are overactive, or "twitchy." Their contraction contributes to the bronchospasm, or narrowing of the airways, which is the hallmark of an asthma attack.

If a child is overweight, it takes more work to breathe, but an asthma attack only makes it worse. These respiratory muscles must not only push air through narrow tubes to facilitate breathing, but layers of fat also challenge the muscles. The more exertion breathing requires, the more frantic the wheezing child becomes. Emotions can play a role in asthma, and when a child is anxious, everything gets worse. Increased airway velocity can also narrow the airway. Imagine sucking hard through a paper straw: suck hard enough and the straw collapses. The same thing occurs when stress significantly increases airway velocity.

Inflammation Links Obesity and Asthma

Obesity also plays a role in the inflammatory component of asthma. Inflammation produces fluid, white blood cells, and mucus, which clog the airway, making it more difficult to move air through it. Obesity appears to cause the body to react to itself by increasing this damaging inflammatory response. When one understands the role of inflammation in asthma, it's not difficult to understand why obese individuals tend to have more frequent and severe asthma attacks. It may take less to set off an overweight child's wheezing episode, and longer to treat it.

Because overweight children are already in this elevated inflammatory state, it takes very little to trigger an attack. Changes in temperature, viral infections, allergens, emotional distress, and even mild exercise can set them off. I'm careful in such cases, however, not to discourage exercise. Nonetheless, establishing a rigorous exercise routine may be a considerable challenge in someone who is overweight and prone to wheezing attacks.

Until the cycle is broken, what a horrible way for kids to live! They may realize they need to get outside and increase their activity, but pollen makes them wheeze, and running makes them short of breath, which may also make them wheeze, and they just don't want to risk it. Instead, they stay inside, play video games, eat snacks, and, all too often, get discouraged and even depressed. In effect, they're respiratory cripples, not because of years of smoking or from working in a coalmine but simply by being heavy.

Joint Problems in Children

My children tease me that I love our yellow Lab, Gracie, more than them. I have to admit that she's far more loyal and never refuses a walk in the woods or the opportunity to retrieve a tennis ball. Everyone who has big dogs knows that they're prone to joint problems, with some breeds more susceptible than others. Often at a relatively young age, they begin to slow down. Jumping up on the bed or running long distances becomes more difficult. Even getting up from a reclining position is a struggle. In the worst cases, their painful joints affect almost every aspect of their lives, and eventually they're unable to perform any of the functions they used to do joyfully.

Our vet is always after us to keep Gracie's weight under control. The heavier she is, the more strain on her joints, resulting in more pain and limited function. So we limit treats and try to keep her active in the hopes of prolonging and improving the quality of her life. Ironically, as a culture, we're more open to dealing with such a situation concerning our pets than we are with our children—or ourselves.

If asthma and obesity create a vicious cycle for kids, obesity and joint problems may be an even clearer example of one. Imagine this: an overweight 13-year-old may have never been one for sports, but he's beginning to feel a little different because of his weight. He decides to take up jogging to slim down. Without any instruction in stretching, weight training, or even running technique, he heads outdoors and starts out running as fast as he can.

Within a quarter-mile he's breathing hard. At half a mile he's exhausted and his knees are killing him. He knew that this might not be fun the first few times, but people have told him to stick with it and it will get easier. However, no one said anything about all this pain! He walks home dejected and in agony. He tries again the next day, but the pain is even worse. By the third day he decides that sitting in front of the television in an air-conditioned room is much less painful—and there he spends the remainder of the summer afternoons.

It doesn't have to be that way. It may take longer, but there are ways to increase activity safely. And as his weight begins to drop, or his height plays catch-up with his weight, your child will experience less strain on his joints, bones, and muscles. Isaiah Truyman, our fitness expert, has produced exercise videos that enable heavy kids to gradually build their strength and endurance—without pain. Let's treat our kids as wisely and as compassionately as we treat our dogs, OK?

Adolescent Gallbladder Disease

Over the last 20 years, I've seen a dramatic rise in the number of teen-agers with gallbladder disease, and most of them are overweight girls. In medical school, we learned that the classic demographic triad for gallbladder inflammation was "fat, fertile, and 40." Nowadays they're fat and definitely fertile, but they happen to 14 instead of 40. In almost every instance, the inflammation is due to gallstones that obstruct the organ, leading to infection, and sometimes perforation. The gallbladder sits at the base of the liver and aids in fat digestion. Stones are made up primarily of fat and sometimes calcium and other minerals. People who eat fatty diets are more prone to stones. When they block the excretion of bile, disease results. Often the only treatment is surgery.

General surgeons are removing more gallbladders in young women (and men) than ever before. Often gallbladder disease will flare up after delivery of a baby. Can there be no more poignant example of the acceleration of adulthood than the rising incidence of postpartum teens with gallbladder disease? We've cared for a significant number of these young women on our pediatric unit. Should a 14-year-old with gallbladder disease still be admitted to pediatrics after having had a child, you may well ask? Different institutions handle such issues in different ways, but the point is that obesity has helped to blur the lines between childhood and adulthood. This is a case in which it's actually more respectful to treat her as a kid than as the accelerated adult she has become. I was struck by the reality of this conundrum through a young lady I once took care of.

A Teenage Mom with Asthma

The 17-year-old—let's call her Tamara—was admitted for asthma. She was also significantly overweight, looked much older than her years, and had borne a child three years earlier. Our hospital doesn't have a specific floor or area for adolescents, so our only option was to admit Tamara to the general pediatric floor. On her last day in the clinic, I checked to see if she was ready to be discharged. The nurse had informed me that my patient's child was with her, and the staff was not happy about it. I reassured them that Tamara would probably be leaving that day, and any discomfort they were now feeling would soon be behind them.

I will never forget what I saw when I entered the room. Our patient was sitting in her bed beside her well-behaved daughter. The TV was on and these two "kids" sat, side-by-side, thoroughly enjoying each other's company as they watched cartoons and colored, sharing crayons. I didn't know whom to feel worse for: the mother whose childhood had been truncated, or the child whose mother was a child herself.

Sleep Apnea and Snoring

Guys like me, well into middle age, snore. Just ask my wife! Snoring is mainly due to a loss of muscle tone in the tissues of the upper airway, the palate, throat, and area around the tongue and tonsils. When we're in deep sleep, these flaccid tissues collapse over the throat, effectively blocking air exchange. As air is forced through the obstruction created by these collapsed tissues, it creates the sound we call snoring. In extreme cases, the airway can become completely obstructed, interfering with breathing—what's called sleep apnea.

This scenario is no longer the exclusive province of middle-aged men. Overweight kids are now experiencing snoring, along with upper-airway obstruction. If this obstruction is severe and long-standing, it causes particular strain on the right side of the heart, and can even cause heart failure. When this occurs, these kids are treated exactly like old people with congestive heart failure. They require diuretics and sometimes medicine to improve the function of the heart. They may even need their tonsils or adenoids removed in an attempt to open their upper airways.

Early Signs of Heart Disease

In 2008, a task force of experts in the field of childhood obesity and nutrition recommended to the American Academy of Pediatrics that beginning at age 2, youngsters should have their lipids (cholesterol and triglycerides) evaluated. Moreover, older children with elevated lipid levels should be considered for treatment with the same statin drugs used to treat high cholesterol in adults.

I lament the fact that this investigation was even necessary. Have we arrived at the point where children can no longer be treated as children, but like adults and dosed with medications with the potential for considerable side effects? I've spent most of my career taking care of kids in general hospital settings, trying to convince my adult-medicine colleagues and hospital administrators that children are not little adults. Apparently this is no longer true.

Because of our history of inaction, pediatricians and others who take care of children's health must also now be trained to handle diseases once thought to strike only adults. At a recent meeting on pediatric critical care that I attended, the speaker told us that we will soon need to be able to identify a heart attack (or rule it out) and know how to treat it. I remind you, we're talking about patients under the age of 18! The current medical educational approach sends us out in the world ill-equipped to handle what may be the greatest public health disaster to face this generation.

Each summer I volunteer for a week at Camp Boggy Creek, in Orlando, which serves seriously ill children. Recently, I met a 14-year-old camper there. Charlie is 5-feet, 9-inches tall and weighs 285 pounds. He suffers from asthma, is on Lipitor (a statin drug) for high cholesterol, and recently started on Metformin to control type 2 diabetes. As if that isn't enough, he's also taking drugs for depression. I saw Charlie in the camp clinic because his gastrointestinal reflux was acting up after eating six (!) spicy tacos. Now he's also on Prevacid for heartburn and acid reflux. One could easily argue that all Charlie's problems stem from obesity; in fact, he could be the poster child for the epidemic!

The Link Between Obesity and Cancer

It's not hard to see the link between obesity and heart disease, high blood pressure, diabetes, and asthma. But a study by the American Institute for Cancer Research published in 2009 quantifies the relationship of excess body weight and the likelihood of developing seven types of cancer. With 49 percent of cases related to excess body fat, endometrial cancers show the largest association. That was followed, in descending order, by esophageal cancer, pancreatic cancer, kidney cancer, gallbladder cancer, breast cancer (in women), and colorectal cancer cases, for a total of 100,000 cases a year linked to obesity.

Researchers still don't understand exactly why obesity increases a person's risk for cancer, but some scientists hypothesize that excess estrogen released by body fat could stimulate certain types of breast cancer. Increased body fat can also lead to inflammation, which could mutate DNA or cause abnormal cell growth, both of which are seen in many forms of cancer. One bright note: the study showed that cancer patients who engaged in more physical activity had better outcomes because activity helps regulate hormone levels.

Premature Puberty

The onset of puberty is occurring sooner than ever before, due in large part to obesity; environmental issues are also a likely cause. A century ago, the average age of the onset of menstruation was more than 17; today, the average age has dropped to slightly more than 12. A study published in the journal *Pediatrics* in 2010 that tracked more than 1,200 girls aged 6 to 8 showed that they were more likely to start developing breasts by age 7 or 8 than they were in the past. This means these children are beginning to think of themselves in a sexual way.

It was once thought that early puberty led to obesity, but we now understand it to be the other way around. Obesity leads to the early onset of puberty. An earlier study showed that girls who are more than 20 pounds overweight have an 80-percent chance of noticeable breast development by age 9. In addition to making it possible for young girls to be sexually precocious, early puberty leaves them open to an increased likelihood of depression and certain types of cancers.

As early as 7, when they should be playing kickball and thinking boys have cooties, these children are thrust into a world where women are seen as sexual objects and sexual innocence is passé. This premature development plays right into the hands of those promoting pop culture and all its implications for profit. The obesity epidemic has helped to sexualize young women, and in turn, make it easy to market sexually provocative outfits, music, and television shows to the "tween" generation. And it's not just girls. Boys are also growing up much faster than they used to, as the rise in teen-age pregnancy evidences. Although male puberty is more difficult to identify, fertility is fertility, and it now happens sooner in both sexes.

Childhood should be savored rather than rushed through. Younger kids almost always want to be older than they are. But ask teens well into their college years who are contemplating careers and other responsibilities how they feel about growing up, and many will tell you they wish that they had had more time to be kids. They may even tell you they miss the innocence they once enjoyed. They appreciate their newfound freedom, but they realize they've paid a price for it.

Compromised Childhoods

For kids plagued with obesity since early childhood, some since birth, their chronic condition may have already taken a huge toll on their health. They could be diabetic or asthmatic. Some may have already had their gallbladders removed. Some may have already had children—who may themselves be on the way to obesity. Although these kids may want to run and play, as they could when they were younger or slimmer, they can't because it simply hurts too much to jog, shoot baskets, or hit a tennis ball. I'm seeing 4- and 5-year-olds who are out of breath from climbing a single flight of stairs. It's not right that a middle-aged adult like me should be in better condition than the children I care for.

I'm committed to saving these kids who have had their childhood robbed by obesity—and I know that with a concerted effort we can do it. What did our society look like before obesity was such a pervasive problem? How did we eat, play, work, and entertain ourselves? Perhaps in examining these activities and then comparing them to the way we do things today, we may find some answers.

In the next chapter, we'll look at the role of physicians in the crisis of childhood obesity and how health-care professionals, and parents must team up to help each and every child with a weight problem—and just as importantly—prevent more kids from having to carry this physical and psychological burden.

Mitchell Achieved Wonders in Eight Weeks

Success Story

I had the opportunity to interview 11-year-old Mitchell and his mom, Mary, before Mitchell began the program. We spoke again two months later, after he had lost 15 pounds. It's hard to believe this is the same boy. Once he brought up the rear in gym class. Now he's keeping up with the other kids. Listen in on our first meeting.

Mary: When he was about 4, Mitchell seemed to puff up. I thought it was baby fat and he would have a growth spurt, but he just kept getting heavier. When he was 9, the doctor said Mitchell had high cholesterol, which runs in the family. I asked the doctor if there was a nutritionist who could help, but instead he said he might put Mitchell on cholesterol-lowering medication and that we'd better watch out for diabetes.

Too Small to Be Big

Ricki: Mitchell, when did you first notice that you were gaining weight?

Mitchell: I'd get out of breath running in PE and playing sports. Everybody was ahead of me, and they were singling me out, like, "Come on, Mitchell, come on."

Ricki: Did they ever call you names?

Mitchell: No one really makes fun of me. I have a lot of friends.

Ricki: I'm glad to hear that. So tell me your favorite foods.

Mitchell: Well, I love spaghetti and I like pizza too.

Ricki: That's my favorite food. If I could live on a desert island with just one food it would be pizza.

Mitchell: I like ice cream and other normal kid stuff. I also like shrimp.

Ricki: And that's high in cholesterol, I know. So Mitchell, why do you want to lose weight?

Mitchell: I want to fit in with my peers and be more active. I want my stomach to be flat. And I want to wear what the other kids are wearing and not have to shop in the adult or teen section.

Ricki: Yeah, we all want our stomachs to be flat. Mary, how do you feel about all this?

Mary: My husband and I were athletic kids and competitive by nature, so we pushed our kids in that direction. When Mitchell was playing soccer, we were screaming, "Mitchell, Mitchell, go, go," but he was lagging behind. He got frustrated and didn't want to play anymore.

Ricki: So you were concerned on both the activity and the food fronts, right?

Mary: I know that you should have six small meals a day with a balance of complex carbohydrates and protein. But I work full time and I travel for business, so meal planning is difficult for me, particularly for six meals.

Ricki: I agree. It's a challenge for all of us and it's our responsibility. Do you feel like you've let Mitchell down in some way?

Mary: I totally blame myself. I was giving my kids breakfast, lunch, and dinner, but they need more than that.

Ricki: Isn't it amazing that in order to lose weight they need to eat more? How tall is Mitchell and how much does he weigh now?

Mary: He's about 4-feet, 6-inches tall and weighs 126 pounds.

Ricki: Did you know he was that overweight?

Mitchell: I didn't have any idea.

Mary: Me neither, I guess because Mitchell never said, "Mom, I don't like the way I look." He was very self-confident and nobody was making fun of him. But I did notice that in the summer he wouldn't take his shirt off for swim team. My husband actually found the program online, and he said, "You should take a look at this."

Ricki: Mitchell, I'm so excited that you're embarking on this great journey. I look forward to seeing you again after you've been following the program for eight weeks.

When I met with Mitchell and Mary the second time, the change in Mitchell was nothing short of amazing.

Ricki: You really look like a different kid. Tell me how you did it.

Mitchell: When we ordered the meal plan, I was kind of shaky about it, but it wasn't hard at all. When I stepped on the scale and I saw I'd lost my first few pounds, I was really happy. I've already lost 15 pounds.

Ricki: What changes did Mitchell make in his eating habits?

Mary: We followed the plan exactly. Portion control was probably the biggest change for Mitchell.

Ricki: Did you feel deprived, Mitchell? Did it feel like a diet?

Mitchell: Not really, because it was the food I liked and there were good new things like edamame and baby carrots. I eat more vegetables and more fruit now.

Ricki: Have your friends noticed?

Mitchell: Yeah, and they're encouraging me to lose more weight. Recently my neighbor said, "Mitchell, you're looking so much thinner. I'm happy for you." It makes my day when somebody says that to me.

Ricki: Wow! How about clothing? Are you a different size now?

Mitchell: When I started the program, I was a small men's size, but now I'm like a medium or large boy's size.

Ricki: That must feel great. And what do you see when you look in the mirror now?

Mitchell: I see a happy, healthy, slimmer person.

Ricki: And a pretty handsome one too. Tell me what it's like in PE these days.

Mitchell: Now I want to go to PE and do more sports and get more active.

Ricki: That's great, Mitchell. Mary, would you say that this program has had an effect on your whole family?

Mary: Definitely. We're all getting into better habits. And we feel good about doing our part as parents to keep him healthy.

Ricki: I'm so happy for all of you. And it has all happened in such a short amount of time. Now, Mitchell, do you pack your own lunch for school?

Mitchell: Yeah. Usually a turkey wrap made with a low-carb tortilla and occasionally cheese.

Ricki: Sounds good. How about for a snack?

Mitchell: Maybe an apple and a string cheese, or after dinner like a smoothie or a fruit parfait, which is really good.

Ricki: What is it?

Mitchell: It's crumbled graham crackers or vanilla wafers and sugar-free or low-fat ice cream or pudding and some raspberries or fruit and Cool Whip®. It's pretty easy to make.

Ricki: So you're not just learning healthier eating habits, you're also becoming more self-sufficient in doing the program on your own. Do you get on a scale every week?

Mitchell: Yeah, at the beginning of the week.

Ricki: And you've consistently lost what, close to 2 pounds a week? That's amazing. Would you say the program is easy to follow?

Mitchell: It's very easy, as long as you stick to the portion control.

Ricki: I'm sure. Would you say that's the hardest part for you, Mitchell?

Mitchell: Probably, but also when some of my friends have chips and offer me some, I'll be like, "No thanks, that has 3,000 calories!"

Ricki: It's hard to say "no" sometimes. So what is your weakness? If you could go home tonight and have your favorite treat, what would it be?

Mitchell: Reese's Peanut Butter Cups®.

Ricki: You and I are like soul mates, Mitchell! That's exactly what I would have. You don't have that much further to go. Do you think you'll stay on this program long term for maintenance?

Mitchell: Yeah. I'll stay on it after I lose the weight just to make sure I don't gain any back.

Ricki: Are there tricks you've learned that you'll probably keep doing forever, like having low-carb tortillas, and other things?

Mary: Yeah, and eating six times a day. That's why he's not hungry.

Ricki: Mitchell, this is an amazing transformation that you've made. I'm proud of you, and I know you're proud of yourself.

Chapter 3

Has the Medical Community Dropped the Ball?

Pediatricians take care of kids from birth until they're 18 or even older, treating everything from diaper rash to drug abuse and ear infections to teen-age pregnancy. It's only recently that pediatricians, whether university affiliated or in private practice, have begun to view obesity as the potentially severe medical condition it is. At the same time, parents are increasingly turning to their children's doctors for solutions. Pediatricians do the best they can, but the issues to be handled with overweight kids are simply insurmountable in a 10- or 15-minute office visit.

A Medical Issue?

As we discussed in Chapter 2, an overweight child isn't just unable to wear the cute clothes her classmates do or run as fast as his friends do. A too-big kid is also at risk for a host of related health problems. Which immediately raises the issue of whether the solution to your child's excess weight (and the epidemic as a whole) is a medical one. I would argue that it might be, but it shouldn't be—and it needn't be. I'll go even further and point a finger at my own profession, and even my own specialty, as being one of the causes. How so? It's because we've failed to prevent a perfectly preventable situation. We didn't put our collective finger in the small hole in the dyke, and now the floodgates have broken and the epidemic threatens to drown us all.

Preventive Health Care, Not

If this sounds dire, it is. Quite simply, the medical industry—and I use that word deliberately—has dropped the ball. If health care in America, and particularly pediatrics, has taken on the commitment to deliver preventive care, then it must receive a failing grade. The whole objective of such an approach is to identify problems before they begin or to solve them when they're still relatively minor. There can be no greater example of how proper medical intervention could have prevented a major problem than the current epidemic of overweight children.

The seeds of failure begin in medical school. I remember that my semester of biochemistry devoted only two weeks to nutrition. This lack of emphasis continues in our clinical training, when we learn how to identify and treat various diseases but not how to deal with obesity, which turns out to be the root cause of many of the problems we now see, including asthma, diabetes, and heart disease. If we could eliminate or mitigate obesity, we might be able to prevent many of these conditions.

Frustrated Pediatricians

One of the reasons university training programs have been far more successful in helping kids achieve a healthy weight than the efforts of community pediatricians is because many of them have given up on those kids. I'd go so far as to say that most private or clinic pediatricians would welcome any alternative to seeing overweight kids in their waiting rooms.

Nor is this frustration limited to my specialty. Doctors who treat adults are equally at a loss—today more than two out of three American adults are overweight—because, in large part, physicians feel that even adults won't take responsibility for making lifestyle changes. When a youngster is heavy, very often the rest of the family is as well, and it becomes very difficult to get everyone to change his or her ways for the good of the child. When I've talked to families in the hospital, there's often great resistance to make even the simplest changes in the way they approach food. No doubt, they're resistant in part because they think a "diet" must deprive them of their favorite foods.

General pediatricians (as opposed to pediatric specialists) give a lot of reasons for their frustration in reversing and staving off childhood obesity. Although many doctors believe it's an insolvable dilemma, many parents clearly live in a state of denial. "I can't even get parents to admit there's a problem," say pediatricians I know, "so how can I help them?" Others remark, "It's the parents' problem; it really isn't mine." For these reasons and many others, pediatricians have pretty much thrown up their hands.

Many pediatricians chart their young patients' body mass index (BMI), as recommended by the American Academy of Pediatrics. (See "Children and the BMI," opposite.) (My staff and I routinely chart BMIs in our hospitalized patients, since so many of them don't have a regular primary-care physician.) But when doctors tell parents that their child's BMI indicates overweight or obesity or puts the child at risk for becoming so, the parents often counter that the BMI is not an accurate indicator of obesity. Despite the tangible evidence, we doctors often hear, "There's simply no way that my kid is obese." Any attempts at helping the child end right there.

Children and the BMI

Body mass index, commonly referred to as BMI, compares weight to height to ascertain whether someone is underweight, normal weight, or overweight for age and gender. A BMI of 25–29.5 is considered overweight for an adolescent who has reached his or her full height. Someone with a BMI of 30 or greater is considered obese. For smaller kids, it's probably better to plot growth curves and look at percentiles for that particular age. In those cases, anything from the 85th or 90th percentile or more is considered overweight; the 95th percentile and higher is considered obese.

With a truly obese child, the BMI only confirms what our eyes tell us. It's obvious these kids need help, fast. But the BMI is a great index to check the status of the child who is marginally overweight, has a tendency to become overweight, or who has a family history of obesity. With these kids you can't always tell if they're overweight just by looking at them. If a child's BMI is trending high but is not yet through the roof, he or she bears watching. An adolescent with significant muscle mass may give a "false" BMI, but a physician can distinguish with a physical exam whether it's fat or muscle that's impacting the BMI.

It's not that doctors are uncaring or don't want to help over-weight kids. It's just very difficult for the average pediatrician to deal with the complex web of factors that can contribute to a weight problem in a short office visit, plus provide advice in a nurturing manner. Moreover, pediatricians simply don't have a pat answer. In the case of an extremely overweight youngster or one who may have additional health problems, most pediatricians refer the child to a specialist. Pediatric cardiologists, pulmonologists, rheumatologists, and endocrinologists report a deluge of overweight kids as patients.

The Role of Specialists

If pediatricians have neither the tools nor the time to help a seriously overweight child, should parents routinely ask for a referral to a specialist? It depends. I would suggest that in the case of a child who's somewhat heavy but not yet showing any other health problems, you tell your pediatrician about *allstride.com*. Explain that it provides both a healthy eating program and a fitness program, as well as the key ingredient of motivation. Clearly, AllStride isn't an alternative to good health care; it's an ancillary tool. Share with your pediatrician this powerful program, which will really work with their young patients, and the doctor's frustration, your frustration, and your child's frustration can all be alleviated.

Chances are your pediatrician will see the wisdom of taking this family approach before you drag your child to a specialist. On the other hand, if your child is obese and already displaying such related health problems as hypertension (high blood pressure) or high blood sugar, a specialist may well be in order. However, there's still no reason not to initiate the AllStride program. Even specialists can find it frustrating to deal with the problem of an overweight child, while also battling the culture of a family and/or ethnic group—and even society in general.

There are individuals in the health-care profession, however, who have taken on a multifaceted, holistic approach, and they are starting to see some success. And by success I mean that first, the parents understand they have to change their lifestyle, along with their child's. This should enable the child to eat in a manner that leads to weight loss and engage in more physical activity, which obviously helps as well. Secondly, and ultimately, success is measured by permanently adopting new habits so that both the kid and the parents take control of their weight and health for good. This approach is akin to what AllStride offers in an online environment.

Kudos to Dr. Janet Silverstein

As a pediatric resident, I was a counselor at a summer camp for kids with diabetes, sponsored by the University of Florida, where I met Dr. Janet Silverstein. I lived in a cabin with seven or eight boys aged 9 and 10 who all had type 1 diabetes. Although I'd already cared for many seriously ill kids, the thought of dealing with these relatively "well" kids with diabetes—getting up with them in the middle of the night to deal with their low blood sugar—was intimidating.

My fears were allayed, however, when I saw Janet for the first time. Kids literally draped themselves around her, fighting for hugs and the chance to hold her hand. Other counselors told me that kids came from all over the state just to spend two weeks in Dr. Janet's camp. Kids who attended her diabetes clinic regularly fell in love with her.

"Love" was the key to everything in the camp. Treatment emphasized the total child, who was never made to feel stigmatized or "abnormal" in any way. Education was also key, but not in a didactic way. Meals and snacks provided good nutrition. Campers engaged in vigorous physical activity all day long, gaining physical confidence and learning that their diagnosis mustn't stand in the way of a healthy lifestyle; in fact, it demanded it! We often discussed issues with the campers, ranging from snacks, to managing insulin during the school day, to the possibility of dating members of the opposite sex. Every aspect of the program revolved around teaching these fabulous kids to deal with their disease in the context of the larger world.

This experience gave me the empathy I would need to care for these kids when I later saw them in the clinic or the hospital. I no longer regarded them as kids with diabetes but each as an individual, whom I would be privileged to assist in navigating a sometimes-challenging childhood. It was no surprise to me that Janet later became the first director of the University of Florida's childhood-obesity program. To do it right would take the kind of approach she had used in caring for kids with diabetes. Not only the food they ate, but also their physical activity, education, family, and social life must be addressed for the program to succeed. And it has.

If a specialist is in order, the obvious choice would be a pediatric endocrinologist. Endocrinology is the study of all things related to glands, which secrete hormones. For example, childhood diabetes is often a disorder of the secretion of the hormone insulin by the pancreas. Pediatric endocrinologists also deal with issues of short stature, which may be related to the secretion of the growth hormone. Thyroid disorders, adrenal-gland dysfunction, and even calcium metabolism all fall under the responsibility of the pediatric endocrinologist. However, if your child is already showing signs of asthma, heart problems, or joint problems, your pediatrician might refer you to a pediatric cardiologist, pulmonologist, or rheumatologist, respectively.

The University Clinic Approach

Almost every pediatric training program in a teaching hospital now has some sort of clinic setting dedicated to the care of seriously overweight children. The clinic attempts to look at every aspect of the child's life and deal with all relevant issues. A clinic in a university setting has many more medical tools available to manage the problem of childhood obesity than does a pediatrician in private practice. The schedule, personnel, and activities can be carefully structured and integrated for this purpose. When kids attend the obesity clinic, they see other kids like themselves, which immediately eliminates the stigma and some of the psychological barriers to accepting recommendations. Dieticians, psychologists, and physical therapists are available on site, and pulmonologists, cardiologists, rheumatologists, orthopedic surgeons, and endocrinologists, among other specialists, are available to the clinic staff, if necessary.

A Disease or a Condition?

Obesity is a medical condition that clearly results in other medical problems. But, unlike traditional diseases, there's not a clear single cause, such as an infectious agent, toxin, or abnormal inflammatory response. The causes of obesity are multiple and primarily nonmedical, which makes it a challenge to treat it as a purely medical disorder. Nor is it a condition that can be handled by a single specialty. Thus a place where multiple specialists are available makes much more sense than the single doctor trying to take care of everything while also struggling to deal with a waiting room full of kids with every other problem imaginable.

The university-affiliated clinic model seems to work best for dealing with all the issues involved in caring for overweight kids. However, not every community has easy access to a large teaching center with such a clinic program, which leaves the private community trying to handle overweight kids who may have related health problems. So while such clinics are making a profound impact on childhood obesity, they cannot solve this problem alone.

For one thing, clinics treat only kids who are already overweight, most of whom are seriously obese. Because they can take a limited number of kids, clinics admit only those with the most severe problems. A child who is simply 10 or 15 pounds overweight and without any other immediate problems probably won't qualify.

Community pediatricians also need to target kids who are at risk for obesity and aggressively work with them, just as we do the kids who are already heavy. In fact, we can overcome the larger issue of childhood obesity only if our efforts toward prevention are as comprehensive as our efforts with kids who are already obese. Also, like doctors in private practice, clinic staff will tell you that they're seeing successful outcomes, but the societal pressures are difficult to overcome. Even the best clinic in the world can't undo the impact of advertising, parents who refuse to change their own habits, and other social forces. On the other hand, if you see your own child heading in this direction, following the AllStride program may forestall the need to take him to a specialist or apply for a spot in a clinic program.

Do "Fat Camps" Work?

I know, it's a nasty name, but that's what everyone calls them instead of the politically correct term of weight-loss camps. Desperate parents may ask their pediatrician about such a program, but even if the child does lose a few pounds, he'll almost certainly regain them when he returns home if he resumes his old habits. Unless the underlying behavioral issues, along with an understanding of the need for a long-term commitment to new eating habits, are addressed, it's unlikely that any program will have lasting impact. I'm aware of only one such network of boarding schools and camps across the country that does take such a holistic approach. The Wellspring Academies program looks at what kids eat, their attitudes about food, and their physical activity. The kids follow a low-fat diet full of fruits and vegetables and whole-grain breads and pasta, but they also learn to prepare food themselves. Intense behavioral training helps kids be in touch with why they eat the way they do and explore their psychological motivations. Kids are also required to keep a journal of what they've eaten, as well as their activity levels and their emotional motivation for eating. Wellspring has two big flaws: it removes kids from home and places them in an "artificial" environment—and it costs about $32,000 for one semester!

Tangled in Emotions and Money

Denial, guilt, and shame make it particularly hard for pediatricians to deal with overweight children. There's also a certain taboo about the subject. One risks offense by insinuating that the child is overweight unless the parent brings it up. There's also an economic incentive: keep the "customer" satisfied by saying nothing. That's one reason why medical care for obesity seems to work better in a university clinic such as the one where I work. We can treat an overweight child as having a clinical problem, rather than some sort of social failing— which is how many parents perceive it. This can be done only if we deal with the problem honestly and objectively. Too much time is spent trying to place blame as to who or what is responsible for the obesity epidemic. If I am guilty of that in this book, I assure you my motivation is to educate, not to blame.

On a personal level, I suggest that parents with overweight children or who are overweight themselves face the facts. You know if you or your children are overweight. If you're not sure, just look at whether his belly hangs over the waistband of his pants. Don't indulge in denial games because you don't want to feel that you've somehow failed your child or yourself. It's not about success or failure, good or bad, beauty or unattractiveness. Put all those things aside. It's all about being healthy or unhealthy.

Would you ignore your child's respiratory infection because you don't want someone to think your house is dirty? Would your pediatrician not treat a child with whooping cough because you hadn't kept up with the immunizations that would have prevented it? Of course not. To address childhood obesity as a society—or help an overweight child achieve his or her healthy size—we have to start by being honest with ourselves.

If getting parents to acknowledge that their child is overweight is a tremendous challenge, it pales next to making dietary or lifestyle changes that would involve the whole family. "How can I get this child to live a healthy lifestyle and eat a healthy diet, when the moment the family leaves my office they head to McDonald's or Dairy Queen to load up on fat and sweets?" I've heard this question, or variations of it, many times from frustrated health-care providers.

Honesty Is the Best Policy

Denial and political correctness both play a major role in why our society hasn't made solving the epidemic of child obesity the priority it deserves to be. But being in denial often hits much closer to home. Our complex relationship with food makes it impossible to separate the emotional from the nutritional, so we react with fear. When kids are overweight, we—and I'm speaking as a physician and a parent—are afraid to tell them so. Understandably, we don't want young people to feel bad; nor do we want them to develop an eating disorder.

We have this bizarre notion that if we tell a heavy kid he should do something about his weight, he will immediately become bulimic and anorexic. So we elect to do nothing because we don't want to risk this horrible consequence.

I've heard many parents voice this concern and, believe it or not, I've heard pediatricians say the same thing. I regularly come across parents of clearly overweight kids who don't want to face the obvious. If we were simply honest about food, weight, and related issues, we wouldn't be faced with such irrational fear and would be able to deal with the issues before they reach crisis proportions.

The Dangers of Denial

I met a young man called Trent who'd read online about a weight-loss camp and wanted to attend. His parents insisted that he was simply "husky" or "big boned" and that his weight would take care of itself. His mother called Trent her "teddy bear." It never ceases to amaze me how many parents cavalierly dismiss what can actually be a very painful situation for a child by giving him a cute nickname. It's a form of denial that delays getting the help he may need. This behavior is no different from discounting chest pain as heartburn, when it's actually a heart attack. When proper treatment is delayed, the result is a bad outcome. In the case of obesity, the end results may not be as immediate, but they are every bit as dangerous.

Although Trent had never been able to persuade his parents to send him to a "fat camp," once he turned 21 he signed up for one run by the one organization of this type that I recommend: Wellspring Academies. He quickly and enthusiastically embraced the camp's principles of a low-fat, low-sugar approach to eating, journaling his food intake and adopting a rigorous walking program. Because he was motivated to lose weight and change his life, Trent became a role model for the campers. In time, he lost 90 pounds and has kept it off. He's now full of confidence and has a whole new outlook on life. Still, one has to wonder if his parents had faced facts sooner, whether he would have succeeded that much earlier. We'll never know, but at least he found help and success on his own terms. Unfortunately, not all kids have the emotional fortitude that Trent displayed.

A Delicate Issue

I once took care of an obviously overweight 6-year-old asthmatic boy. Once we got him over his attack, I asked his mother if his weight bothered him. She said, "No. He just likes his food!" And she laughed the nervous laughter I so often hear from parents of chunky kids: it's a combination of embarrassment, denial, and a dose of "Isn't he a cute little cherub?" When his mom left to make a phone call, I asked him if he was bothered by his weight. As tears welled up in his eyes, he buried his face in his pillow and wouldn't look up. Sometimes kids want to talk about their weight with their parents, but they get a very strong signal that their parents just don't want to hear about it. Or the parents may tell their youngsters that they take after Aunt Bessie or they have an appetite like Uncle Joe. Or they may just laugh and move on. The child is left with the sinking feeling that no one understands, and perhaps no one really cares.

Nothing Funny About Being Fat

I wasn't obese as a kid, but I definitely was plump. I don't think my family meant to be mean, but there were plenty of jokes at my expense. My nickname for a while was "Crisco," because I was "fat in the can." I still remember, with disturbing clarity, one summer day when I was 11 or 12. I was already embarrassed about being chubby. My mother had bought me a hideous new bathing suit with orange and white vertical stripes in a polyester fabric that hugged my body and caused my belly and thighs to flow over the elastic, making me look like a sausage.

I'm still not sure why my mother did this, but one day she had me get out of the car on the way to the neighborhood pool to show our neighbor my new swimsuit. When I dropped my towel, my mother and our neighbor broke into laughter. If I was so plump as to be amusing, why didn't my parents talk to me about it and perhaps try to work with me to do something about it? To date, I have never gotten over the embarrassment of this experience, and probably never will!

Not all parents are in denial, of course. The mere fact that you're reading this book means that you're not one of them. We doctors also see the opposite situation when parents obsess about their child's weight. Parental emotions with regard to an overweight child are complex, often complicated by guilt and sometimes the desire to blame another person or outside factor.

A Quick-Fix Mentality

Compounding these issues, we live in a culture hooked on instant gratification and quick fixes. We physicians have trained patients to expect a pill or an immunization for every problem, and an instant solution for issues that may have taken a lifetime to establish. This quick-fix mentality extends to most weight-loss diets, which involve a short period of deprivation, after which most people revert to their old way of eating—with predictable results.

Such quickie diets rarely work, as legions of yo-yo dieters will attest. As Ricki and I will discuss later, a real, sustainable lifestyle change is a gradual process, unlike a crash diet, and demands the mentality of a tortoise rather than a hare. (Just remember who won that race!) Becoming overweight doesn't happen overnight; it may take months or even years to solve. Patience and perseverance are essential, but these qualities usually aren't present in medicine these days, or in our society as a whole. One of the many virtues of AllStride is that it teaches a way of eating and living for the long term.

What Doctors Can and Cannot Do

Physicians must recognize childhood obesity as the health disorder it is. This is what we are best trained to do: place all disorders in the "disease" model, with a cause, a treatment, and a proposed result. In the case of obesity, there are numerous causes, and although physicians cannot impact some causes, there are others we can. Much of the challenge is educational:

- **Help people better understand what they should eat, rather than learn about nutrition from advertising.**

- **Impress on our patients and their parents how important any kind of regular physical activity is for a healthy lifestyle and a future unburdened with ongoing health issues.**

- **Refer parents and children to programs with demonstrated results, such as AllStride.**

It's a cop-out for health-care professionals to treat obesity as some sort of "social disease" that's the responsibility of the family and can be treated only in the home. If our commitment is to give children the highest quality of life possible, we doctors must not ignore this problem. As a parent, you also have responsibilities (see "What You Can Do Right Now," on page 60). If the health-care community can do anything for you, it's to take emotions out of the discussion. Further, physicians and patients need to be honest with each other and engage in an open exchange about what can be done to resolve the problem.

Society needs to treat childhood obesity as the health emergency it really is, much as we did with the public health problem of smoking. In some ways the obesity epidemic is even more tragic than smoking was. Given all the information, people can choose to smoke if they like, but kids often have little choice as to the food they are given, the environments in which they live, the schools they attend, or the activities in which they participate. They don't even have much to say about what goes on in their household. How can they be blamed for watching four to five hours of television a day when their parents are doing the same thing?

If you are worried about your child's health, diet, activity level, or weight, you must:

- *Push your doctors and other health-care providers to partner with you to help your child.*

- *Be emotionally prepared to accept the reality that your child is overweight and needs help.*

- *Not let avoidance, guilt, blame, shame, and other emotions entangled with having a heavy child stand in the way of seeking help.*

- *Be prepared to make changes in your family's lifestyle.*

Hope on the Horizon

Given my concern and strong opinions, I was excited when Ricki asked me to become part of AllStride. The program has all the components included in my first book, but with stronger nutritional underpinnings. Importantly, it adds the crucial component of family involvement and community support to food and to fitness—or, as we refer to it, fun. The AllStride Community enables parents to "talk" with other parents and kids to "talk" with other kids. Parents can also join in discussion forums and watch "webinars" hosted by our nutritionist, physical fitness expert, family coach, or myself. Also key to the program are personalized meal plans that include only the foods the child likes, and numerous fun activity videos.

We'll get to all the details of the program in Part II. I have every confidence that AllStride can be a major influence in turning back the tide of the obesity epidemic—child-by-child and family-by-family—and thereby saving a whole generation of kids.

Nonetheless, we have our work cut out for us. Because it wasn't proactive about nipping the epidemic of overweight kids in the bud, the health-care system must now play catch-up. Parents also clearly have a responsibility to do everything they can to ensure their children's health. But it's not that simple. Many of this generation of kids are overweight for a complex and related set of causes. In the next chapter, we'll begin to explore some of the many reasons your own son or daughter may not be the slim and trim picture of health you envisioned— and how it may have started even before birth.

Together, Amanda and Caleb Lost 92 Pounds

Success Story

Ten-year-old Amanda lost 32 pounds and whittled 3½ inches off her waist and another 4½ inches off her hips. Meanwhile, her 15-year-old brother, Caleb, lost a whopping 60 pounds, trimming 8½ inches from his chest and 9½ inches from his waist. But the good news doesn't stop there. The whole family lost an amazing 180 pounds! Let's get the scoop from parents Gail and Phil before talking to Amanda and Caleb.

Ricki: Gail, what made you decide to do AllStride?
Gail: We all struggled with weight issues and the kids weren't healthy. I wanted to find something on which they could succeed. I asked them if they'd be willing to try the program, and they were both very excited. We figured it would be easier and work better if we did it as a family.

Ricki: Phil, were you on board from the start?

Phil: I was. Quite frankly, I felt guilty that I was passing on my heritage and it wasn't a good one. I needed to break the chain of being overweight. So far, I've lost about 50 pounds.

Ricki: How about you, Gail?

Gail: I've lost between 30 and 35 pounds and kept it off. We stay away from fried foods and we don't eat junk stuff with empty calories. It's just the way that we eat now.

Ricki: Gail, were you convinced it would work from the get-go?

Gail: I was excited, but I have to say I was a little skeptical. Could this program really be what would help us become healthier? There were weeks where we didn't lose weight—what's called a plateau—but it's not always about weight. Inches count too. More importantly, both Amanda and Caleb now know how important it is to eat right!

Ricki: Wow, that's quite a buildup. So let's hear from Amanda. What made you want to try the program?

Amanda: When I was turning 8, I already weighed 127 pounds. I got teased about my weight a lot, and most of the girls in my class were really mean to me.

Ricki: Did it make it easier to follow the program because the whole family was on it?

Amanda: It did.

Ricki: Gail, what kinds of changes have you seen in Amanda?

Gail: I remember when she was only 8 years old I'd take her into stores where she would see all these great things kids her age were wearing. She'd try them on and they wouldn't fit. It was so discouraging for her. She's finally able to wear cute clothes made for her age.

Ricki: Phil, you talked earlier about feeling guilty that your genetic predisposition to being heavy was being passed down to your kids. Can you talk a bit more about that in relation to Caleb?

Phil: One of the hardest things was seeing him and comparing him to myself. Everybody has always said that we looked a lot alike. And I've been heavy since I was a young kid, but not as heavy as Caleb was. I knew that as hard as it was for me to cope with things as a kid, it was going to be just as hard if not harder for him.

Ricki: Was that what made you comfortable talking to Caleb and Amanda about the program?

Phil: They were ready. They were tired of being teased because they were overweight, tired of not being able to keep up with the other kids. People shouldn't be judged on the way they look, but they are. Children can be brutally honest in an innocent sort of way, but it can still hurt feelings.

Ricki: Caleb, did it make it easier to do the program because the whole family was on it?

Caleb: Yes, because we all ate the same things.

Ricki: Gail, tell me how things changed for Caleb.

Gail: He's become so much more confident since he lost 60 pounds and is determined never to go back to where he was before. Our kids have broken down the barrier. Not just the barrier of being overweight and unhealthy, but also the barrier in their minds that there's nothing they can do about their weight. I hope more and more families realize that this program is attainable—and sustainable.

Ricki: Gail, do you have any advice for other parents struggling with similar issues?

Gail: My kids are living proof that you can do it. Success is all about being involved: getting out every day and finding fun ways to get more active together as a family. You want your kids to feel good about themselves. Now that Amanda and Caleb are eating the right foods and getting the right exercise, they're much more confident. In terms of their health, I think we saved their lives because now they see that there's a better way to live and feel great.

Chapter 4

It Starts in Infancy— and Even Before

When the parent of a child asks me or another physician the painful question, "Why is my child overweight?" there's no simple answer. There are multiple reasons why your child is heavier than he or she should be. A child may be part of a family in which nutritional education is poor or nonexistent. Or the parents may know better but lack the time and/ or money to practice good nutrition. Other youngsters may eat well yet are sedentary. Some kids eat well but simply eat too much. Even more complex are the psychodramas in the heads of insecure, fearful, or love-starved children who are overeating for reasons unrelated to the need for nutrition.

Then there are the societal pressures. Advertising bombards kids daily with images of what foods they should eat to give them the biggest lift or the happiest disposition, with little or no attention paid to these products' potentially harmful effects. Meanwhile, the larger media engine beams forth the nonstop message that physical appearance, not health, is what counts. "It is more important to look good than to feel good!" was once a tongue-in-cheek statement made by Fernando, Billy Crystal's character on "Saturday Night Live." Sadly, it's become the underlying message of many advertisers.

Ironically, the obsession with body image and thinness is at an all-time high, even as more than two-thirds of adults are overweight. Both are manifestations of our culture's fixation on food. We'll discuss this complex situation later. In this chapter, we'll focus primarily on the first few years of a child's life.

Scary Statistics

Recent estimates reveal that almost 40 percent of all children are overweight or obese. According to a 2007 report from the Robert Wood Johnson Foundation Center to Prevent Childhood Obesity:

- One in 10 toddlers under the age of 2 is overweight.
- Among preschool kids (ages 2–5), 12.4 percent are clinically obese. The figure was 5 percent in 1980.
- Among kids aged 6 to 11, 17 percent are obese, compared to 4.2 percent in 1970.
- Eighteen percent of teen-agers (12–19) are obese, up from 4.6 percent in 1970.

These numbers are horrifying in of and of themselves, but the trends they indicate are even scarier. Pediatrician and epidemiologist Matthew Gillman of Harvard Medical School has been tracking the statistics on babies born in eastern Massachusetts for more than 20 years. He notes, "Excess or accelerated weight gain even in the first four or six months of life may be setting up kids for overweight, for higher blood pressure, maybe even for asthma over the first years in childhood." Statistics may seem impersonal, but we know that you're probably reading this book because someone you love is overweight—or at risk for becoming so. So let's look at what could be impacting your own child's health and weight. Please understand that none of this discussion is meant to induce guilt about anything you have or have not done. It's only now that we can step back and look at how life has changed in the last 50 years with the perspective that allows us to see where our culture has taken many missteps.

Nature Vs. Nurture: It's Not that Simple

Many great minds have puzzled over the issue of whether an individual's weight is genetically predetermined or is just a matter of how many calories he or she takes in and how many are burned by activity and the body's natural processes. Some people metabolize calories more efficiently than others. An active 16-year-old boy will naturally burn a lot more calories than his sedentary grandma. Perhaps one of your kids is overweight and another one or two aren't, despite eating the same diet. If I had the answer to the question of genes vs. environment, I'd probably be short-listed for the Nobel Prize!

Unquestionably, genetics determine our height (assuming we receive adequate nutrition), and some people are naturally petite while others have a bigger frame. Some people also have a genetic predisposition to obesity, but it can be overcome with diet and activity. It's a mistake to use genetics as an excuse for a child's being overweight. In fact, knowing that a child has such a predisposition should only motivate us to address the problem. But genetics and normal variances aside, something in our recent history—or a perfect storm of such things—is impacting the weight of adults and children alike.

Seeds Planted Before Birth

It's not surprising that if a mother consumes too many calories during her pregnancy, it could increase her infant's likelihood of later becoming overweight. However, it turns out that consuming too few calories can have the same result. It appears that the genes of babies born to starving mothers program them to pack on fat so they'll have a better chance of survival in a famine. And it's not just future weight that's impacted; both groups of infants are at higher risk for later developing diabetes and heart disease. Children born to women after they've developed type 2 diabetes have a higher BMI and a fourfold chance of developing the disease themselves as adults, compared to siblings born before the onset of the mother's diabetes. (See "The Impact of Maternal Diabetes," opposite.)

Researchers at Penn State Center for Childhood Obesity Research have found that a child's genes inherited from either parent can be turned "on" or "off" by environmental factors while the fetus is developing, as well as early in an infant's life. In this case, the answer to the old question of nature vs. nurture would appear to be both. Obstetricians recommend that an overweight woman planning to get pregnant lose weight first so as to reduce the risk that her infant will become overweight and develop diabetes.

Twins Provide Proof

Some of the strongest evidence that genes control our metabolism comes from research on identical twins (who have the same genetic makeup). In one study, when multiple pairs of identical twins were put on the same weight-loss diet, the number of pounds lost varied significantly across the whole group. But when they looked at the pairs of twins, the researchers found that each pair's results were similar. This means that individuals with the same genes respond to dietary changes in a similar fashion, but individuals with another genetic makeup may lose more or less weight and may lose it more or less quickly. The researchers found that each pair of identical twins also responded to a vigorous exercise regimen (burning 1,000 calories a day) in a similar way: each pair of twins lost similar amounts of weight, but again there was great variation from one pair of twins to another.

Influences in Infancy

Researchers have also found that by the time a child is 2, his or her propensity for being overweight may be determined. Overfeeding and lack of activity can, of course, play a role; and so can sleep patterns. Babies who sleep less than 12 hours in a 24-hour period are more apt to grow up to be obese. If they don't get enough sleep and spend more than two hours in front of the television each day, their risk for obesity increases. Many of these findings come out of a long-term (and ongoing) study at Harvard Medical School, in which researchers have been following more than 2,000 women and their infants since pregnancy. One fascinating finding: if a mother smokes during pregnancy, her infant has a greater likelihood of a very low birth weight, but also a greater chance of being overweight in childhood.

The Impact of Maternal Diabetes

Groundbreaking research published in The New England Journal of Medicine *in 1983 looked at the relationship of obesity in the offspring of more than 1,500 women of the Pima Indian tribe to their mother's health status during pregnancy. Among the women who were already diabetic, a higher percentage of their children were obese at 15 to 19 than were those born to women who subsequently developed diabetes (meaning they had prediabetes during the pregnancy) or to women without either condition. As teen-agers, 58 percent of the offspring of diabetics were obese, as compared to 25 percent of children of women who had prediabetes during pregnancy and 17 percent of the offspring of women with neither condition.*

Don't Confuse Chubby with Healthy

Pediatricians routinely see newborns triple their birth weight within six months. A generation ago, this milestone usually occurred around a child's first birthday. I regularly see four- and five-month-olds who weigh nearly 20 pounds, the

It's Never Too Early to Instill Good Habits

Include your baby in family meals as soon as he or she is eating table foods (usually between six and nine months). Eating together as a family has been shown to reduce the risk for being overweight, and the earlier it starts, the better. Here are more tips to get your baby on the right track:

- *Wait until at least four months to introduce any solid food.*

- *Wait until six months to introduce juice (not juice drinks, which usually have added sugar in one form or another) and give no more than 4–6 ounces daily.*

- *Feed juice only from a sippy cup, not a bottle.*

- *Introduce vegetables before fruit.*

- *Don't put the baby in front of the television.*

- *Take your infant out regularly from the get-go. Later, when he or she is mobile, encourage outdoor play in a supervised environment. Both activities will foster enjoyment in being outside.*

expected weight for a year-old baby. Every time Suzy so much as whimpers, mom plugs a bottle in her mouth. "How much does she have at a time?" I may ask the parent. "Oh, she eats really well," is the reply, "5 or 6 ounces each time." This would represent a good intake at four- or six-hour intervals, but these babies are consuming this much perhaps every two or three hours. When I offer the very obvious suggestion that perhaps if Suzy didn't eat so much and so often, she might not be as fat, there is disbelief. I see the excess weight, the nurses see it, but more often than not the parents just don't see it! Until they do, the infant will almost certainly go on to become an overweight child, and later an overweight adolescent, and most likely an overweight adult—perhaps with a shorter life span.

The old idea that a roly-poly baby is a healthy baby has now been challenged. There's also evidence that once fat cells develop they'll never disappear. While a breast-fed baby will stop nursing when he's full, mothers who bottle-feed may encourage their infants to polish off the bottle, whether or not Junior is full. Habits such as offering a bottle whenever a baby cries or putting her to bed with a bottle may foster an association between food, particularly sweet food, and solace. Giving even diluted apple juice may cause baby to develop a sweet tooth before she even has teeth. On the other hand, don't cut back on a baby's calories and fat too soon. The American Academy of Pediatrics recommends that after babies are weaned from the breast, they continue to drink whole milk until they're at least 2 years old.

Too Sweet for Comfort

Take a look at the list of ingredients and the Nutritional Facts panel on baby and toddler foods to understand one reason most children eat too many sweets. We humans are programmed to find sweet foods appealing, but introducing puréed fruit as the first food after cereal gets infants hooked on sugar from the get-go. Nor does it stop there. Why is there added sugar in the form of pear juice concentrate in a major manufacturer's chicken noodle baby food dinner? Sugar converts quickly to calories, but offers no other nutritional benefit. Larger question: why are we in such a hurry to spoon solid food into a baby when breast milk or formula is fine until they're at least four months old?

The Decline of Vegetables

All too many of our children have decided that they hate vegetables or that the only vegetables worth eating are French fries and ketchup. Vegetables are valuable sources of hundreds of vitamins, minerals, antioxidants, and other nutrients, as well as heart-healthy fiber. How did this happen? One needs only look at the suggestions of some of the old-time pediatricians to understand how to approach vegetables. Typically, babies took only breast milk or formula for the first four months or so before cereal was introduced. At about six months, fruits and vegetables were introduced.

I remember working with an elderly pediatrician who would always tell mothers to introduce vegetables first. Once you introduce fruit and babies get used to its relative sweetness, you'll have a hard time getting them to eat vegetables. Even the marketers for V8® juice understand this fact. They try their hardest to get Americans to consume more vegetables in the form of their famous juice. Recently the company came out with a formulation that essentially "hides" the vegetables by combining them with fruits. Advertisements even say that the best way to get your kid to eat vegetables is to make them think they're eating fruit.

Tips on Raising Toddlers

Once your child is between 2 and 3, continue to see that he or she gets outdoors in a safe environment and joins in family meals. In addition:

- *Provide healthy snacks without excess calories.*

- *Don't offer junk food.*

- *Avoid or limit snacking in front of the television, video games, etc.*

- *Restrict television and other electronics to one or two hours a day.*

- *Set mealtimes yourself.*

- *Provide choices at meals.*

- *Let your child determine fullness.*

- *Limit intake of juice and any other sweetened beverages to 4–6 ounces a day.*

Vegetables are absolutely essential to good health. We have a better chance of getting kids in the habit of eating and perhaps even enjoying them if we introduce vegetables early in life. So let's enjoy them because they're vegetables, not simply because they're substituting for something else. The best way to do that is to find out your child's favorite veggies and then come up with delicious ways to serve them. Some kids just like their veggies raw, which is certainly simple enough to handle. You'll find the *allstride.com* meal plans are full of kid-friendly ways to serve veggies.

In the next chapter, we'll get into the role played by sweetened food in the epidemic of childhood obesity. We'll look at the increasing use of the now-controversial sweetener high-fructose corn syrup, as well as a dangerous form of fat to avoid at all costs. When you finish reading the chapter, I suspect you'll be shocked at how much sugar your children are routinely sipping and eating each day—from their breakfast cereals and toaster tarts washed down with fruit drinks to the late-night bags of chips and cans of cola you may find under their beds. But you'll also learn how to steer clear of such unhealthy foods.

Connor Got a Little Help from Grandma

Success Story

At 14, Connor lost 20 pounds, thanks to some coaching from Jeffrie, his grandmother. Daily calls to check on his progress and the occasional delivery of homemade dishes, plus a big dose of love and concern, helped her grandson slim down in just two months. He also trimmed 3 minutes off his time to run a mile, and his self-confidence has soared. A proud grandparent and grateful grandson look back on their shared experience.

Ricki: Jeffrie, I understand you got the ball rolling.
Jeffrie: I kept seeing Connor getting bigger and bigger, and I knew he wasn't happy. Sometimes I would stay over with him, and I remember one night he said his prayers and then he said, "And please make

me skinny." It was so hard to hear. Yet several years went by before we reached the point of doing something about it.

Ricki: What did his pediatrician say?

Jeffrie: He kind of pooh-poohed the questions my daughter would ask. He'd say, "Well, you know, he's a little borderline." Yeah, right. Then he added, "But I don't think you need to worry because he'll have a growth spurt." There was no recommended plan, just, "We'll watch it." For five years we watched it.

Ricki: So you decided to take things into your own hands. How did you approach Connor?

Jeffrie: I found the program online, showed it to him, and asked whether it was something he'd be interested in doing. He was, so I said, "When do you want to start?" He said, "Tomorrow!" He was committed immediately.

Connor: All the kids were calling me mean names, so I wanted to do this program even more. I don't think they realized what pain they were causing. It's hard to think about now. I was just glad that I had somebody to help guide me through it.

Ricki: Jeffrie, how did you actually coach Connor since you don't live together?

Jeffrie: I helped him get started with an understanding of how to figure out serving sizes. We printed out everything from online. We'd talk on the phone and see each other periodically. I would look up recipes and make them for him. Then he'd put them in the freezer so he'd have something in case he needed it. Once he learned how to do the program, he just took off on his own.

Ricki: And he began to see results?

Connor: I lost about 2 pounds in the first three days. It was really significant.

Jeffrie: All of a sudden the weight started dropping off of him. His face reappeared and it was just so great. I kept saying, "Connor, you look so wonderful. Are you sick of me saying that?" And he said, "No."

Connor: You still say it!

Jeffrie: I still say it. The highlight of my life, next to the birth of my children and the birth of my two grandchildren, was seeing Connor lose weight.

Ricki: Connor, how about you? Do you feel different now?

Connor: I felt more outgoing as I lost more weight, and it made me like a happier, more self-confident person. I think it helped me a lot making friends.

Jeffrie: This week Connor had a project at school dealing with events that had had a personal impact on students, and he stood in front of his classmates with pictures of himself before and what he looks like now and talked about the changes he's experienced. So he really turned it around.

Ricki: What did your doctor say?

Connor: When I went in for my checkup a year later I'd lost 20 pounds. They didn't even recognize me and were like really surprised. It was a good feeling.

Ricki: How did you feel about your grandmother getting involved?

Connor: I'm just thankful for what she did for me. My stepdad's usually out of town and he's the main cook. My grandmother called me every day. I told her how much I lost. I never gained at all, because I just stayed with the program. I don't even know what to say because I'm so glad.

Jeffrie: I'll always be there. I'll always be there.

Connor: You changed my life.

Jeffrie: Parents don't always have time to do everything, and I'm just glad that I was there. I would encourage anyone who sees a child needing help in any way, whether it's about weight or otherwise, to step in.

Ricki: That's so true. Most families are pretty much on their own nowadays, and Connor is very lucky to have you nearby and so committed. So, Connor, what other changes did you see beyond trimming 20 pounds?

Connor: I play baseball and now I can keep up with the other kids better. Before I did the program I ran a mile at 10 minutes and 30 seconds, and after being on the program, I ran it at 7 minutes and 30 seconds.

Ricki: Wow! That's a huge difference! What was the biggest change in your eating habits?

Connor: The main thing was I didn't eat school lunches anymore. That was really affecting me. I started packing my lunch with sandwiches and fruit. I also found out that I could eat a whole lot of certain foods that filled me up.

Ricki: What are some of your favorite foods you got to eat?

Connor: It's hard to believe, but pizza, quesadillas, turkey sandwich, chicken and rice casserole, and a breakfast burrito.

Ricki: With yummy foods like that, were you ever tempted to go off your meal plan?

Connor: Every time that I thought about eating something that was off the meal plan, I always thought, "Would I rather eat this for 5 or 10 seconds or would I rather be happier for the rest of my life?"

Ricki: And the answer was always, "No." Right?

Connor: Right.

Ricki: Jeffrie, how do you feel after the fact?

Jeffrie: I'm grateful to the point of tears every single day. It's been a year and a half and I still feel that way.

Too Small to Be Big

Chapter 5

What Kids Eat: A Recipe for Excess Weight

Remember how the wicked witch fattened up Hansel and Gretel? First she offered them foods that they couldn't resist—her house was made of gingerbread and candies—filling them with sugar. She prodded them to eat more even when they weren't hungry. And she kept them in a cage where they couldn't get any exercise. Her method worked so well that Hansel had to make the sight-challenged hag think she was feeling his arm when he was only extending a finger.

Of course, real-life parents don't lock their kids in cages, but for perfectly understandable reasons, many parents do confine their kids to the house when they're not home. In general, today's youngsters aren't running, jumping, and generally roughhousing nearly enough. And all too often, they're eating products that are a poor excuse for real food. It's no wonder that millions of children are as supersized as the soft drinks they consume.

That Was Then, This Is Now

Many researchers who have studied the childhood obesity epidemic maintain that it has blossomed over the last 20 or 30 years. I would say that it had its roots in the second half of the 20th century, with the post-World War II baby boomers. In short, my generation was given the tools for making our children fat, and we were highly successful at implementing them. During my childhood, snack foods became ubiquitous and part of most people's everyday diet. When my parents were kids, snack food was unheard of. Of course, there was fruit and maybe you got some fresh-baked cookies or a bowl of homemade popcorn after school, but that was it. I remember my father, who is now in his eighties, telling me how he would sneak down to the tavern on the corner to steal pretzels off the bar. That's what a novelty snack foods were in those days. Now I dare say that nearly every household in America has a cupboard filled with pretzels, chips, and cookies.

The Food Revolution

The pace of change has accelerated rapidly since I was a child, for good and bad. There was less choice than there is today, particularly in terms of produce. Families that lived on farms or had a backyard garden may have eaten as their parents and grandparents did, including fresh or home-canned vegetables and fruits. And some mothers still regularly baked cookies, apple pies, and other treats. But in many a household, salad was synonymous with iceberg lettuce, with the occasional head of romaine making an appearance. It may not have been the heyday of whole foods, but processed, prepared, heat-and-serve foods hadn't yet come to dominate the market. Margarine appeared in 1955—at least the kind colored to mimic butter—so artificial trans fats (hydrogenated and partially hydrogenated oils) were not yet in wide use. However, many people baked with Crisco® because it was supposedly healthier than butter. And it would be almost 20 years before high-fructose corn syrup (HFCS) burst onto the scene.

The Arrival of Junk and Convenience Food

Which product deserves the dubious distinction of being the first junk food? My vote is for Twinkies®, which appeared in 1930. Tang® famously circled the Earth with the first American astronaut, John Glenn, in 1962. (Another significant historical moment was the invention of Pringles®, but that wasn't until 1970.) By the 1960s, junk food was well ensconced, reflecting an overall change in the nation's eating habits. And as home baking became less common, many a freezer harbored Sara Lee® frozen cakes.

Next came the addition of "convenience" foods. The first microwave ovens appeared in home kitchens in 1967. However, the precursor of the microwave dinner, the Swanson TV dinner, appeared more than a decade earlier in 1954. (Remember Ricki telling us that her nightly meal was one or two Hungry-Man® TV dinners?) This invention brought together two emerging trends that have contributed to the epidemic of obesity: time-strapped families turning to packaged foods and the national pastime of watching television. More than 10 million of these aluminum trays with dividers filled with fried chicken or Salisbury steak, sweet corn or carrots, and mashed potatoes were sold during the first year of national distribution. The seeds of change in our current dietary habits had sprouted, although their far-reaching implications were not yet understood.

One the biggest changes in food today is that it is designed—and I use that word consciously—for pleasure and convenience, which often take precedence over nutrition. When you go to the supermarket, most of what you see is packaged and preserved in plastic. All too often, it's filled with salt, sugar or

HFCS, and white flour to make it taste better; preservatives to give it a longer shelf life; and dyes to make it look more appealing. When kids take products like Lunchables® instead of lunch to school, it's a clear indication that there's something wrong with the way we eat. (See "Lunchables Don't Make the Grade," below.)

In the last 50 years, the snack-food industry has been the single fastest growing component of the food economy. By definition, a "snack" is a food that comes between meals. Therefore, it's not essential for nutrition. But there are snacks and there are snacks; and sugary, doughy, fat-filled snacks don't build slim, healthy bodies. We're spending a huge proportion of our food budget on items that don't contribute to our children's nutrition.

Lunchables Don't Make the Grade

The Lunchables® concept is brilliant. Appeal to time-starved parents with a package that includes everything a kid supposedly needs for a healthful lunch, from beverage to sandwich to dessert. Problem is, a Lunchable meal isn't healthful, not by any stretch of the imagination. Nor is it necessary. Once you have the right ingredients in your fridge and cupboards, you can put together a truly healthful lunch in just a few minutes. Better yet, your child can do it. And let's not even get into the price tacked on for the convenience.

So what's in a typical Lunchable meal? Along with a turkey and Cheddar cheese sub is applesauce, a packet of cookies, bottled water, and Kool-Aid®. Although there's nary a fresh fruit or vegetable in sight, it all sounds innocuous, doesn't it? But what about the more than 100 ingredients listed on the package? Many of them are artificial colorings and flavors and preservatives, along with nitrates, which have been shown to cause cancer. Also present are high-fructose corn syrup and partially hydrogenated cottonseed oil (a trans fat), plus a staggeringly long list of chemicals. Of the 370 calories, 128 come from sugar! No growing body should have to suffer this "Frankenfood."

Fast Food Here, There, and Everywhere

It's not just the foods we're putting in our grocery carts that are making our kids plump. The superstitious believe that bad things come in threes, so let's add fast food to junk food and convenience food. There seems to be a fast-food restaurant, or several, on every corner. In most cases, we don't even have to get out of our car to order, pay for, pick up, and eat our food. Then we can hurry to the next drive-through for dessert or coffee. And how does this affect our kids? A 2004 study published in *Pediatrics* examined the effects of fast-food consumption on more than 6,000 American kids aged 4 to 19 and revealed that a horrifying 29 to 38 percent of them subsist primarily on fast food! It's no surprise that compared to children who didn't eat fast food, those who did consumed more calories, more total fat, more saturated fat, more total carbohydrates, and more sugary beverages. The few things they ate less often, unfortunately, were fiber, fruit, and nonstarchy vegetables.

According to the study's lead author, Shanthy A. Bowman, Ph.D., of the USDA, the fast-food group also ate more food throughout the day because the tastes of these fatty, sugary, salty foods stimulate more eating. Moreover, because fast food is low in fiber (unlike whole foods), it doesn't produce a feeling of fullness, prompting the desire for more food later. Finally, the large portions typical of fast-food places also contribute to overeating. On average, kids who regularly eat fast food consumed 15 percent more calories than other kids. And here's the clincher: the study showed that a child who eats a lot of fast foods can gain an extra 6 pounds a year. Not surprisingly, Bowman believes that marketing fast food to kids should be limited. I couldn't agree more.

These results have been echoed in other studies, including one published in 2005 in the *Archives of Pediatric Adolescent Medicine*. This study looked at the diets of more than 2,300 girls over a period of up to 10 years. The girls were aged 9 or

10 at the beginning of the study and 19 at the end. Over all, they increased their use of fast food over the decade; and those who ate more fast food consumed an average of 187 more calories a day. They also took in more fat, saturated fat, carbohydrates, added sugar, and salt. The only thing they ate less of was dietary fiber. It's apparent that fast foods also often displace more healthful foods. The researchers concluded, "Dietary intake of fast food is a determinant of diet quality in adolescent girls. Efforts to reduce fast-food consumption may be useful in improving diet and risk for future cardiovascular disease."

In a study published in late 2010, the Yale Rudd Center for Food Policy and Obesity (see Resources on page 256), indicted fast-food restaurants for aggressively marketing their products to young people, among other vulnerable groups, and failing to offer enough healthy options. According to the study, one-third of American children and teens eat fast food every day; and fast food accounts for more than 16 percent of their daily caloric intake. Here are some other distressing findings from this study that will likely give you pause:

- Preschoolers saw an average of 2.8 television ads a day for fast food; older kids viewed 3.5; and teens 4.7. This doesn't include the online and radio ads.
- In 2009, the fast-food industry spent $4.2 billion on advertising.
- Forty percent of parents report that their children ask to go to McDonald's at least once a week.
- Fifteen percent of preschoolers ask to go every day.
- Eighty-four percent of parents take their kids to a fast-food restaurant at least once a week.
- Sixty-six percent reported going to McDonald's in the past week.

Separate and Unequal

If growing up in the 'burbs manifests itself in latchkey kids who chill in front of the television and the computer screen while eating junk food, then inner-city children (who do the same) face additional situations that influence their weight and health. Visit almost any disadvantaged neighborhood and you'll notice the absence of the grocery store chains full of fresh fruits and vegetables, fresh meats and fish, and other whole foods. Instead, convenience-type stores that service poor neighborhoods concentrate their sales on snack foods and soda, not to mention cigarettes and beer.

Such food may be cheap, tasty, and desirable, but it's devoid of good nutrition. It's no coincidence that African-American and Latino children are far more likely to be overweight than their white and Asian peers who live in more affluent suburban and urban areas. The inner-city kids simply don't have the availability of healthy alternatives to processed foods and junk-food snacks. A recent article in the *New York Times* suggested that the 1946 debut of 7-Eleven convenience stores—now the largest chain store, with roughly 38,000 outlets worldwide—has played a major role in increasing the consumption of fast food and junk foods.

Steer Clear of Trans Fats

Manufactured trans fats, which appear on food labels as "partially hydrogenated oils" or "hydrogenated oils," are among the most damaging chemicals present in our foods. Trans fats consumption has been linked to heart disease because it elevates LDL ("bad") cholesterol and lowers HDL ("good") cholesterol. Trans fats probably play a role in obesity as well, although the direct link is disputed. Coronary heart disease in children is on the rise, particularly in those who are overweight. One of the culprits may well be the explosive growth of snack foods and the presence of trans fats in many of them.

Blasting liquid vegetable oils with hydrogen atoms changes their chemical structure, making them solid at room temperature. This biochemical process reduces manufacturing costs and adds shelf life, a desirable trait for snack foods that are designed to sit on grocery store shelves and in home pantries for extended periods of time. Trans fats were once almost omnipresent in many commercial baked goods and most snack foods. Fortunately, starting in 2006, the U.S. Department of Agriculture (USDA) mandated that food labels note the amount of trans fats in packaged foods, which has significantly reduced—but not eliminated—their use.

Researchers have also linked trans fats to Alzheimer's disease, cancer, liver disease, and infertility. Among the many dangers of promoting snack foods as a significant proportion of our diet is their trans fat content, albeit generally lower than it was several years ago. Still, the safest amount of trans fats to consume is none. (To learn how to detect trans fats in processed food, see "When None Means Some," below.)

When None Means Some

Since 2006 manufacturers have had to list trans fat content on labels. So does that mean that these manufactured hydrogenated and partially hydrogenated oils have disappeared from our foods? Not quite. A loophole allows manufacturers to claim "no trans fats" when a standard serving contains less than 0.5 grams.

So they remain in many foods, although in smaller amounts. However, eat a whole bag of most potato chips or a significant amount of many foods and you'll definitely consume some trans fats. You'll know that a food contains these dangerous substances if the ingredients list cites partially hydrogenated or hydrogenated oil, even if the Nutrition Facts number of grams of trans fat per serving is listed as zero. Once again, it pays to read foods labels carefully. (See "Required Reading: Food Labels," on page 175.)

Portion Distortion

Fast food and monster portions go hand in hand. It's not just the type of food that we're eating that's making us all plumper. That corn muffin is bigger than it once was, as is that slice of pizza and the amount of ice cream in that cone. The 5-ounce box of popcorn once typically sold at the movies contained 270 calories; today a huge tub of that addictive snack can total

630 calories. (For more of these disturbing comparisons, see "You've Come a Large Way, Baby," below.) Enormous portions are typical fare in the family restaurants like T.G.I. Friday's or Applebee's, some of which offer "all-you-can-eat" meals. Of course, your child doesn't have to eat the whole thing, but studies show that when you put more food on a kid's plate, more gets eaten. Duh!

You've Come a Large Way, Baby

Look what's happened to portions in the last 20 years:

- *Once a bagel was typically 3 inches in diameter with 140 calories; today's 6-inch bagel packs about 350 calories.*

- *A typical cheeseburger has ballooned from 333 to 590 calories. A soda used to be 6.5 ounces with 85 calories; today a 28-ounce soda contains 250 calories.*

- *A half-cup portion of pasta with spaghetti sauce and three small meatballs once totaled 500 calories. Today, it's likely to include two cups of pasta, sauce, and three large meatballs, tallying 1,025 calories.*

- *A 2.4-ounce serving of French fries contains about 210 calories; today's typical portion is a hefty 6.9 ounces, packing 610 calories.*

- *The Double Gulp® sold at 7-Eleven, containing 64 ounces, logs in at 744 calories, all from sugar!*

What ever happened to the advice to never eat anything bigger than your head?

Hooked on Sugar

In Chapter 3, I discussed how infants get hooked on sugar. So is it surprising that "sugar babies" grow into "sugar kids" who will grow up to be sugar daddies and sugar mommies? Like more than two-thirds of adults, our children are consuming more calories than their bodies need for energy. Many of those calories come from sugar in one form or another, all of which lack any nutritional value other than calories. The sweet stuff is in sodas, cereals, baked goods, snack foods, barbecue sauce, and even things you don't regard as sweet, like breads, salad dressings, ketchup, mayonnaise, pickles, and frozen pizza dough. Start scanning the list of ingredients on packaged foods and you'll be amazed at how often sugar turns up.

Sugar and Weight Control

We all know that eating sugar can cause dental cavities, but fewer people understand its role in weight control and over-all health. It's not just a matter of calories, although they're important too. First of all, repeat after me, "It's not just fat that makes kids (or anyone) fat." When you eat food filled with sugar, it turns quickly to blood sugar (glucose). What your body doesn't use immediately for energy must be stored, as it's dangerous for too much glucose to remain in your blood. Without getting too detailed, some of that glucose winds up stored as glycogen in your liver and muscles, where it is read-ily available when your body needs a boost of energy. Guess how the rest is stored as? As fat! That's right, your liver transforms excess glucose to fat and stores it on your tummy, rear end, thighs, or wherever. Just to be clear, what starts out as sugar winds up as fat.

Sugars occur naturally in dairy products, fruits, and vegeta-bles, as well as in other carbohydrate foods. For example, the sugar in dairy products is called lactose. Humans have always consumed natural sugars in these foods. In the olden days, sugar in the form of honey, maple syrup, or sometimes cane sugar was a rare treat. Today, sugar is added to an astound-ing array of foods. (See "What Are Added Sugars?" opposite.) What the food industry has done (and we have been complicit because we love the sweet taste) is to convince us that we can-not live without sugar. And perhaps the biggest impact has been in the increased consumption of sweetened drinks— soda, vitamin water, energy drinks, sweetened ice tea, and fruit drinks—all of which our kids happily lap up.

There's sugar and then there's sugar. Sugars in whole foods such as milk and fruit are integral to the food. But added sugars, as the name implies, boost the level in other foods. Some added sugars are natural, such as honey added to mustard or breakfast cereal. Others are manufactured sugars like the high-fructose corn syrup in most sodas. But don't assume just because they're natural, certain added sugars are OK. According to the USDA, each person in the United States consumes an average of 154 pounds of added sugars per year, up from an average of 123 pounds in the early 1970s. This translates into nearly 750 calories a day! I'm willing to bet that some kids consume even more.

To figure out whether there's added sugar in a packaged food, first check the Nutritional Facts panel. There you'll see the number of grams of carbohydrates and specifically how many grams of sugar (which is a carbohydrate). Then look at the list of ingredients, which are listed in descending order of volume. To figure out if a sugar is added or integral, check out its name. If you see fructose instead of fruit, for example, even though the sugar has a natural source, you'll know it's an added ingredient. Many ingredients ending in "ose" are also sugars, although exceptions include sucralose (a noncaloric sweetener) and cellulose.

Soda Is the New Water

When soda pop first hit the market, it was sweetened with sugar. Today, high-fructose corn syrup (HFCS) has replaced sugar from sugar cane, which is a kind of grass, as the predominant sweetener in soda (and many other foods). In a study published in 2004 in the *American Journal of Clinical Nutrition,* public health officials linked the doubling of obesity in the last 40 years to the growing use of HFCS to sweeten soft drinks. In 1970 each American consumed about 8 ounces of HFCS a year. By 1997, the amount was a staggering 62.5 pounds! Meanwhile, from 1975 to 2000, average annual soda consumption doubled to an astounding 50 gallons a year! In case you're wondering, an average 12-ounce can of nondiet soda contains at least 12 teaspoons, or one-quarter cup, of HFCS. (Soft drink manufacturers offer numerous alternatives. In addition to conventional "diet" sodas sweetened with saccharin and aspartame, many are now sweetened with one of two other non-nutritive, noncaloric sweeteners: sucralose and stevia.)

We can rail at manufacturers, the advertising industry, and the fast-food restaurants that push huge portions of sodas at low prices, but we parents buy this "liquid sugar" and drink it ourselves. I leave it to each family to decide how to minimize intake. There's no question that being too restrictive with children can backfire. You may find that what works best for family harmony is to not allow soda in the house, but let kids have it if they wish when you're eating out. Water is always a better alternative, and I'm not talking about fancy-schmancy bottled water, or fruit-flavored water, or vitamin water, or anything else. Just plain old tap water is all you need. (We'll talk more about beverages in Chapter 12.)

Sweeter Than Sugar

Why does HFCS now dominate the market? Part of the reason is that gram for gram, it's much sweeter than traditional sugar. (And because it is sweeter, it's higher in calories.) It's also considerably cheaper than sugar, helping soda manufacturers' bottom line. To think of the difference between sugar from a grass and sugar from corn, think of how a corn-fed steer has far more fat on it than a grass-fed animal. For that very reason, beef cattle are fed corn in feedlots to fatten them up before they're taken to market. Keep that image in your mind every time you or your child consumes a can or bottle of a sweetened soft drink. High-fructose corn syrup has a more severe impact on blood sugar than sugar does, which in turn triggers the release of more insulin. Insulin is a fat-producing hormone. Quite simply, the more soda you and your kids drink, the more fat is being packed into your fat cells.

As a member of the American Academy of Pediatrics, I recently received a huge, glossy brochure with a personalized letter and patient handouts from the corn industry. The mailing was in response to recent research that implicated HFCS (and even corn itself) as a major culprit in the obesity epidemic. Amazingly, the whole point of the literature was to say that HFCS, as well as any other type of sweetener refined from corn, is as safe as sugar from any other source. The letter was even signed by physicians. The corn lobby has missed the point. Regardless of its source, sugar is aging our kids before their time. For example, high sugar intake can lead to out-of-control blood sugar, which is the first sign that diabetes may be in a child's future. Over the years, glucose and its metabolites accumulate in cells that can't handle it well, including the eyes, kidneys, and tiny blood vessels that affect the heart. Eventually every organ system can be damaged, likely leading to an early death.

Snack Time, All the Time

If families are spending less time together at meals, kids and adults alike are spending lots more time snacking. It's not that snacking itself is inherently a problem. Healthy snacks are a key component of the AllStride program, and two or three small snacks a day can help control hunger. However, our culture's consumption of chips, crackers, popcorn, and pretzels tripled from the 1970s to the 1990s. All these snacks are high in calories and many are also high in fat. Some even contain trans fats.

The snack phenomenon is one of biggest societal changes in the last 50 years, paralleling the rise of obesity in general and of kids' obesity in particular—just as the consumption of soda has done. And like soda, the best bet is simply not to have these foods in the house or to cut back significantly. In Part II, we'll go into detail about all the great snacks kids can enjoy on AllStride without threatening their health.

Marketing Food and Beverages

The advertising for soda is difficult to ignore: it's powerful, convincing, and effective. You and your youngsters are subjected to the messages hundreds of times a day. We can barely walk into a ballpark or multiplex or pass a billboard without being subliminally or directly told to stop as soon as possible and get ourselves a soda. But soda advertising is only the tip of the iceberg. There aren't many people on the planet who don't like chocolate, and now we know that dark chocolate is loaded with antioxidants. (Most chocolate is also full of sugar.) But chocolate for breakfast? Afraid so. Dozens of breakfast cereals marketed to children are full of the stuff! And it's there because we buy it. That in a nutshell describes the problem with the food and beverage industries: they're in business to make money, not to promote good nutrition. To make money, they have to advertise, and we consumers eat it all up, if you'll excuse the pun.

The good news is that watchdog groups are beginning to force some results. The American Heart Association's "Healthy Choices" program, which allowed foods of dubious nature to display that honorific, has been shelved. That's the program that allowed a Cheerios® package to display a heart-healthy symbol. Manufacturers have been under significant pressure to make their advertising more responsible. For example, only cereals with sugar content of less than 12 grams per serving can appear in commercials on children's TV shows. This is still an incredible amount of sugar, but limits have to be set somewhere. Not surprisingly, there is now a bumper crop of cereals out there with 11 grams of sugar per serving! (See page 174.) The food industry knows that we, and especially our kids, are as good as addicted to sugar, and they're going to do everything they can to deliver as much sugar to us as possible—and still be able to advertise these products.

However, neither the food and beverage industry nor legislation regarding the contents and labeling of products or how they are marketed to children (or adults) will save us from unhealthy ingredients. We drive the market and we are responsible for what we feed our kids. Fortunately, there are plenty of other choices. Whether you opt for organic foods is a personal and financial choice, although even Walmart now sells organic produce and other foods. Or you may simply opt to avoid conventional foods with added sugar and trans fats. (And by the way, many organic products are full of added sugars—although they aren't HFCS or other manufactured sugars.) If you and enough other people stop buying unhealthful foods, believe me, the industry will stop producing them. Most importantly, we must become more educated about nutrition as a culture. And AllStride is a great way to start.

In the following chapters, we'll continue to discuss how our children eat, and we'll offer concrete suggestions for how to improve their diet for good health and weight control. We'll also look at the flip side of the coin, the importance of physical activity. By the time you finish this book, you'll know how to find the tools you need to help your kids achieve total wellness. Ricki and I also believe that you'll have a better understanding of how, as a society, we can change our collective focus, realign our priorities, and look honestly at ourselves. Together, we can craft an all-encompassing strategy to help all overweight kids, once and for all. I hope you'll join us in this crusade. But first, let's look at a few more factors that have, in effect, robbed so many of our children of their childhood.

Megan Is No Longer Just the "Fat Girl"

Success Story

Before 12-year-old Megan lost 24 pounds, she could barely make it around the track at school. But now she's winning ribbons, and inspiring her friends and family—including her brother, Westin. She's also bursting with energy and self-esteem. Once Megan realized she had to do something about her weight, there was no stopping her.

Ricki: Megan, why did you decide to make some changes in your life?
Megan: I just didn't feel comfortable with myself. In the morning I'd put something on and look from every angle, but it was impossible to find something that made me look good. My self-esteem was zero. When I'd go to school, I'd constantly compare myself to the other girls and think, "I wish I had that body or those clothes or I looked good

in that." I felt like I couldn't make any friends. That's when I realized I needed to do something.

Ricki: Believe me, I know what it's like to be in such pain, and I'm so sorry you were feeling that way. Was it all in your head or were the other kids teasing you?

Megan: I got a lot of "fatty" or they'd be like, "Who's Megan? Oh, that fat girl." That was the worst thing. After all those years of having no confidence, I just looked at myself in the mirror and said, "This has to stop. I need to do something, to take charge." And so I went on the computer, I typed in "diets for children," and found the program.

Ricki: You definitely took charge, and it must have felt great. What happened when you told you mom you wanted to do this?

Megan: My mom was on the phone and she said, "Not now, Megan." So I got a piece of paper and wrote, "Mom, please get this for me, please, please, please." And I stuck the note on the computer and she saw it when she checked her e-mail. She said, "I'll talk to your dad about it."

Ricki: What did you think of your meal plan?

Megan: I was so excited. It was "real" food and it kept me full and it was for my age level. Because you get to pick the foods that you like, that makes it easier to stick with it and lose weight. It makes the whole experience joyful.

Ricki: Did you see results quickly?

Megan: I remember losing 2 pounds the first week and going to school and asking my friends, "Did you notice? Could you tell?" And they'd be like, "You look great, Megan." After three months, I'd lost 24 pounds.

Ricki: So you feel better about your appearance now?

Megan: I waited until I lost a certain amount of weight to get new stuff. When I went to school wearing them, my friend, he's like, "Megan?" I'm like, "Yeah?" And he's like, "You look stunning." I was like, "Really?" I just remember the warmth in my heart from hearing that.

Ricki: What else is different in your life now?

Megan: I used to dread PE. I'd ask my mom to write me notes so I didn't have to run. I remember being a seventh-grader with the whole class watching while I finished running a lap. It was just terrible. I'd always get tired halfway through and have to walk. And if anyone walked, the whole class had to run again. Now I love to run. In eighth grade, I joined the track team. I even got some ribbons in competitions with other schools. And I'm like, "Yes, I get to run today."

Ricki: Are you treated differently at school now?

Megan: When you're not heavy anymore, everyone seems to be your friend. It's sad that they judge you on your appearance. I now have more friends, and there's more than just "the fat kid" attached to my name. Before I didn't have the confidence to talk back to other kids, like saying, "That's not fair" or whatever. Now when I see that happening to another kid, I tell the kid who is teasing her, "Don't judge people" and "How would you feel?" They usually just walk away. But at least I stood up for the other kid.

Ricki: So you've become a role model.

Megan: Westin told me, "I want to be like you and lose weight like you." I helped him through it. He lost like 3 pounds in the first week, and his confidence level went way up. A lot of my friends want to start the program now. Like they say, "You inspire me." That's just the best feeling.

Ricki: Now that you're slim, self-confident, a role model, and an athlete, what would you tell other kids?

Megan: I would tell them that anything that you feel is impossible, you have to make it possible. No one's just going to wave a magic wand over you to make you thin. You have to be committed and follow the meal plans. You have to be ready because nobody can make you do it. It has to be a personal choice. But once you make that choice, it's the easiest thing.

Too Small to Be Big

Chapter 6

The Perfect Storm

We now know much more about childhood obesity than we did a bit more than a decade ago, when the topic first surfaced on the national scene. The surgeon general has referred to it as one of the most important public health issues of this generation. Experts have been quoted as saying that this could be the first time in recorded human history in which children won't live as long as their parents. Susan Dentzer, the editor in chief of *Health Affairs,* which recently devoted an entire issue to the topic of childhood obesity, wrote in her editorial, "America is guilty of child abuse." She was referring to the fact that we have allowed one in three children to be overweight or obese, including "kids entering Head Start programs at the ripe old age of four."

Officials have scrutinized school lunches; some schools have removed soda machines; and trans fats must now be quantified on food labels and have been banned in restaurants in certain cities. Yet look around you. Are there fewer overweight youngsters? Hardly. The epidemic of overweight children not only threatens our health as a nation, it also puts our economy, our vitality and even our national defense in jeopardy. If we don't recognize this crisis for the danger that it presents, it could do more to bring our country down than the terrorist threat, the struggling economy, and the deteriorating environment combined.

I deeply believe in the evolution of all things, including the science and technology that have impacted the way we eat, work, play, and get around. However, I do worry about the acceptance of all advances as "good" simply because they are "new." And I think that most people would agree that the hard evidence showing that about 15 percent of our children are clinically obese and almost 40 percent are garden-variety overweight means that we've gone off the track somewhere. Over the last 50 years, three interrelated happenings—the explosive growth of the suburbs, the way we eat, and our activity patterns—have directly impacted our health and weight.

Time Travel

Let's take a little trip back to the late 1950s and early 1960s. Perhaps by seeing where we've come from, we can understand a little bit better why we are where we are today—and formulate better solutions. Most of you are probably too young to have any personal recollection of that era, but I'm sure you've heard stories, and television and movies have documented the period fairly well. Sitcoms can reveal a lot about the pop culture of the time and give us a glimpse of the way life was back in the "dark ages," when I was a small child.

Of course, the TV shows of that era idealized much of what life was like, and happy, cohesive families were part of that ideal. No mythical family was more "real" to my generation than the Cleavers of "Leave It to Beaver," which debuted in 1957 and ran through 1963. These were relatively prosperous years in the United States, and everybody was having babies. Madison Avenue had just realized that children were an untapped market for their clients' products. Television was in its black-and-white infancy—well, perhaps its toddlerhood—but certainly not the force it is today. Three networks dominated the airwaves, so a significant percentage of the viewing public might be watching the same show on any given night.

The Era of Stay-at-Home Moms
Even though she rarely left the house, June Cleaver was always decked out in a dress, heels, full makeup, and jewelry. The women's movement had not yet awakened. Betty Friedan's groundbreaking book, *The Feminine Mystique,* would not be published until 1963. It was June's job to make sure the house and laundry were clean and that Beaver, his brother, Wally, and their father, Ward, sat down to a nice home-cooked meal in the dining room every evening. The kids never took seconds without first asking; before agreeing, June would survey their plates to see if they'd had the proper amount of each food.

Mothers of that era usually learned the basics of nutrition from their mothers or in home-economics classes. Back then, girls were required to take home economics, while the boys took shop. (In some enlightened school systems, a one-semester swap enabled boys to learn to cook and girls to try their hands at woodworking.) Today, most young people are sorely lacking in such practical skills. Is it any wonder then that many people don't have even a rudimentary knowledge of basic nutrition— or how to make a grilled cheese sandwich and tomato soup, for that matter? Our kids often assume that these comfort foods turn up on the table only if they open a can or Tetra-pak or pop a package in the microwave oven.

The Pivotal Sixties
Let's continue our sociological study of the 1960s. As kindergarteners in 1960, a friend and I walked the three-quarters of a mile to school and back each day. Now I would no more send two 5-year-olds out on a city street than I would let them play with a loaded gun! In fact, child protective services would probably turn me in to the authorities if I did. Like the kids in my neighborhood, the Cleaver boys played outside after school

in mostly unsupervised, imaginative, active ways. Neighborhoods were safe and well lighted. Everyone knew their neighbors and watched out for one another's kids. There were no websites that identified sex offenders in the neighborhood. After dinner, Beaver and Wally would go upstairs, where there were no television sets, computers, or video games to interfere with their homework. Nor did they take bags of chips and cans of soda with them, although the boys might sneak one of June's homemade cookies before bed.

Couch Potatoes and Web Surfers

Not only do our kids not play outside as much as children did in earlier eras, but many of them also spend hours connected to their favorite electronic devices. If he's not watching MTV, today's "couch potato" has a far wider array of sedentary diversions. Much has been made of the seductive powers of the Internet, computer games, Xbox, MP3s, cell phones with multiple apps, MySpace, and, of course, Facebook. With ear buds in their ears, a mouse at their fingertips, and their thumbs madly texting, kids spend much of their lives tuned out of the "real" world. Technology has kidnapped our kids.

Research confirms that kids are less active than ever before and become less active with every passing year. The average 9-year-old American gets about 2 hours of physical activity a day at school and home, while the typical 15-year-old gets much less than an hour. In an era of reduced school budgets, curtailed physical-education programs, and elimination or shortening of outdoor recess, is it any wonder that our kids are putting on weight? If you don't believe me, consider this: kids aged 8 to 18 spend a staggering average of $7\frac{1}{2}$ hours a day plugged into one form or another of electronic media. That's right, $7\frac{1}{2}$ hours!

Changing Society, Changing Food

The fabric of society has frayed. We now drive everywhere and rarely rely on our feet for basic transportation. A suburban lifestyle means that dad and, increasingly, mom are spending most daylight hours working and commuting, while their latchkey kids are at home. When someone is minding the "store," she's likely to be a mother taking care of another family's kids so she can stay home herself, or a teen-ager. Neither has any investment in seeing that your kids eat healthfully. And a teen-age sitter will likely let your kids eat the same "junk" she's eating. With no one around to keep watch, many parents won't allow their kids to play outside. Add to that the fact that reduced school funding has curtailed or eliminated phys-ed programs and athletics, only compounding the problem.

With these social changes come inevitable nutritional changes. We've discussed the growth of fast food, convenience foods, and junk foods. During the afternoon and often into the evening, older kids fend for themselves food-wise, often by heating up microwave meals. Even when mom is home or gets home early, she's less likely to cook from scratch than her grandmother or even her mother did. All too often, putting dinner on the table (or in front of the TV) means picking up takeout on the way home from work.

In general, kids have more say in what the family eats or simply make purchases themselves. And needless to say, left to their own devices, most kids aren't spending their allowances on apples and oranges. The family dinner is practically an extinct event. Instead, the habit of grazing on sugary beverages and starchy junk foods at home, in school, and at social and sports functions creates a situation in which people unlearn the body's hunger cues and eat instead out of habit or boredom. Not only does this approach to food impact quantity—as in too much food—it also usually affects quality. Without an eagle eye like June Cleaver sitting at the dining table, it's easy to lose track of what your kids are eating—or not eating.

The Changing American Family

The concept of what defines a family has changed a lot in recent decades. There are two huge entwined changes from when I was growing up in the 1960s: divorce and women in the workplace. According to the 2000 census, a single parent heads about 30 percent of all families. When we see the results of the 2010 census, I suspect that number will be even higher. Divorce is no longer something to be embarrassed about, and that's a good thing. But the simple fact is that parents can't be in two places at once. If you work to support your family you usually can't be at home during the day. That definitely affects family life, including what your kids eat and do after school, contributing to the increase in the number of kids who are inactive and/or overweight. Even when there are two parents in a household, both are often employed full time. Seventy-two percent of mothers of young children now work outside the home. Many of the social changes we've discussed are linked to this seismic shift.

Ironically, despite these changes, the responsibility for child rearing remains pretty much all on parents, whether they're living together or not. Many people are geographically distant from their close relatives—the very people who might once have lent a helping hand when kids got home from school before mom or dad. Or grandma may be close by and dearly love her "grands," but she's holding down a full-time job herself and simply isn't on call when a delicately balanced childcare situation totters.

A Hopeful Note

A recent study published in *The New England Journal of Medicine* reported a slight drop in obesity rates among 4,500 students in a study that followed sixth-graders for two years. Half were enrolled in a program that taught healthy behavior, increased the length and intensity of the physical-education program, and introduced healthier school lunches and snacks; the other 2,250 students didn't experience any such modifications.

When the study began, half of the kids in both groups were overweight, with 30 percent of them clinically obese. By eighth grade, the rate of overweight in both groups had dropped to 45 percent. Of students who had participated in the enrichment program, the obesity rate had dropped to 24.6 percent; interestingly, even those in the control group showed improvement: 26.6 percent were now obese. The difference between the two groups was not that large.

According to the lead author, Gary D. Foster, "Something is going on in the environment that is leading kids to become less overweight or obese. We need to find out what that is and do more of it." Dr. Foster, if you could get these results in school regardless of what is going on at home, we suggest you take a look at the AllStride program. The combination would be powerful!

This isn't the first study that seems to indicate that the epidemic has slowed its advance. Some of the things we are doing must actually be working. But is the problem solved? Absolutely not, and even these modest signs of leveling off provide little reassurance to the close to 40 percent of kids who are still considered either overweight or obese. And if you have an overweight child, you know how great the impact is on every aspect of his or her life.

You've heard the dire warnings and now have a good idea of the entwined reasons so many of our nation's kids are unhealthy, unhappy, and unfit. Now it's time for the good news. In Part II, Ricki will introduce the AllStride program—a unique lifestyle with the potential to eliminate childhood obesity in one generation.

Ricki, over to you.

Part 2

The AllStride Solution
for Total Wellness

By Ricki Lake

Chapter 7

AllStride Is About Food, Fun, Friends, and Family

Welcome to the first truly complete program that enables kids to resolve weight issues for good. But the moment I mention weight, I must immediately stress that AllStride takes the emphasis off weight and focuses instead on total wellness. Once again, that's why the AllStride program isn't a diet; instead, it's a lifestyle for the whole family. Total wellness includes not just how your child looks, but also how he feels physically, how well his body functions, and, of course, his self-image.

Every child needs a support network. And guess who's the most important champion of your child's cause? That's right: mom and dad. Also on the team, or at least cheering loudly from the bleachers, is the AllStride Community, which offers peer support on both a practical and an emotional level. Children also want and need the friendship of their contemporaries. That's why AllStride's three "Fs"—food, fun, and friends—are key to success on the program. And behind the scenes is always the fourth "F" of family, meaning you and any siblings, grandparents, aunts, uncles, and anyone else who has the child's best interests at heart.

AllStride Is Unique

Unlike the pediatric obesity programs or camps where kids slim down for the summer (but usually not for good), the AllStride program takes place within the family and encourages permanent lifestyle changes for everyone. Here are more key points that set AllStride apart from other programs:

- It's designed specifically for kids from age 4 and up—although people of any age can benefit.
- It's a permanent lifestyle, not a quickie weight-loss diet. Let me say that again. Diet, no way; lifestyle, yea!
- It's about choices—lots of choices—not denial.
- A team of experts in pediatrics, nutrition, fitness, and child psychology partner with you and your child.
- Kids get to choose their favorite foods to create easy-to-follow, nutritionist-approved meal plans.
- Learning how to determine portions is easy.
- Yummy snacks are integral to the program.
- There's no need to count calories, although kids do need to check the calories listed on packaged snacks.
- A wide array of fun physical activities allows kids to choose the ones that fit their interests and skills.
- Kids can easily understand the simple approach to nutrition and metabolism.
- The program provides kids with the knowledge and tools to track progress, take control, and build self-confidence.
- An online community links kids with similar issues.
- Likewise, a parent community encourages online communication.
- A toolbox full of aids includes more than 150 easy, family-friendly recipes.

Now let's look more closely at the four pillars that support the AllStride program.

PILLAR #1: Kid-Approved Food

At the core of the AllStride program is the premise that kids get to choose the food they eat—or at least weigh in on it. "Tell a youngster that she must eat this and must not eat that, and you could be setting her up for failure and/or a lifetime of food issues," explains nutritionist Robert Ferguson. He further recommends removing the words "must," "can't," "have to," and "got to" from all child-parent dialogue—they're counter-productive. He also advises that you not make any big, sudden changes. "Start with where you are, rather than imposing a whole new way of eating on your kids," he suggests. "Most weight-loss programs expect people to make a 180-degree change." No wonder most "diets" crash and burn when people return to their original way of eating.

The customized AllStride meal plans start with each child and don't require any drastic changes from previous eating habits. However, the number of times a kid eats certain foods in a week or the size of the portions will likely change. A kid of 12 or older will almost certainly want to input food preferences online. A very young child will definitely need help. Discuss with kids in the middle age range which approach they prefer, keeping in mind that the more they have their own say, the more they'll be invested in succeeding on the program.

It's simple to set up a personalized meal plan. First, you or your child indicates age, gender, height, and weight, as well as activity level. This generates a basic meal plan from a database of thousands of items, which can produce an almost limitless number of combinations. Each child or parent can then customize the meal plan by entering preferred foods (and omitting disliked ones). This also allows you or your child to deal with food allergies and the like. It's important for your child to be an equal participant in this process. "Initially it's all about kids eating whatever they want, but as they become more educated about food and how the body responds to it," explains Robert Ferguson, "they'll probably make some other changes."

Your child's meal plan tailors portions to age and size, and includes three snacks as well as meals. (Yes, eating snacks reduces the likelihood of overeating at the next meal, making them key to appetite control, as you'll soon understand.) Does this mean that your daughter or son has a different meal than the rest of the family? No way. You can opt for a family meal plan with meal and snack offerings suitable for parents and kids, although portion sizes will vary, as we explain in Chapter 8. Remember, this isn't a diet and it isn't about denial; it's a lifestyle that allows a child to eat his favorite foods.

Does that mean that the whole family has to eat green beans or carrots every night at dinner because they're the only two veggies your son will eat? Of course not. You and your other kids are entitled to enjoy your favorites as well. But it may mean that you make extra portions of those "safe" veggies and serve them repeatedly, while the more adventurous members of the family have broccoli, bell peppers, and other vegetables. In Chapter 12, Robert will talk more about nutrition and metabolism.

PILLAR #2: Fun with Fitness

If the meal plans are one crucial side of the AllStride coin, the flip side is the fitness component. And it's no surprise that the two share the same philosophy: if kids get to choose which activities and exercises to pursue, just as they decide what they want to eat, the odds are significantly greater that they'll stay the course. Additionally, fitness guru Isaiah Truyman makes physical activity so much fun that kids will have a hard time resisting. He has a huge gym bag full of ideas to get kids hopping, jumping, running—and generally acting like "real" kids. Isaiah will share them with you in Chapter 9. As your child begins to feel more competent and in control of his life, chances are he'll come to enjoy being physically active and ramp up

Five Ways to Get Your Kid on Board

How do you get your son or daughter to consider the AllStride program without hurting feelings and creating resistance? Family coach Robert Ferguson suggests some gentle but effective approaches:

1. Let her create an opening. If your daughter says she's being teased about her appearance or is upset that she can't find cute clothes that fit, first assure her that she's beautiful just the way she is. If the time seems right, add that if she wants to make some changes, you've heard about a program that sounds fun and effective. If she seems responsive, explain that a number of kids have achieved good results and you'd be happy to help her with it. Or if she's old enough to go online alone, give her the AllStride URL. Be careful not to use words like "fat" or "diet." Then drop the subject and see if she brings it up again later.

2. Take the third-person approach. If your son says nothing but is clearly unhappy with himself, wait until the two of you are comfortably talking about something else. Casually add that you recently saw an interesting TV show in which a doctor mentioned that most parents aren't comfortable talking to their kids about their size. They don't want to hurt feelings, but it turns out that kids often really do want to talk about it. Ask whether he feels that way. The moment he seems offended or clams up, switch to another topic. Wait until he brings up the subject later or until a significant amount of time has passed before broaching it again.

3. Lead by example. If you need to slim down or shape up, begin AllStride yourself. When your daughter sees the results, it may prompt her to ask if she can do it too.

4. Suggest a partnership. If you sense an opening, say that you're not pleased with how you look and feel, but you've just heard about a plan designed specifically for families and wonder if he'd like to do AllStride together.

5. Start with activity. Although food and fun (fitness) work in tandem, your child may be more receptive to becoming more active before he's willing to change his eating habits. If so, introduce him to the fun component of AllStride first.

You can gently suggest and act as a role model, but until a child's ready to do the program, it's futile to push it. The chances are, when he sees the benefits, he'll come around. You really want to be responding to initiative rather than initiating yourself.

his routines. But Isaiah also has "sneaky strategies" for kids who freak out the moment they hear the word "exercise."

More than 40 videos featuring Isaiah show how developing endurance, power, and strength—in that order—can be lots of fun. Or kids can choose a balanced program that integrates all three fitness goals. (Also integral to the program are what Isaiah calls PlayOuts: simple, fun activities such as jumping rope, skating, or swimming.) The whole family is welcome to join in some or all of these activities. There's no doubt that seeing mom or dad doing jumping jacks, bear-crawls, or the downward dog has a positive influence on kids. No matter how much kids may resist us, they tend to imitate their parents. According to Robert Ferguson, "What mom, dad, or another caregiver actually does, instead of just talking about it, is the most powerful influence on a child. Parents have to walk the walk and not just talk the talk."

PILLAR #3: Friends

The AllStride Community is critical to success on the program. After becoming a member of *allstride.com,* your son and daughter is "friended" by Dr. John, Isaiah, Robert, and me. Kids can also friend other members. They'll be able to chat (in private—no parental eyes and ears allowed!) about anything they wish. They can share tips on how to deal with birthday parties and Halloween or going out for fast food with friends. They can motivate one another to stay with the program when they're not in the mood. Or they can boast about a cool new pair of jeans in a smaller size, share how a member of the opposite sex is flirting with them, simply crow about how fabulous it is to see results on AllStride, or in kid-speak, whatever!

Likewise, AllStride parents can support one another. While the younger generation is chatting about snacks, bullying, or the latest cool Wii game, adults can vent or crow with their peers (again, in private) about their hopes, concerns, joys, and frustrations. Here's where you can discuss how to reward kids for good results and boost their self-esteem, find ways to make time for family activities, swap recipes, or share tips on quick snacks. Other parents who have "been there, done that" can offer advice on how to gently encourage kids when progress is slow, avoid showing impatience if a kid goes off track, and generally be less judgmental. (After all, they're just kids. Remember, we have a hard enough time ourselves always doing what we know we should be doing.)

Finally, AllStride's team of experts is always there to answer questions from you or your child, lead forums, write informative articles, and generally help in any way possible. Remember, support encourages compliance, which leads to success, pride, and self-confidence—a powerful combo that promotes transformation.

Support You Can Count On

When you become a member of the AllStride Community, you'll get:

- *Access to a dream team of experts in the fields of pediatrics, nutrition, sports psychology, fitness, and child behavior*

- *Personalized meal plans based on your child's food preferences, using "real" food and simple ingredients your kids already like*

- *A shopping list based on the meal plans*

- *Forty-plus video-training sessions with Isaiah Truyman*

- *A safe social community for your kid, complete with a place to create his own profile, a message board, an album to post photos to share with others, and a private journal in which to record his progress and his feelings*

- *A separate community for parents*

- *E-mail and phone support*

- *A monthly e-newsletter*

- *All the tools necessary to ensure success*

PILLAR #4: Family

The AllStride program—or any wellness program—works best when the whole family is on board. That way your child doesn't feel different or singled out because there's "something wrong" with him or her. How parents eat and how active they are can definitely impact a child's habits, and therefore results. That's why at its heart AllStride is a family program. If you choose to continue to eat one way and expect your child to eat another way, it's highly unlikely that he or she will stick with it and achieve success. And even so, other issues with food could develop with long-lasting implications. Your love, patience, and concern will also go a long way to supporting your child.

How Does AllStride Work?

Changing one's body and way of eating can take several months or more. Every time your child veers away from the meal plans, it slows progress. In following a personalized meal plan, a kid will consume just slightly fewer calories each day than are burned for energy. (Neither of you will be counting calories—just follow the meal plans, using a simple method to determine portion size we'll explain shortly.) This means that drinking one full can of sugar-filled soda or eating a piece of cake could undo an entire day's work. That doesn't mean a kid can't have soda or cake, though. He can have everything, and that includes starchy foods, meat and other protein sources, vegetables, fruit, and some fat. In fact, your child needs to eat all these foods every day.

We'll go into the details of what's on the menu in the next chapter, but a balance of different food groups in appropriate portions, in tandem with sufficient physical activity, guarantees success on AllStride. Progress may be slow—or may slow down after an initial burst—but that's a good thing. As you well know, if you lose weight fast, you almost always gain it back, often with the penalty of a few extra pounds. The same holds true for your child. By making a lifestyle change and removing the focus from the scale, you're giving her the essential tools to be slim, fit, healthy, and self-confident—for life.

The AllStride Community also offers an easy way for your child to track progress—using an online journal. There, she enters foods eaten each day (which may not be the same as what's on the meal plan), activities engaged in, and weight and measurements (which are actually a better indicator of progress than weight alone). There's also plenty of space to enter thoughts and feelings. With younger children, parents take on the role of tracking food and activity. Because AllStride also brings together nutrition, activity, and loving support, kids often see results fairly quickly. And good results are a powerful motivator to stick with the program.

In the next chapter, Robert and I will look more closely at all the yummy foods your kid can eat on the AllStride program.

Michael Shed Depression, Along with Pounds

Success Story

Before 14-year-old Michael pared 40 pounds from his body and 5 inches from his waist, he struggled with depression and anxiety, and often didn't want to leave the house. Now he's a captain of the football team and an honor student. Parents Mike and Michelle were once frustrated that they couldn't help their son, but today they're proud of his resolve and accomplishments. As a bonus, the program brought everyone in the family closer together.

Ricki: When did you notice that Michael was putting on pounds?
Michelle: In third grade he was having a hard time with some activities. Portion control was a problem, and he really liked pizza, other

really high-carb things, and fast food. A lot of that was our fault for bringing him to places that served such food.

Michael: I didn't notice that I was gaining weight until around sixth grade. I stuck out and felt like I was the only one who was heavy. Kids would laugh at me in the gym.

Ricki: How was Michael coping with this sense of being different?

Michelle: The summer between sixth and seventh grade he became very depressed and developed anxiety. It made me very anxious too.

Mike: I felt like a failure as a parent. I asked myself, "What did we do wrong and what could we do to help?" It was extremely frustrating.

Ricki: How was the depression and anxiety manifesting itself?

Michelle: Michael wanted to sleep all the time and he didn't want to leave the house. He'd have panic attacks and his heart would race and he'd be sweating. He thought he was having a heart attack, and a couple of times we took him to the ER.

Ricki: Michael, what was going through your head at this time?

Michael: I felt like what was wrong with me was causing problems in the family.

Ricki: That must have been really hard for you, Michael.

Michael: It was. The week before seventh grade got out, I just decided it's time to do something about this. I wasn't happy with myself and I didn't want to live the rest of my life like this. I wanted to go back to eighth grade a new person.

Michelle: He came to me and said, "Mom, I really want to lose weight." We'd told him all along, "We'll help you any way we can, but you've got to want this for yourself."

Michael: We went online and found the program. "Mom, I want to do this," I said. And she said, "Well, I'll do it with you because I need to lose some weight too."

Ricki: Michelle, you could have picked any of a dozen weight-loss programs out there. Why this one?

Michelle: It was the only one designed for kids and that can be customized to the foods they like. And I could feed my whole family the meals. The meal plans were awesome. Even my younger kids were saying, "Oh, this is really good, mom."

Mike: We could eat meals as a family and it didn't seem like you were on a diet.

Michelle: It was a buddy system. We'd go for walks and bike rides, and it kind of brought us closer as a family.

Ricki: So how did you guys do?

Michelle: We both started the program in May of 2007. Michael lost 6 pounds the first week. I lost 10 pounds in about four weeks, which is what I wanted to lose. By December Michael had lost 40 pounds.

Michael: I liked that it was easy to stick to. Each week, I'd weigh in and

Too Small to Be Big

I'd have lost more weight, so I'd just want to keep going. Plus I was feeling great and I wasn't hungry. Eating this way is like getting up in the morning. You know, it just happens. When I went back to school, people were like, "He's a new person." It was like I started my life all over again.

Ricki: Any other changes?

Mike: On the seventh grade football team, Michael played right guard. Then the eighth grade, they moved him to outside linebacker because he was so much quicker, and made him defensive captain.

Michelle: He never wanted to go out for track, because he felt too heavy to run, but that changed in eighth grade, when he was in the long-distance 800-meter run.

Michael: I have the confidence to get out and go do things with my friends now. When I used to go swimming, I didn't want to take my shirt off, but now I do. That's the best.

Michelle: When he's happy, I'm happy. He exercised every day when he was losing weight, and he continues to exercise and lift weights. It's become part of his normal routine. And once you're at your goal weight, you can use this program for maintenance with slightly bigger portions.

Ricki: Any other changes?

Mike: We're proud that in eighth grade Michael made the honor roll for the first time.

Chapter 8

What's for Breakfast, Lunch, and Dinner?

For any way of eating to become a permanent lifestyle, the food must be tasty, filling, and comforting. That's why most "diets" fail. They expect you to eliminate the very foods you love or dramatically reduce one type of food, often carbohydrates or fats. Pretty soon your body, your mind, and your emotions are screaming out for the very foods you're not eating. It's hard enough for an adult to endure this, and it's even more unlikely that a kid is going to hang in there. Fortunately, that form of torture bears no resemblance to the AllStride program.

So what do AllStride meals look like? Pretty much like any well-balanced meal. Based on the guidelines of the USDA Food Guide Pyramid, each meal contains the three macronutrients: protein, carbohydrate, and fat. And because your child gets to choose the specific foods he wants to eat, there should be no surprises or unfamiliar foods. There may be

Too Small to Be Big

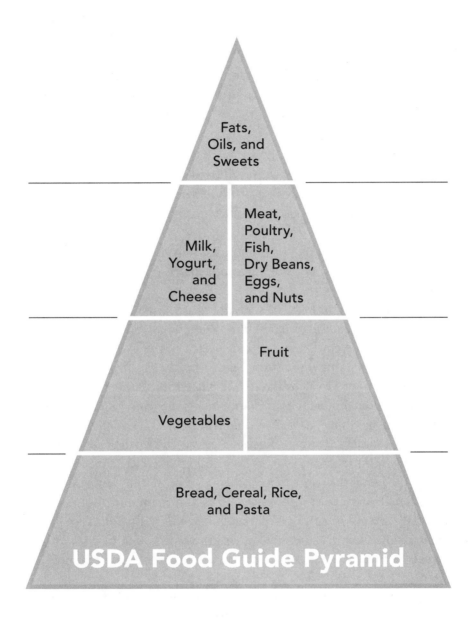

The *AllStride* meal plans are based upon the U.S. Department of Agriculture (USDA) Food Guide Pyramid. Consume more of the food groups at the base of the pyramid and eat sparingly of those at the top. Personalized meal plans specify the appropriate number of servings from each food group, depending upon a child's age.

larger portions of certain foods and smaller portions of other foods—the program minimizes added sugars and discourages the consumption of foods that contain trans fats (hydrogenated and partially hydrogenated oils)—but no foods are forbidden outright. AllStride is not into denial, restriction, or guilt trips. Instead, it's simply about enjoying eating and feeling satisfied.

Back to Basics

Eating well starts with knowledge. Before we take a look at some of the yummy meals an AllStride follower can enjoy, let's review some of the basics about food and metabolism. And who better to instruct us than nutritionist Robert Ferguson?

Ricki: Why has something as simple as eating become so complicated?
Robert: I think most of us know in our heart of hearts how to eat. Many years ago before I became a nutritionist, I was asked to lead a seminar on weight loss. I'd been doing seminars on empowerment and self-defense for women for years, but I felt uneasy about doing one on weight loss, since I suspected many of the attendees would already know more than I did. I finally decided to take what I call a "Sesame Street" approach. I placed 10 plates of food on a table and covered them with a cloth. Nine of the plates contained a lot of green vegetables, as well as a protein source. The tenth plate was mostly meat and all brown. I asked the women to watch as I pulled the cloth off the table. As soon as they noticed what was different about one of the plates they were to raise their hands. All the hands shot up at once. My point is that everyone in that room intuitively knew what she should be eating. The real question is not what to eat but how to close the gap between what we know and what we actually do.
Ricki: I think all the books on different diets based on different theories have actually confused people.
Robert: You're so right. That's why it's important to have a basic understanding of nutrition. The experience in that seminar many years ago convinced me to go back to school to get my master's in nutrition. How could I coach people, who on some level already knew how to eat well, without being educated about nutrition myself?
Ricki: And how can you coach your kids if you don't know the basics?

Robert: So let's start with protein, carbohydrate, and fat. These are macronutrients, and foods are their sources. (Micronutrients are vitamins, minerals, antioxidants, and the like.) So fish, poultry, meat, tofu, and eggs are all sources of protein. Bananas and green beans are sources of carbohydrate. Olive oil and avocado are sources of fat. But it's not quite that simple. Eggs also contain fat and a little bit of carbohydrate. Meat, poultry, and fish contain fat, along with protein. Vegetables contain small amounts of protein. An avocado also contains carbohydrate. We call a food a protein source when it is made up primarily of protein. Likewise we call a food a carb source when it's primarily composed of carbohydrate. Ditto with a fat source. Very few foods are the source of only one macronutrient.

Ricki: Can you give some examples?

Robert: Well, table sugar is all carbohydrate. Olive and other oils are 100-percent fat. I'd be hard put to come up with many others.

Ricki: And none of these macronutrients are eliminated or drastically reduced on the AllStride program.

Robert: That's correct. The meal plans contain an adequate amount of protein at every meal, as well as both of what we call "fast carbs" and "slow carbs." Fat is also essential for human health. There's fat in many of the foods, such as fish, meat, poultry, peanut butter, nuts, and salad dressings. Because fat contains more than twice as many calories as a gram of protein or carbohydrate, the meal plans minimize additional fat. The important thing to understand is that eating the right combination of these three macronutrient sources at the right time plays a large role in fat loss.

Ricki: I notice that you referred to fat loss, rather than weight loss. Could you explain that?

Robert: I also use the term "overfat" instead of overweight because it's more precise. When someone is trying to slim down, the objective is to lose excess fat, not lean muscle mass. This is even more the case with children, who are still growing. Eating adequate protein (which almost always contains some fat), in combination with carbohydrates, provides a steady supply of energy. That way, your body doesn't poach on muscle.

Ricki: And eating enough protein also keeps your blood sugar on an even plane, which helps moderate your appetite, right?

Robert: Yes. The other two pieces of the puzzle are eating at frequent intervals—that's where snacks come in—and consuming proper portions (see "Right-Sizing Portions" on page 122). When you moderate swings of blood sugar by eating this way, you're less likely to stimulate insulin production, which plays an important role in storing body fat, as Dr. John discussed earlier.

Ricki: How much protein does a child need to eat at each meal?

Robert: Unlike an adult, a growing child requires extra protein, and individual needs vary. Kids also need to get sufficient protein at each meal to maximize fat burning. For a 4- to 8-year-old, that means at least 6 grams of protein at breakfast, lunch, and dinner. Nine- to 12-year-olds require at least twice as much—12 grams—and teen-agers at least 15 grams.

Ricki: How does this connect to portion sizes?

Robert: Each ounce of meat, poultry, or seafood contains 6–8 grams of protein. The amounts above are minimums. Eating up to twice the minimum is fine. The Children's Nutrition Research Center at Baylor College of Medicine in Houston offers a handy calculator based on your child's height, weight, and age (see Resources on page 256). But you needn't obsess about this. Whether a child is at home following his meal plan, at school, or elsewhere, rather than worry about grams, which are meaningless to most Americans, he can simply have a palm-sized or open fist-sized portion of a protein source.

The Difference Between Fast and Slow

Now let's talk to Robert about the importance of carbohydrates, including how to distinguish between "fast" and "slow" carbs and why both of them are part of a healthy diet.

Ricki: When kids follow the AllStride meal plans, how much carbohydrate are they consuming?

Robert: It's important that the majority of our daily intake of calories comes from carbs—about 45 percent to 65 percent. Children and adults need a minimum of 130 grams of carbohydrates per day for proper brain function alone. For a fat-burning meal, I recommend a minimum of 30 grams of carbs for both kids and adults, but no more than 45 grams of net carbs for girls and 50 grams of net carbs for boys.

Ricki: *Please explain what net carbs are.*

Robert: *Fiber is a form of carbohydrate, but it doesn't impact blood sugar the way other carbs do. Net carbs represent the number of grams of carbohydrate remaining after subtracting the number of grams of fiber from the total number of carb grams. For example, a half-cup of steamed, sliced carrots contains 8.2 grams, but after you subtract the 2.6 grams of fiber, the net carb count is 5.6 grams. There's no need for you or your child to do these calculations. The meal plans provide the proper ranges. By the way, the only time net carbs are important is when large amounts of carbohydrates are consumed without sufficient fiber or protein at the same meal. That's because a heavy dose of carbs can provoke the fat-storing hormone, insulin.*

Ricki: *Got it. I suspect that fiber is related to my next question. What's the difference between "fast" carbs and "slow" carbs, and when do you eat one rather than the other?*

Robert: *Fast carbs are metabolized quickly and therefore elevate your blood sugar level fast. Slow carbs are usually higher in fiber and protein—remember that a carbohydrate source usually contains some protein as well—and therefore metabolize more slowly. While you don't want to eat too many fast carbs, when they're eaten with protein or slow carbs, the impact on blood sugar is blunted. A good example would be having some blueberries (a slow carb) with breakfast cereal (a fast carb).*

Ricki: *Does a breakfast of cereal and milk provide sufficient protein?*

Robert: *Yes, as long as the proportions are right. Both the milk and the cereal contain some protein—check to make sure the milk contains at least 5 grams of protein per serving. Although both are fast carbs, together they contain enough protein to make a fat-burning meal. The serving of cereal should be accompanied by no more than a cup of milk.*

Ricki: *When would you want to have just a fast carb?*

Robert: *Sometimes a fast carb food is exactly what kids need to forestall a meltdown after they've expended a lot of energy, (For food sources of each type of carb, see "Fast Carbs, Slow Carbs" on page 124)*

Right-Sizing Portions

Obviously, a 4-year-old has smaller portions than a 10-year-old. And a 14-year-old's portions clearly must be larger. Robert Ferguson explains a way to determine portion sizes that eliminates having to count calories, weigh food, or measure it out in cups. We all have a built-in measuring device: our hands. The smaller and younger a person, the smaller the hands, and therefore the smaller the portions. On average, a 5-year-old's hand is about half the size of a 14-year-old's hand. Here's how to use this "handy" measuring device for different foods—plus a few other visual cues in the few cases when a hand doesn't do the trick.

Protein Food Portions

Measuring from the wrist to where the fingers begin, use the palm of the hand to determine portions of a protein source high in fat, such as salmon or steak. The thickness of the portion should also correspond to the hand. On average, a 4-year-old's palm is the equivalent of about 1½ ounces; for an 8-year-old, it's about 3 ounces; for a 12-year-old, it's about 4 ounces. If the protein source is lower in saturated fat, say chicken breast, tofu, tilapia, or another white fish, measure from the wrist to the top of the first knuckle (open fist). This slightly larger portion is about 2 ounces for a 4-year-old, 3½ ounces for an 8-year-old, 4–5 ounces for a girl 12 and older, and 5–6 ounces for a boy 12 and older.

The hand doesn't work when it comes to other protein sources such as milk, cheese, or eggs. A 4-year-old would have one egg at a meal; a teen-ager may have two. For example, a 1-ounce serving of cheese (a slice or a piece the size of an egg yolk) provides as much protein as an ounce of lean meat, fish, or poultry. So does a cup of milk, an extra-large egg, 2 tablespoons (each tablespoon is the size of an egg yolk) of peanut butter, or a half-cup (half an adult's fist) portion of cooked lentils or other legumes. There's some protein in breads and cereals and most vegetables, but it takes more portions to get to the recommended intake. It's perfectly possible for a vegetarian to follow the AllStride program and get enough protein.

Carbohydrate Food Portions

For carbohydrate foods, instead of the palm, use a closed fist as the measuring device. In the case of slow carbs, a child can have at least two to three fist-size portions at a meal. Or if he's having both fast and slow carbs at the same meal, a fist-size portion of each will do the trick because the fiber in the slow carb helps to put the brakes on the fast carb. That might translate to a hamburger on a bun served with some cooked carrots. You have a fast carb (the bun), a slow carb (the carrots), and the protein, which also slows down the impact of the carbs, making it an ideal fat-burning meal. If you don't have a fast carb in a meal, you can have up to three servings of slow carbs.

Fat Portions

It's recommended that fat intake be 25–35 percent of daily calories. Most of the fat your child will consume is in the protein sources he eats and the oils used in cooking. But when she has a slice of cheese on a sandwich or as part of a snack, this counts as a fat portion. A thumb-size piece (from the top of the knuckle to the tip of the thumb) of butter is an age-appropriate portion to put on a baked potato or slice of bread. In the case of an avocado, a portion is an eighth or a quarter of the fruit, depending upon the age of the child. When it comes to salad dressings, a portion is 2 tablespoons (the size of two egg yolks) or 1 tablespoon (the size of one egg yolk) of extra-virgin olive oil, plus vinegar.

"Fusion-Food" Portions

Blended food like casseroles, lasagna, chili, and shepherd's pie, to name a few, can contain a mix of foods. For example, a casserole might include protein (ground turkey), a slow carb (string beans), a fast carb (pasta), and fat (cheese). Here the portion size would be two fists.

Snack Portions

The only time you have to concern yourself with calories on All-Stride is when it comes to packaged snacks, and even then, you don't have to count them. A snack for a 4-year-old should be no fewer than 50 calories. Snacks for children ages 8 to 12 should be closer to 150 calories. A snack for a teen-ager will come in about the same as for an adult: 100–200 calories for girls and 100–300 calories for boys. The meal plan will list an appropriate snack, but if a kid wants to substitute a packaged food, he can check the calorie count for one serving indicated on the Nutrition Facts panel to make sure it's within the range suitable for his age. For younger kids, parents can do this. When kids snack on whole foods like fruit and cheese, they should follow the advice for portions above.

Fast Carbs, Slow Carbs

Here are just a few examples of the two different kinds of carbohydrates. For a more complete list, go to allstride.com.

Fast Carbs	Slow Carbs
Bread	Carrots
Cereal	Tomatoes
Tortillas	Grapefruit
Baked Potato	Celery
Watermelon	Raspberries
Apples	Strawberries
Bananas	Blueberries
Pasta	Zucchini
Corn	Bell Peppers
Rice	Spinach
Pancakes	String Beans
Chickpeas	Lettuce

Kid-Friendly Food

We'll drill deeper into nutrition in Part III. Now it's time for the nitty-gritty of the food kids get to eat on AllStride. Remember I told you that all the food on the meal plans is "regular" food? Well, you're about to see how kid-friendly it is:

- There are no unfamiliar ingredients or special foods you have to buy. Everything you need to start the AllStride program is either already on your shelves, in your fridge, or at your supermarket.
- There are no AllStride-brand foods you must purchase in order to follow the meal plans.
- While there are many recipes at *allstride.com,* you don't have to be a great cook or have a big food budget to put together satisfying meals. (See "Timesavers for Busy Families" on page 186 and "Dollar-Conscious Meals" on page 129.)
- You also can rely on many packaged foods—we'll tell you which ones—to feed the family without spending hours in front of the stove.

Breakfast Is Ready!

You and your kids will be wowed by all the possibilities for that first important meal of the day. How about these for starters? Actual meal plans typically provide details on serving size and types of bread, jelly, butter, etc.

- Any cereal low in sugar, such as Cheerios®, Kix®, or Wheaties®
- Bananas, berries, oranges, and other fruit
- Bagels, toast, muffins, and English muffins
- Canadian bacon, turkey bacon, and pork or turkey sausages
- Pancakes and waffles
- Peanut butter
- Cheese
- Eggs, whether scrambled, in an omelet, or in a breakfast sandwich
- Breakfast burritos with onion, mushrooms, and salsa
- Oatmeal and grits
- Orange juice and milk

The Open-Plate Club

One of the reasons your child will never go hungry on AllStride is that she can eat most raw vegetables to her heart's desire, thanks to their high fiber and water content. Serve them at meals or as part of a snack with a chunk of cheese or some peanut butter, hummus, or ranch dressing. Older kids are more likely to eat salads than younger ones. Robert calls these free vegetables members of the "open-plate club." They include leafy salad greens and the following:

- Bell Peppers
- Cauliflower
- Celery
- Cucumbers
- Mushrooms
- Peppers
- Radishes
- Sprouts

Snacks Aren't Optional

Change your mindset on snacks. Instead of regarding them as something extra, see them as an integral component of a healthy eating program—and essential to weight control. By going no longer than three hours without eating, your child's blood sugar level remains on an even keel, which keeps his appetite and emotions under control. So two to three hours after breakfast, lunch, or dinner, it's time for a snack. (Hold off on snacks for an hour before bedtime because they may interfere with sleep.)

The food on AllStride is pleasurable, and snacks are no exception. That means that your child can eat almost anything—whether a protein, fat, or carbohydrate source—as long as it meets the following guidelines:

- Whole-food snacks—such as raw veggies, fruit, or a slice of ham—must contain fewer than 50 calories and can go up to 200 to 300 calories, depending upon age. A cup of sliced carrots provides just about 50 calories, but combine this with some cheese or ranch dressing and the snack will fall within the recommended calorie range.
- The same applies to packaged foods, but items like granola bars can contain a huge range of calories. Cookies, crackers, or even chocolate are fine as long as the calories are on target. Actual meal plans specify portions and specific products.
- If your child is cranky or low on energy in the early afternoon, cookies, pudding, fruit juice, or another fast carb is likely to restore her energy and equilibrium quickly.
- An evening snack that's primarily protein, such as Greek yogurt, is less likely to interfere with sleep than a fast carb like a candy bar.

Here are just some of the snacks on the meal plans:

- Fruit, including an apple, applesauce, a fruit cup, cantaloupe, grapes, mango, orange, peach, pear, and plum
- Pudding or gelatin dessert
- Yogurt, ice cream, or sherbet
- Granola bar or granola
- String cheese, cream cheese, Cheddar cheese, etc.
- Nuts, including almonds, cashews, walnuts, and nut butters

- Popcorn, Gold Fish®, crackers, pretzels, cookies, graham crackers, and animal crackers
- Angel food cake
- Beef or turkey jerky and cold cuts
- Protein shake or banana or peach shake

Lunchtime on AllStride

OK, here's the big test. Can your child eat an AllStride lunch in the school cafeteria and not stand out from his peers? Does having a grilled cheese sandwich with tomato soup label him as weird? No way. How about a roast-beef wrap and baby carrots? Pretty normal, right? And when you look at other possibilities below, the answer is a resounding yes! (By the way, the meal plans include lots of foods that work for packed lunches.) Once again, the actual meal plans will go into detail—how many nacho chips, for example, or a specific brand of soup—and include vegetables, condiments, and fruit or another dessert. Show me a kid who won't find his appetite whetted by several dishes on the following list:

- Sandwiches made with bread, a pita, or a wrap: ham and cheese, turkey and Swiss cheese, chicken, steak, chicken salad, tuna salad, cold cuts, and roast beef
- Baked chicken and rice or Chinese stir-fried chicken
- Nachos, burritos, fajitas, quesadillas, and tacos
- Chef salad
- Hamburgers, turkey burgers, and hot dogs
- Mac and cheese, fettuccini, pasta salad, spaghetti and meatballs, ravioli
- Peanut butter and jelly (or banana) sandwich
- Sushi
- Chili
- Vegetable noodle, chicken noodle, vegetable, or tomato soup and clam chowder

Let's Sit Down to Dinner

Many lunch options work just as well at dinner. Meal plans include cooked veggies—including corn on the cob and mashed potatoes—or a salad, plus a beverage, and a main dish. In addition to pizza—yes, pizza is acceptable (See "How to Eat Pizza," below)—the following main dishes are just the tip of the dinner iceberg:

- Meatloaf
- Grilled chicken, fish or steak, or chicken strips
- Hamburger, cheeseburger, or veggie burger
- Pork chops, roast pork, and barbecued spare ribs
- Grilled shrimp with angel-hair pasta
- Scallops and linguini
- Baked turkey breast
- Baked salmon, halibut, tilapia, or cod
- Turkey sausages
- Fried rice with chicken or shrimp

How to Eat Pizza

No, we're not discussing the relative merits of hands versus a knife and fork. Here's the real question: can your child (or you) occasionally eat pizza and stay on board with her meal plan? After all, pizza is a favorite takeout or family-night-out option. It's also about the most inexpensive way to feed the gang. No child on AllStride should ever feel deprived of a certain food or guilty because of eating it. According to pizza lover Robert Ferguson, portion size is more important than whether a pie is made with whole-wheat flour or organic ingredients. You've already learned how to use a hand to estimate portion sizes. Check out nutritionist Robert Ferguson's suggestions for how to enjoy pizza without overdoing it:

- For regular pies, your kid can have a piece the size of both his hands (with fingers aligned).

- For deep-dish pizza, he can have a piece the size of both open fists.

- Ask for a pie that's light on cheese and topped with vegetables and/or chicken, rather than sausage and pepperoni.

When making pizza yourself, follow the recipe for Lisa's Pizza at allstride.com.

Money is as important as time when it comes to feeding a family. Fortunately, there's nothing inherently costly about following the AllStride program. There are no exotic ingredients or fancy cuts of meat. You can get everything in the same store where you currently shop. Here are some of Robert's tips to stretch your food budget:

- Club stores like BJ's, Sam's Club, and Costco offer good value. Walmart is also a great place to shop. I did my own comparison-shopping at Target, Trader Joe's, Whole Foods, and Walmart. The last was the price winner in almost all categories. Almost everyone lives near a Walmart, and there's no membership fee as there is with club stores.

- If you shop late in the day, you can often get baked goods and other perishables at a significant discount. Just eat them that day or the next or freeze them. Some supermarkets offer a discount to seniors one day a week. If you ask, most stores also extend that discount to shoppers of any age.

- Many supermarkets offer a discount card that takes a percentage off your order no matter what you purchase.

- Many of the 99-cent stores sell food and even produce. I've found some fantastic deals there.

- Buy foods when they're in season and prices are lower. Freeze berries and other seasonal fruit and veggies for later use.

- Stock up on meat and poultry cuts when they're on special and freeze what you cannot use immediately in single-portion servings.

- Purchase nonperishable items when they're on sale as well.

- The Internet has put a whole new spin on coupons, with several sites dedicated to searching out the best deals to save you money and time. Check out couponmom.com, which compares coupons from the three main insert flyers you find in your mailbox or newspaper to get you the best deal. The site then compounds the savings by comparing local retailers' prices.

- Visit the websites of manufacturers whose products you regularly purchase to download coupons, whether Kellogg's, General Foods, or many others.

Make It Personal

In the lists of foods on previous pages, we didn't include gluten-free, kosher, or vegetarian meals, but rest assured that they're all in the AllStride meal planner database, to which your child's favorites can also be added. Likewise, if your son or daughter is allergic or sensitive to soy, peanuts, eggs, dairy, or any other foods, that data too can be fed into the program.

Customization also extends to cultural preferences. If grits, black-eyed peas, barbecue, and turnip greens are often on the menu, you can personalize your child's meal plan to include them. Likewise, if tortillas are more common than bread in your cuisine, and kidney beans, plantains, calabaza, cassava, and taro are among your child's favorite vegetables, her meal plans can reflect that. Robert told me an instructive story about when he began his practice as a nutritionist. He asked a Filipino client to refrain from eating white rice (which is integral to her culinary heritage) for three weeks before her next appointment—and she never came back! As an older and wiser Robert says, "You need to meet people where they are."

Robert's belief in meeting people where they are continues into Chapter 9, where Coach Isaiah Truyman will help explain the fun-filled fitness component of the AllStride program. As we say at AllStride, not only do you have to eat, you have to move!

Brieanne Stars in Her Own True-Life Story

Success
Story

It starts with her losing 37 pounds at age 11. If you catch "Kit Kittredge: An American Girl" at the movies or on DVD, you'll see a plump little girl playing one of Kit's friends. That's Brieanne, but you'd never recognize her now. Her mother's defining moment occurred on the movie set when four girls were all sitting on the floor. After several takes, they'd repeatedly gotten up and sat down. The other girls could do it easily, but Brieanne was having a hard time. Watching her, she suddenly realized her daughter's weight could be impacting her health. (We'll talk to Brieanne here and pick up with the rest of the family on page 144.)

Ricki: Brieanne, what do you think was going on with your weight?

Brieanne: At first I wasn't aware of it. It just happened. I used to eat whenever I felt sad, mad, or even just bored. I always found comfort in eating. But after I ate junk food, I felt horrible and hated myself for it. I'm not dumb. I knew that eating like that was going to ruin my life, but the stress of knowing that made me eat even more!

Ricki: What you're saying rings so true, but most people don't realize this at your age. You're really lucky you've dealt with it now.

Brieanne: Today I see myself in the movie and I have a hard time believing that's really me on the screen. When it was filmed, I weighed 137 pounds. Now I'm 100 pounds. I was so happy when my mom found this program. We talked it over and decided to do it together. She'd do the shopping and cooking and I'd make my snacks, and of course, clean up after myself. I couldn't get out of that! Making that decision to start made me feel more grown up. I felt I was finally going to get serious and lose the weight for good.

Ricki: Taking responsibility is key to success; no wonder you achieved such great results. I didn't get serious about my weight until I was an adult. At least I always enjoyed physical activity.

Brieanne: I'm not what you'd call a sports girl, but the activities in the program are fun. I'd tried other exercise videos and they were either frustrating or boring or hard to do—or all three! These videos give me a sense of accomplishment, and the whole family could do them.

Ricki: Of course, the combination of being active and following the meal plans is unbeatable. How quickly did you see results?

Brieanne: My first week, I lost 6 pounds. I was so happy! I finally began to feel a little hope. The best part is the program isn't a "d-i-e-t," so you don't feel you're gong to "d-i-e." It's a program that gets you into a healthy way of eating you can stay with for the rest of your life!

Ricki: How was this different from other programs you'd tried?

Brieanne: It was awesome. At first, I thought I was going to starve! But I didn't even finish the stuff on my plate at the first dinner. I loved that there were tons of different meals. Not having to change my whole life was also great. It's just so flexible.

Ricki: How *has* your life changed since losing all that weight?

Brieanne: I have loads of energy and I feel better than I ever have before. Who knows where life will lead me next? I'm ready. I've recommended the program to many people, because I'm living proof that it works! I've also decided to give back to those who are less fortunate by holding a fund-raiser and food drive for the Second Harvest Food Bank. I know what it's like to overeat, but I don't know what it is like to under-eat.

Ricki: Did the other actors in the film recognize the slim new Brieanne at the premiere?

Brieanne: I got to meet Jada Pinkett Smith and also almost the whole Smith family on the movie set. A year later at the premiere party, Jada walked up to me, gave me a hug, and said, "Brieanne, you look awesome!" I didn't think she'd remember my name because I've never done anything in the business before. But she did, and she recognized the change in me. I knew that was really special.

Ricki: It sounds like an unbelievable journey for you.

Brieanne: When I think about what I was like, say, a year ago, I'm amazed that I could change myself the way I have. I'll never be the same girl I was a year ago.

Ricki: Any parting words of advice to other kids?

Brieanne: Never give up on yourself and always believe that you can accomplish your task. Without faith in yourself, you'll go nowhere.

Brieanne's brother, Shawn, tells his story on page 144.

Chapter 9

Kids Just Wanna Have Fun

A toddler's "job" is to play and by playing learn about the world. Educator Maria Montessori incorporated this concept into her nursery-school curriculum. A child might even be lucky enough to find that by the time "real" school rolls around, play continues to serve an important role in learning. Unfortunately, for many children school isn't much fun. And for some kids, gym class is no exception.

Kids who are agile and naturally active may love physical education. It certainly allows them to blow off steam and settle down to school "work." But the one-size-fits-all environment of gym class and the competitive nature of team sports can intimidate a child who feels clumsy or is heavier than classmates. Gym becomes just an extension of the educational system instead of an opportunity to be playful.

If you want a kid to do something with enthusiasm and joy, it must be fun—and the impetus has to come from within. After all, who wants his activities imposed by another person? Not me. It's a sign of maturity to accept that we may have to do something regardless of how we feel about it. But why expect kids to be mature? We at AllStride believe that kids should be treated as kids as long as possible—which includes giving them reasonable choices, instead of imposing ultimatums from on high. Besides, as any parent knows, if a youngster doesn't want to do something, he'll find one way or another to wriggle out of it. That's why your son or daughter will cast the deciding vote in picking activities, as well as influencing meal plans.

Fun, Not Fitness

I love to be physically active, but I'm not much of an athlete. I was the slowest kid on the track team and the shortest kid on the basketball team in high school. But at least I was out there—if only to be with my best friend! I wish I'd had our expert on physical activity, Isaiah Truyman, in my life when I was a kid. Let me remind you of some of his qualifications. He's an accredited coach, trainer, and the developer of EZIA Human Performance in Southern California. Oh, yeah, he's also an accomplished surfer.

Isaiah tells me that when he was very young, he learned that sports gave him self-reliance, as well as strength. This understanding made him want to help others to help themselves. Isaiah is particularly attuned to the needs of the family, and is committed to fostering health and fitness as family values. Let's hear about the AllStride approach to play from him.

Ricki: I guess the most basic issue is whether a kid enjoys being physically active or not. And if he doesn't already enjoy it, how can a parent make it fun?
Isaiah: The moment you start using words like "fitness" or "exercise" or even "physical activity," a kid who may not feel physically

confident begins to get nervous. That's why I prefer to talk about play. Whether I'm coaching kids or adults, we start out by just running around the block, jumping, skipping, throwing, twisting, rolling over, climbing, and following an obstacle course. We don't use any equipment, unless you call balls or resistance bands equipment. It's all about having fun and becoming comfortable with our bodies. Building skills, strength, and endurance come later. Because if a kid doesn't enjoy the activity, he'll never get to that point, or he'll simply do it to please someone else like a parent or a coach.

Ricki: When you put that spin on it, it sounds weird to ask, "How can a parent encourage a kid to have fun?"

Isaiah: Exactly. Humans and all other mammals are programmed to play, which is one way they learn. All you have to do is watch kittens, puppies, or any other young animals romping around. So our first objective is to create an environment that encourages playfulness. This can be as simple as taking a toddler to a playground or getting out in the backyard with an older child. You don't even have to go outdoors. It could mean roughhousing on the family room floor, playing tag in the garage on a rainy day, or playing Wii Sports Resort.

Ricki: When does parental encouragement turn into parental pressure?

Isaiah: That's a really important distinction. You don't want to pressure your child to do something just because you enjoyed it when you were young. Nor should you promote something that you feel would make your kid "well rounded." The perfect example is the father who insists his son toss a baseball around with him, when the boy is far more interested in swimming or paddleball—or playing the trombone. Motivation always has to come from within. A coach can help, but at the end of the day, the kid has to want to play and transform himself. Unless he's self-motivated, his commitment collapses once the program ends. Your child needs to be doing all the components of the AllStride program for himself, not for his parents.

Ricki: But the parent can help make it fun to do these things, right?

Isaiah: I call it natural consequences. You make sure your kids brush their teeth every night, but at a certain point they just start doing it themselves because it's yucky not to. They want to have

Too Small to Be Big

clean teeth, which feels good—and this just happens to help prevent cavities. It's the same with physical activity. You can certainly gently encourage a child to get out there and play, and ultimately, he realizes that he enjoys it.

Walk the Walk

Dr. John and Robert Ferguson have both already made the point that parents have to walk the walk, and not just talk the talk. My mother was interested in staying thin, but she was never one for exercise, and my father was always working, so my sister and I didn't engage in physical activities as a family. That's probably why it's so important for me to be active with my sons. Let's first talk to Isaiah about the hows and whys of family activity before we move on to the program itself.

Ricki: Why is it important for a family to do fun physical things together?
Isaiah: Sometimes parents want me to change their kids' habits, but they don't want to get involved. What kind of a message does that transmit? Often a kid will think, "There's something wrong with me that needs to be fixed." Kids who see their parents enjoying physical activity find it natural to be active themselves. If a child grows up playing games, tossing a ball around, and playing tag with his family, he just naturally adopts an active lifestyle. I've also seen instances in which one member of the family—it's often the mother—begins a transformation and then it spreads like a virus to the rest of the family. But when parents send a kid out to play to get him out of their hair, he may regard it as a punishment rather than pleasure.
Ricki: So just as the family needs to participate in the meal plan the child is following, parents need to get out there and roll around on the grass or jump in puddles or whatever. But what if a kid cringes the moment the mere idea of exercise comes up?
Isaiah: We learn how to crawl first, then walk, and finally to run and skip and jump. These are all fundamental, primal movements. Sometimes you meet a 14-year-old who never learned some basic skills and may be at the level of a 5-year-old in terms of fundamental movements. And likewise, sometimes you meet a 5-year-old who

already has the fundamentals of a typical 12-year-old. When you don't have these basic skills under your belt, it undermines your sense of self. But teach these things young—and clearly, the younger the better—and a kid develops tremendous confidence in his body. It's like savings: the sooner you start putting money in the bank and interest compounds, the more you'll have in your bank account.

Ricki: If a kid gets a late start, can he still learn the fundamentals?

Isaiah: No one is ever too old to learn new things. Some of the adults I work with have never mastered certain basics. And that raises another point: you can't succeed without experiencing failure. A toddler has to fall down in order to learn how to walk. Parents aren't helping their kids if they don't let them make mistakes. I frequently have to send parents away because mom or dad is standing around yelling at the kids to do this or that. I have to say, "Look, you're the parent, but I'm the coach. Take a walk around the block, and we'll show you what we've learned today when we're ready."

Get Moving with AllStride

Now let's have Isaiah go into detail about the fun-filled AllStride activity program.

Isaiah: This program was developed specifically for youths who aren't super athletes right out of the gate. And, of course, kids have a wide range of abilities. Each child can pick his activities and with time increase his performance level. The website includes videos in which I demonstrate all sorts of fun ways to inspire and instruct kids on how to get moving. Each kid also gets to choose from among many other activities, or "PlayOuts," as we call them.

Ricki: So in effect, each child can create an individualized program?

Isaiah: Yes. But the mix of activities selected is less important than establishing the habit of regular movement. In fact, the first way in which the program is tailored is that the kid can pick between the online videos and the PlayOuts. If a kid doesn't take pleasure in being active, we can really downplay the exercise approach of the videos and focus initially on the movement and games embodied in PlayOuts. On the other hand, if a child enjoys activity, but needs a mentor to help him optimize his potential, he can get involved with the fitness videos from the get-go. (And that's not to say that everyone can't enjoy the PlayOuts. Ideally, kids will engage in both the online video activities and the PlayOuts.) Once those kids who didn't initially enjoy activity attain some skills and confidence just in moving and playing, they can move along to the online videos.

From Frustrated to Focused

About six years ago I met a 15-year-old boy I'll call Jonathan, who was about 30 pounds overweight. He asked me to coach him, not because he enjoyed working out, but because he wanted to get fit so he wouldn't be teased. I didn't talk to him about his size, what he should eat, or how we were going to fix it. Instead, I asked him what he liked to do. His answer was surfing. So first we just played around on a surfboard. Then I said, "Give me 20 minutes in the gym and then let's go surfing." I kept increasing the time in the gym before the surfing session, and he grew to enjoy the workouts. Not only did Jonathan slim down, he completely changed his body and now travels around the world surfing. I saw him recently and he's clearly a successful, functioning member of society with a whole network of friends, including a girlfriend. If Jonathan had remained overweight, he might have been trapped in his lonely world and slipped through the cracks as a troubled, friendless youth. My experience with him reminds me that sometimes it takes more energy to run from your fears than to actually face them. They needn't be that big a hurdle when you face them, as Jonathan did. Although his initial goal was to be more popular, he's achieved far more.—Isaiah Truyman

Ricki: How would you engage a reluctant child?
Isaiah: First of all, never make it about the child's weight, clumsiness, or lack of confidence. In fact, shift the emphasis to yourself. You might say, "I get lonely when I walk the dog and I'd love it if you'd come with me." Or ask for help: "Could you help me carry these potted plants from the car to the garden?" Or "I found this old croquet set in the basement. Let's set it up and see if we can hit the balls through the hoops." Every kid wants to be successful, make parents proud, be popular, and have fun. Something may

have happened at an early age that is making a child fearful or uncomfortable about physical activity, but by turning movement into a positive experience, the parent can help the kid get beyond this.

Ricki: But at a certain point, most children realize that there's an "agenda," right?

Isaiah: As long as the agenda is about having fun, that's fine. Once he or she is clearly enjoying this special time, you can begin to be a bit more direct. But if your daughter is still feeling shy or nervous about moving her body or your son is self-conscious about his size, it may be better to keep things one-on-one for the time being. You don't want everybody and his mother to know your overweight child is starting a fitness program. As a parent, do your thing together in the backyard instead of a public place, so you can create an emotionally safe environment, free from the judgment of others, whether it's a nosy neighbor or a competitive sibling.

Ricki: What are some of the activities you might start with to eliminate any "whiff" of fitness?

Isaiah: Among the PlayOuts are nature walks and a treasure hunt. Both are great ideas for kids who are not that active. The kid is so focused on spotting squirrels, frogs, and birds or finding "treasure" that he isn't aware that the walk is good for him. Other low-key activities might be romping in a swimming pool, throwing a ball around, riding a bike, climbing a tree, jumping on a trampoline, or twirling a hula-hoop. With time, you'll want to coax your child by saying things like, "How many times can you touch your toes (or hop on your pogo stick)?" Or "I bet you can't skip 20 times." Or "Let's race to the garage." There's a distinction between pressure and gentle challenges. Believe it or not, your child will begin to enjoy the movement and will certainly love your undivided attention.

Ricki: Tell me a bit more about what the PlayOuts include.

Isaiah: An 8-year-old girl might keep plenty busy jumping rope, roller-skating, and playing paddle tennis. Her 12-year-old brother might be into mountain biking, shooting baskets, skateboarding, and karate. Or vice versa! (For a more complete list, see "Fun Comes in Many Flavors" on page 142.) The goal would be to work up to five PlayOuts a week.

Ricki: Now let's move on to the more structured activity program on allstride.com. What does this involve?

Isaiah: When we're talking about just movement, there's no time expectation. If a kid spends 5 or 10 minutes doing something that gets the heart pumping that otherwise would have been spent in front of the TV or computer, that's great. One online video activity a week would be the minimum; better yet are three half-hour sessions. The child gets to choose which to follow, decide how often to do them, and how far to develop skills.

Ricki: Important as play is, it's not the sole purpose here, though, is it?

Isaiah: Play—and the pleasure it provides—is always a goal in itself, but it also builds such skills as strength, flexibility, endurance—and, of course, self-confidence. The online videos promote three fitness goals: stability and endurance, strength and coordination, and speed and power. A kid can work on one goal and then move to another or opt for a mix of goals.

Ricki: Do you or your kid have to keep a log of his or her progress?

Isaiah: There's no need for this, although you should note what the kid could do the first time she tried something, where she is after a couple of weeks, and then again in a month or so. That way you both know Sherrie was able to do 18 jumping jacks at first, and after a couple of weeks is up to 29. Or that James initially ran 40 yards in 20 seconds and has now cut 5 seconds from his time. Such evidence of progress is very motivating. Of course, if your child wants to keep his own log, that's fine. But until about age 14, most kids need a coach to encourage them to keep improving their performance.

Ricki: How would a kid consciously improve her performance?

Isaiah: Once a kid is seeing the sort of improvement I mentioned above, she is usually really into it. She's seeing the results in how she looks, how she feels, and how much energy she has. At that point, she could pick up the pace, whether in intensity or duration. She might continue with the same online videos or PlayOuts or move to other ones, or some combination of the two. All the while, she's building her skills and self-confidence—and burning more calories.

Fun Comes in Many Flavors

All "PlayOuts" are designed to be simple, fun, and short—30 minutes or so—but effective. Even before beginning the AllStride program, here are some fun activities your child can pick from—right now:

- **Walk!** This could be walking the dog, going bird watching, hiking in the woods, or exploring a city park. To ramp it up, your kid can try skipping, hopping, jogging, and dodging objects. Or carry a backpack filled with books or bottles of water, starting with one or two and working up to several. Next, switch the backpack from chest to back and from one shoulder to another. Or bounce a ball while walking.

- **Run!** Up a hill, around a track, on a football field, at the beach, in the park, on a treadmill, or wherever. To ramp it up, a kid can time herself or race against a friend or a family member. Running is a great way to spend quality time with someone, but take it slow at first.

- **Bike!** Depending upon where you live, this may not be safe on the road. If so, find a bike path. Try mountain biking or BMX/freestyle too.

- **Swim!** Jump in a pool, pond, river, or the ocean. In cold weather, check out the pools at school or the YMCA or YWCA. Take it to the next level by adding diving, surfing, wake boarding, and windsurfing.

- **Skate!** Kids can hop on a skateboard or lace up their inline skates, roller blades, or ice skates. Many communities now have outdoor skate parks.

- **Ski/Snowboard!** Chill out with cross-country skiing, sledding, and tobogganing.

Too Small to Be Big

Make the Most of PlayOuts

- *Encourage your child to be creative and have fun.*

- *Team up with other parents to get several kids involved.*

- *Encourage kids to do the best they can, but avoid being judgmental or showing you have certain expectations.*

- *Be patient. Progress comes over time through consistent effort.*

- *Stay focused on the small improvements that are likely to occur in each session, rather than on the end result.*

- *Encourage your child to understand that if he takes good care of his body, it will take good care of him.*

- *Remind kids that how they feel is more important than how they look, and who they are is more important than what other people may think of them.*

In the next chapter, we'll explore how the AllStride Community has taken a page from Facebook, enabling kids to meet other kids with similar interests and issues, and provide mutual support.

A Lifestyle Change for Shawn and His Family

Success Story

Brieanne's 10-year-old brother, Shawn, lost 14 pounds on the program, so let's catch up with him and his parents, Christine and Bruce. In addition to Brieanne's 37 pounds that are now history, Christine lost 15 pounds, and Bruce 40 pounds. It all adds up to an amazing 106 pounds!

Ricki: What made you decide to do the program as a family?
Christine: We needed to make a lifestyle change in our house. I had to stop enabling the children. When I found the program, we sat down and looked at it together and decided it was doable. From there, it was up to Bruce and me to set the example, so we decided to do it as a family. If we're to teach our children something new, we should lead the way.

Bruce: I'd gained weight as well. As parents, we hadn't led by example.

Ricki: Christine, how were you enabling the kids?

Christine: They were eating in an unhealthy manner because of the way we were shopping. Some of the foods in the house weren't conducive to a well-balanced diet.

Ricki: Shawn, did you think you needed to slim down like your sister?

Shawn: I looked big and I felt slow and slumpy, like my feet were pasted to the ground. I played baseball, but it was really hard for me to bat and play catcher and stuff. My weight would just slow me down.

Ricki: How did you feel about your parents' decision to stop buying and serving certain foods?

Shawn: After you've eaten so much junk, you kind of get addicted to it, but after a couple of weeks of eating healthy, I got used to it. Now I love the food that my mom makes.

Ricki: Shawn, how long did it take for you to lose 14 pounds?

Shawn: About a year. When I was losing, I would ask people if I looked slimmer. And they would always say, "Yes." It made me feel much better about myself. Now I feel healthier. I think I look much better too.

Ricki: You know you do! Are sports easier and more fun now?

Shawn: Yeah. I run faster, bat better, and catch better. I'm just a better baseball player.

Christine: The program has been a godsend. I can't express how proud I am of Brieanne and Shawn! I see such a difference in their self-confidence and their overall outlook on life! They walk with a little pep in their step. I hadn't realized just how much I allowed food to comfort my kids. Now new, healthy habits are here to stay in our family.

Ricki: What do these changes mean in terms of shopping?

Bruce: There's no need to buy special prepackaged foods. The customized meal plan includes all the basic food groups. We just go to the grocery store and buy what's on the shopping list.

Christine: I used to buy the week's specials to try to manage our grocery budget, but a lot of them are convenience foods that are detrimental to our kids' health.

Bruce: We now spend more time together in meal prep.

Ricki: Does it take longer to get meals on the table now?

Christine: No dinner takes more than 30 minutes to fix.

Bruce: There wasn't a thing that was for mom only or dad only. Each person could partake in any aspect of it.

Shawn: It was cool because we got to experience it all together, and we could help each other. And we could just bond—that was the best part of it.

Christine: Shawn's right. If you choose to do this program together, it will definitely bring your family closer together.

Chapter 10

Making New Friends Online

In less than a decade, the phenomenon of social networking has changed how millions of people communicate with one another. Unlike texting or instant messaging, online communities like Facebook, MySpace, and Twitter (along with blogs) allow one person to simultaneously speak to an unlimited number of others. As early adopters of technology, our kids have made social media integral to their lives.

Dr. John and I have cast blame on electronic media and entertainment devices for their role in helping promote inactivity and weight gain. However, there's obviously another side to the wired (and wireless) world we now inhabit. I, for one, would be lost without my laptop. And when I find out something, I can instantly share it with thousands of people via Twitter and Facebook. Thanks to Skype, far-flung grandkids can chat with their grandparents online, show off their artwork, or even read a book together. Kids research school assignments online. Our computers, cell phones, and smart phones don't just allow us to keep up with the news, pay bills, and gather information. They open the door to virtual communities.

My 8-year-old recently told me, "Mom, I need to be on Facebook." His words echoed something I read recently in a fascinating book aptly entitled *Hanging Out, Messing Around, and Geeking Out: Kids Living and Learning with the New Media*. It was written by Mizuko Ito, Ph.D., a cultural anthropologist of technology use at the University of California (Irvine), and multiple coauthors. One of them, danah boyd (as she spells it), Ph.D., a social-media researcher at Harvard University's Berkman Center for Internet and Society, reports that one 18-year-old girl she interviewed told her, "If you're not on MySpace, you don't exist."

Teen Scene

The authors of the book make the point that social media has not intrinsically changed kids. It is only the latest in a series of forces that converged, starting in the 1950s, to create the culture of youth. Back then, high-school students were often called the rock-and-roll generation, segregating themselves from their parents' generation with their own music, fashion, films, and television shows. Younger kids also increasingly identify with their peers more than their families, pursuing their own interests and preoccupations. This division has only increased over the last decade, and all the forms of new media have played into it. Tweens and teens are far more inclined to use instant messaging than e-mail, and to text instead of speaking on the phone. Social networks have become central to kids' daily lives.

The Digital Generation

Although parents may worry that kids are too involved with social media, it's important to realize that they hang out online, much as they did in parking lots and shopping malls in earlier decades. This behavior is simply an adaptation of an existing practice, although it takes place in a different environment. Likewise, instead of passing a note behind a teacher's back, today's student is more likely to text his friend across the classroom. The new technology enables kids to interact with their friends, regardless of physical boundaries. Online communication is changing how they do the things they've done for generations—if not forever: gossip, flirt, joke around, and hang out. Most of their interchanges are about keeping tabs on one another.

This first generation of kids who've grown up taking digital media for granted is variously referred to as the "digital generation," the "Net generation," "generation M" (for media), "digital natives," and the "gamer generation." Take your pick. A recent study by the Pew Internet & American Life Project on the use of technology by kids 12 to 17 found:

- 94 percent use the Internet.
- 89 percent have Internet access at home.
- 66 percent have broadband Internet access.
- 71 percent own a mobile phone.
- 58 percent have a social-network profile.
- 51 percent own an iPod or MP3 player.
- 63 percent go online daily.

For more statistics, go to *pewinternet.org*.

Online Communities

Facebook has more than 500 million active users worldwide and MySpace more than 200 million. Twitter is a distant third, but there are other social networks for every age and interest. Kids can also pick from Neopets, Nick, VMK (Virtual Magic Kingdom), Zwinky, Gurl, SparkTop (for kids with ADD or dyslexia), and countless others. To be sure, this freedom to explore virtual worlds has its risks, and we parents need to be attuned to what our kids are up to. (See "Three Steps to Protect Your Kids Online" on page 151.) You can be assured that *allstride.com* employs both technology and humans to monitor the site to keep your kids safe.

Online communities let members have far more friends and acquaintances than they could juggle in the real world. (For most kids, social media appears not to be used as a replacement for actual relationships but as another layer of communication with existing friends.) Ito and her colleagues report that kids see face-to-face interactions, Facebook, and instant messaging as a seamless part of the same dynamic, with technology reinforcing social relationships. For example, one kid might meet another at school and then check him out on Facebook so he can talk to him more easily the next time they meet. But the new media also has the power to change relationships. Because kids can keep in closer touch with one another, strengthening existing affiliations, the culture of youth is stronger than ever.

Social media also enable kids to define themselves and therefore influence status among peers. When a kid creates a page about herself, she decides what to include and how to say it. She decides whom to list as friends and which photos to post. She selects which interests, favorite music, films, and television to list. Making these choices allows her to shape and polish her image.

When Kids Feel Different

While most kids use social media to complement "real" relationships with their peers, some kids use it to develop connections with kids they don't already know. According to the authors of *Hanging Out, Messing Around, and Geeking Out*, kids who have been marginalized because they feel they are different in some way are more open to finding new "friends" online. Our children's technical prowess and receptivity have the potential to help them face sensitive or embarrassing issues by "chatting" with kids they don't know who may also be struggling with body image, poor self-esteem, bullying, or gender identity. Or perhaps a "different" kid simply doesn't know anyone nearby with whom he can identify on such matters. Online interactions enable such kids to give one another ongoing feedback, support, and validation they can't find locally. (Other kids, who identify as computer geeks, freaks, dorks, musicians, artists, or gamers, are more likely to seek out online communities that address their interests.) By the way, many kids belong to more than one community and may therefore have multiple online identities to fit particular groups.

In addition to the meal plans, personal profile page, journal, and other features, the AllStride Community provides the valuable gifts of encouragement and feedback to kids who want to feel valued for who they are—right now. Other kids who may be slimming down on AllStride but haven't encountered social difficulties at school may still find it helpful to be able to openly discuss issues they might not want to bring up with classmates or on their other social networks. They may also be able to support kids who are having a more difficult time at school socially.

Being part of a social network also gives kids a chance to interact with adults who aren't their parents, relatives, or teachers. AllStride enables kids to talk with a pediatrician, nutritionist, fitness trainer, and family coach, all of whom they will come to know on the website. Teens pose special challenges to health-care practitioners. All too many teens adopt health-risk behaviors even as they move toward establishing separate relationships with health-care practitioners. Studies show that teens want to discuss issues with health professionals, but often they don't actually do so. Meanwhile, health-care researchers are looking at how technology could improve dialogue with kids. We believe AllStride will serve as a powerful example of how to reach kids and teens.

A Powerful Personal Experience

A few years ago I produced a documentary film on childbirth. Directed by my friend Abby Epstein, it was called "The Business of Being Born." We created a website with the same name to promote the film and an accompanying book. Soon the

Three Steps to Protect Your Kids Online

1. Be sensible. *Place the computer where it's readily visible, so you can monitor Internet use without appearing to snoop. A family room is an ideal spot, rather than a child's own room. Most social networking sites have age restrictions. Know which chat rooms your kids are using and make sure youngsters (and teens) use only well-monitored and age-appropriate ones.*

2. Employ technology. *Block instant/personal messages from anyone you and your kids don't know. Install or activate software to block unsuitable content or sexual predators. Microsoft offers detailed advice on free, downloadable parental control software that's built into operating systems such as Windows 7 or Windows Vista. Go to http://65.55.21.250/protect/parents/social/predators.aspx.*

3. Establish trust. *Spend time with your kids online. Discuss the potential online risks in an age-appropriate fashion. Role-play certain situations that could arise in online discussions. Make it clear that they should bring to your attention any situation that makes them uncomfortable. Set up rules about Internet use at home, school, and elsewhere. Protectkids.com has a contract you can adapt for your kids to sign.*

community members were touching on issues beyond the scope of the film and book, so Abby and I launched *mybestbirth.com* on Mother's Day 2010. It took off immediately, attracting thousands of members all over the world who have clearly been helped and inspired. Women share birth experiences they've enjoyed because of the information they've gotten from the movie, the book, or their "sisters" in the community. Members share their joys and offer advice and information. The site includes video interviews with new mothers, videos of home births, member blogs, and a bulletin board to show off photos of new family members. On the forums, members discuss everything from the reasons for the high rate of C-sections to nutrition during pregnancy to the best diapers for preemies. We all learn from and support one another.

My point is that being part of a virtual community is not just about meeting others with similar issues. It can also be a powerful force to effect change. When a critical mass of individuals gets behind a cause or an issue, change is far more likely to happen. We're seeing this in the political world. There's no question in my mind that a large, strong online community like *allstride.com,* particularly in partnership with other compatible online communities, can play a huge role in helping our children achieve total wellness in the years to come.

The First Weight-Loss Community for Kids

Thousands of virtual communities center on particular health conditions or on good health in general. Their chat rooms have helped men and women take charge of their health, fitness, and nutrition—and learn how to cope with specific diseases and conditions. The Web has certainly changed how people deal with their weight. Among the thousands of sites on weight control for adults are the biggies like eDiets and Spark People. Sites focused on a particular diet include Weight Watchers, Jenny Craig, South Beach, and many others.

All these sites have communities and although the particulars differ, they have one powerful thing in common: community members provide valuable support to one another. They celebrate successes, offer a virtual shoulder to lean on when another person experiences frustration or a setback, and hold out a virtual hand when another is tempted to throw in the towel—or eat a whole cheesecake!

But until *allstride.com* offered families and kids an opportunity to become members of a virtual community centered on nutrition, fitness, and health, there was no such support group for young people. Community, or as we call it, friendship, is one of the four powerful pillars that support AllStride. Once more, the purpose of the AllStride Community is to provide a safe haven for kids to commune with one another, as well as find information they can trust. Because experts drive that information, parents can feel equally comfortable that *allstride.com* is a trustworthy source for their kids to use.

Information and Inspiration

I'd like to close this chapter by focusing on how information and support can come together when kids use the Internet to explore health issues. I will be talking to Andrea Grimes Parker, a doctoral candidate in the Human Centered Computing program at Georgia Institute of Technology. Her research centers on the interaction of technology and sociology, and how the former can improve the health and nutrition of various cultural groups. Although her research has focused on adults, Parker is familiar with the research on teens and technology. Here she shares some insights that are relevant to AllStride.

Andrea Grimes Parker: A lot of times physicians will give people generalized support on cutting fat or the number of servings of vegetables they should eat each day. But often they are not given the detail they need to actually follow these recommendations.
Ricki: How does that relate to your research?
Parker: I look at how technology affects eating habits and how communities can organize to improve these habits.
Ricki: By support, do you mean primarily information?
Parker: Providing information on ways to eat better is crucial, but it turns out that providing emotional support is just as important.
Ricki: That's exciting to hear, because it mirrors what the AllStride Community does. Kids and parents learn from experts in the appropriate fields how to eat properly and get fit. But the opportunity to get and give support from peers is equally important, both for kids and parents.
Parker: We always hear that people are eating poorly, that they are getting diabetes and suffering from other health problems. Unfortunately, there is not as much positive dialogue out there. We are hoping that with technology people will be able to find strategies that lead to success.

Ricki: Do you think kids are as likely to do this as their parents?

Parker: One study shows that kids are looking for health and nutrition information online as much as elderly folks do. Half of the kids and teens interviewed in this study were looking online for such information.

Ricki: How about the emotional support part of the equation?

Parker: The Internet is an amazing resource. Researchers found that kids were checking out sites about body image, sexuality, STDs, nutrition, and exercise. By doing so they got information, but the kids also realized that they are not "freaks" because all kids have such concerns.

Ricki: How about those kids who may feel marginalized or different because they are overweight?

Parker: Kids who are different, whether they are victims of bullying or who may be struggling with social or sexual identity issues, can find the Web helpful. It also provides a wider community. A kid may not know another very overweight kid at his school, so being able to "friend" someone of his age who's also overweight can be extremely helpful. When people go to online sites that address such issues, they may be trying to validate their own feelings. It also gives them new opportunities to interact with peers.

Ricki: Do you think that the virtual nature makes it easier for kids to talk about uncomfortable issues?

Parker: Yes. The impersonal nature of the Web allows people to act differently. For example, a girl who is too shy to flirt with a boy in person might be able to do it online.

Ricki: The Internet does give kids more control over their lives, which one would hope builds confidence.

Parker: Absolutely, both the content they consume and image they present about themselves give them a sense of control. When they set up their Facebook or MySpace profile, kids can choose what they want to include. They can create their own persona, their own online presence.

Ricki: How about confidence?

Parker: Here's an interesting example of how kids who are "different" can benefit from the new technology. Researchers at Stanford University Medical Center created a video game for kids with diabetes called "Packy & Marlon." It lets them create and then take *care of an avatar with diabetes. The researchers found that the game gave the kids information, boosted their confidence to handle and manage the disease, and led to better communication with their doctors and parents. Before they were introduced to the game, the kids averaged 2.4 diabetes-related emergency visits to the hospital each year. After six months of playing the game, they were down to 0.5 annual visits. A control group of kids who didn't play the game showed no reduction in emergency visits over time.*

In the next chapter, we'll look at the fourth "F" of the AllStride program: family. Although the world is changing at warp speed and family life is unquestionably different than it was when we parents were kids, family is still front and center in raising happy, healthy kids, as Dr. John and I will discuss.

Mom Heard Alexandra's Cry for Help

Success
Story

Both of 8-year-old Alexandra's grandfathers are diabetics, and it looked as though she might be heading in the same direction. Fortunately, a white lie alerted her mom, Maria, to her distress. Today, a happier (and 14-pounds lighter) girl is able to once again fit into clothes that she'd outgrown a couple of years earlier.

Ricki: Maria, when did you notice Alexandra was having a problem with her weight?

Maria: She was always heavy, although she's into sports and very active. The doctors would tell us that she was in the 99th percentile for her age and height. But it wasn't until she came home and told me about kids teasing her that it came to a head.

Ricki: What was the incident that precipitated things?

Maria: When Alexandra wasn't invited to a classmate's birthday party, she told me it was because he'd said she was going to eat all the pizza and cupcakes. I went to see her teacher the next day and asked if she could get to the bottom of it. It turned out that the real reason was that the family was on a tight budget and could only invite a few kids. When Alexandra admitted she'd invented the story, I realized it was her cry for help.

Ricki: How did that make you feel?

Maria: I felt really bad for her because I was always heavy too. I didn't want her to fall into the same trap of being sad and not being able to buy certain clothes. Plus both my dad and my father-in-law are diabetics, and I was afraid she was headed down that path. So I went online and found the program.

Ricki: What did you like about it?

Maria: It seemed workable for a child, but I didn't start it right away. I'd revisit it and then I told myself, "OK, once she's out of school in summer, I'm going to dedicate myself to working with her."

Ricki: Had you tried other things with Alexandra before?

Maria: I'd encouraged her to eat slowly, cut back on bread and other starches, eat more veggies and fruits, and avoid fast food. But I'd never tried a specific program. This one lays everything out for you, word for word.

Ricki: Alexandra, did other kids ever say anything about your weight?

Alexandra: One of my friends from kindergarten until second grade used to say I was too fat and stuff. It made me sad.

Ricki: How much weight did you lose and how quickly?

Alexandra: I've lost 14 pounds in about three months. When I started this program, I didn't think that I'd lose this much. It took almost a week but I was so happy when I lost my first pound.

Ricki: How did you feel about that gradual weight loss, Maria?

Maria: It works because she's been able to keep it off. I've tried quick-weight-loss programs myself and it comes right back on. This is a healthier option.

Ricki: How did you incorporate the program into your lifestyle?

Maria: I would look at the menus for the week, make my shopping list, and head to the market. I'm a teacher so we started after the school year ended. It was easy to follow then, and once school started again, I used a lunchbox with ice packs. Alexandra travels with her food when she has extracurricular activities.

Ricki: Alexandra, what are your favorite meals and snacks?

Alexandra: Lisa's Pizza and hamburger casserole are my favorites, and I like the smoothies and the banana split parfait.

Ricki: Did Alexandra learn about portion control and healthy food choices?

Maria: Definitely. She's now taking control of her food. Just this week, my friend kept her after soccer practice. I packed Alexandra's food for dinner. My friend told me, "Oh, my gosh, she's so good. She measured out her hamburger casserole. We were eating something else, and she didn't even budge."

Ricki: What else is she learning?

Maria: She knows that her snacks should be about 100 calories, so she'll look at something and say, "Mom, this only has 90 calories, so I can have it instead of what it says on the meal plan." She's learning how to substitute and figure out portion sizes. Instead of heading for sweets, she knows maybe carrots or broccoli are better. This program has shown her how to make good food choices for the rest of her life.

Ricki: Do you feel that the program is worth your investment?

Maria: Definitely, because those 14 pounds have changed her life. The little girl who made fun of her all those years has stopped. And we've brought out clothes we'd put away that fit again.

Ricki: Do you do the program with her?

Maria: We've all switched to help her. We're now more aware of what we eat and portion control. I've lost 12 pounds.

Ricki: Good for you. As a teacher, what do you think about the obesity problem in this country?

Maria: I see so many kids and every year they're getting bigger and bigger. It's heartbreaking when they don't fit under the desks or can't participate in PE or certain activities because they get tired. We do a Christmas program every year, and some kids don't fit into the generic costumes. I'm so grateful that I've saved my daughter from being one of them.

Too Small to Be Big

Chapter 11

All in the Family

I like to think of each family as a piece of a huge jigsaw puzzle. All the family pieces fit together to create communities, which are the larger pieces that form our society. If a jigsaw puzzle suggests an earlier, slower-paced era, don't be fooled. As we've just learned, the 21st-century phenomenon of online communities has the potential to bring us together. At AllStride, we strongly believe in the transformative power of the family. You already know that the best thing a parent can do for her children is to be a good role model. By upgrading your habits—and doing so with the right attitude—you'll indirectly help your children change their own habits.

Let Kids Be Kids

With kids' worldliness and technical prowess, it's easy to forget the obvious: that kids are kids. Dr. John has discussed how childhood has changed since we parents inhabited that territory. He'd like to share some of these concerns and how All-Stride can help families strengthen their bonds.

Dr. John: I think a really important point is that years ago, kids were kids, and they stayed that way until well into high school.

Ricki: I'm teasing you, but haven't kids always been kids?

Dr. John: Historically, the idea that children are different from adults is a relatively recent construct. Until the last 100 years or so, once they were a certain age most kids had to work to help put food on the table. Once that was no longer necessary or socially acceptable—although it still is in certain parts of the world— there's been a clear delineation between youth and adulthood.

Ricki: And now you see that changing?

Dr. John: Obesity, among many other societal phenomena, is blurring the lines between childhood and adulthood. I've already discussed how being overweight subjects kids to problems that only older folks used to face. But changing social customs have played an equally damaging role. The two have worked hand in hand to eliminate the freedom kids had in earlier generations to just be themselves. They've also lost a certain innocence, which may be liberating in certain ways, but it's also stressful.

Ricki: What's a parent to do?

Dr. John: We can never go back to the way things were, but we can learn from earlier generations. If we simply rein in our families, feed them good food at slightly more structured times, and let them run and play freely, we'll be going a long way toward helping prevent them from becoming overweight and sexually developed before their time. These concepts are inherent in the AllStride philosophy.

Ricki: So I hear you saying to let kids be kids—but also to supervise them more.

Dr. John: Yes. I firmly believe that kids want to feel that adults are in charge—that their parents set limits because they love them and are concerned about them. Too many busy, stressed parents are ceding control to their children. Don't get me wrong. I'm not talking about a return to a Victorian approach to child rearing. Kids are incredibly smart, and when parents create an environment in which their children know they're respected and listened to, family life can be a form of teamwork.

We're the Adults

Dr. John has raised the issue of parental responsibility. It's easy to blame food companies, the advertising industry, the government, the schools, and the medical community for making so many kids overweight. But we as parents have the most at stake.

Ricki: Dr. John, how does that manifest itself for parents?

Dr. John: It means taking full responsibility for your child's health. If your child had a high fever, you'd do everything in your power to bring it down and seek medical help if you couldn't. Being heavy also threatens a child's health, so a parent's response should be just as immediate. It also means educating yourself about good nutrition, as AllStride encourages. Finally, it means leading by example.

Ricki: But you're not letting health professionals off the hook, are you?

Dr. John: No way. We, and by that I mean doctors, nurses, and nutritionists, need to be proactive with heavy children (and their parents). We must make every effort to help parents learn the basics of nutrition and avoid overfeeding infants and toddlers. And by the way, doctors also need to know more about nutrition themselves.

Ricki: Would you agree that at the end of the day, it all comes down to our families and our own personal dynamics?

Dr. John: Yes. Each family is responsible for the health of its children. This seems pretty obvious, but unfortunately, from my perspective, families rarely want to take responsibility.

Ricki: That seems so hard to believe. Is it a reflection of the denial syndrome you've talked about earlier?

Dr. John: A pediatrician friend recently told me about a teen-age boy in her practice who weighed close to 300 pounds. The mother came to my friend with her son and asked what the pediatrician would suggest. The pediatrician began by asking the mother what the boy ate in a typical day. Of course, the amount of food was enormous and the quality of the food simply abysmal. When my friend heard that he downed two double cheeseburgers every day after school, she suggested, "Why don't you cut down to only one cheeseburger or perhaps find an after-school snack alternative that's healthier?"

"Oh, I can't do that," the mother replied. "He would get mad at me if I didn't let him have his cheeseburgers!"

"So, what can I do?" the pediatrician asked me. "How can I possibly help this kid if his mother is not willing to stand up to him and teach him what is healthy and right!"

I had no answer for her. Changing the schools, the advertising industry, what's on TV, and even the content of food won't solve this problem, if parents aren't willing to work with their children to make hard decisions necessary to ensure their health.

Ricki: Has this generation of parents ceded too much power to kids by giving them everything they want in order to make their kids like them?

Dr. John: This is a very difficult time to be raising children. No matter how good the home environment, most kids are exposed to all sorts of influences. Parents want to do what's good for their kids, but sometimes their work and other commitments get in the way of just spending "quality time" with them.

Ricki: And then there is the social dynamic at school of who has what. Most kids don't want to be different. If the rest of the gang is having a cheeseburger and fries, they want to have them too.

Dr. John: In a loving way, parents have to make it clear that when necessary, they'll take responsibility for making decisions in the child's best interest.

Ricki: Let's go back to denial for a moment. Perhaps the reason that so many parents are in denial about their child's excess weight is because they have failed to control their own weight and don't want to be reminded of that.

Dr. John: That's an excellent point. We all have a very difficult time accepting failure in ourselves, and parents certainly don't want to set up their kids for failure. One way to avoid the feeling of failure is by discouraging your child from trying something you failed at. But we all have to stop treating obesity as failure. Yes, parents could have done things differently, and perhaps they should have done so sooner. But at a certain point, parents need to look at their children's health and say, "OK, this is where we are and this is what we can do to help the matter. So let's do it."

Ricki: Another way to put this is that loving your children takes sacrifice. In this case, a family may have to give up the pleasures of eating junk food for the long-term health of the child.

Dr. John: Loving your kids also takes objectivity, humility, and the willingness to accept the fact that occasionally we have to change course and do things differently. Making a commitment to change bad habits is good for everyone, and taking it on as a family project can enhance family bonds. Believe it or not, children really want their parents to act like parents, not peers.

Ricki: I'd like to add patience to the list of things that being a good parent demands.

Dr. John: Absolutely. A kid didn't become overweight overnight and the problem won't be resolved overnight. Nor should it be. Rapid weight loss is never the goal, particularly with children, and rarely results in permanent weight loss. Parents must give their child permission to take the necessary time to slim down and get healthier. Equally important is to make it clear that you're always there to serve as a sounding board.

Ricki: How would you do that?

Dr. John: We owe it to our kids to be honest with them. Naturally, we to want to protect our children, but it's better to help them shed those extra pounds and the ills that go with them once and for all. By approaching the topic gently and respectfully, you're actually showing how much you love them.

Raising the Subject

Dr. John has just identified the 700-pound gorilla in the room. For some more expert advice on how to bring up this topic gracefully, let's talk to family coach Robert Ferguson.

Ricki: Many of the kids I've interviewed who've been successful on the program came to their parents for help. But how do you talk to your kid about your concerns if he doesn't ask for help?

Robert: First of all, eliminate such words as "fat," "overweight," "heavy," and "too big" from your vocabulary. Just talking about weight loss can cause your kid to become fixated on the scale and develop a "diet" mentality and a poor self-image.

Ricki: But most kids hear about diets on the news and online. Or

*their parents have been on and off diets. They'd have to be quite
young to have not been exposed to this mindset.*

Robert: *Of course, but if you focus on weight, you'll magnify the
problems they'll have later on. Instead discuss how to maximize
their metabolism, as we will in the next chapter. A byproduct of
enhanced metabolism, of course, is fat loss. If your child says something like, "You're putting me on a diet because you think I'm fat,"
you can explain that your real concern is that he feels good about
himself and gets to do all the things he dreams of doing. When I
work with overweight adults and ask them when they first became
aware of a problem, they usually say it was between the ages of 8
and 12. So we have to be really careful about not watering those
seeds that our culture has already planted.*

We owe it to our kids to do everything we can to prevent their
becoming overweight, as I was when I was in my "tweens"
and teens. Or if your kid has already packed on some extra
pounds and inches, you'll want to help him or her to slim
down. If you've felt powerless, you'll soon learn how AllStride
enables you to introduce changes in a frank and loving way.
Nor does it stop there: once your kids take responsibility for
their own weight, they'll inspire others to do the same. As
kids who've participated in the program tell us, friends and
acquaintances take one look at them and immediately want to
know the secret of their success. No wonder self-esteem soars!

In Part III, we'll delve deeper into nutrition at home and away.
We'll also look at the other ways you can help your child succeed on AllStride—and in life.

Part 3

Educating and Motivating

By Ricki Lake

Chapter 12

Help Kids Maximize Their Metabolism

In Part I, Dr. John gave us an overview of the childhood obesity epidemic, using his perspective as a pediatrician to explain how being overweight puts a child's health at serious risk—now and in the future. He also delved into many of the reasons why so many children are overweight today. In Part II, we introduced the four components that make AllStride work—food, fun, friends, and family. In this section of the book, we'll delve deeper into the specifics of the program, starting with nutrition. In later chapters, we'll look at other ways to motivate kids to take responsibility for their health and happiness.

We've already touched on a few of the basic principles of nutrition—including the idea of "fast" and "slow" carbs. Nutritionist Robert Ferguson, Dr. John, and I are in total agreement that until we parents have some understanding of nutrition and metabolism, we can't give our kids the guidance they need.

But we also know that this subject can be an immediate turn-off to some people. That's why we've put our heads together to make this a bit more fun. I'm going to act like the talk show host I once was to poke and prod Robert to make nutrition easy to understand. Fortunately, he's great at that. Dr. John will chime in too. We suspect that many of you already know a fair amount about nutrition. If so, please regard this chapter as an opportunity to brush up on your skills. Let's start by delivering on the promise in the title of this chapter.

Big Word, Simple Concept

As a parent and a family coach used to conversing with kids, Robert has the gift of simplifying even complex concepts. "I always make my best effort to use age-appropriate examples that people can understand," he says. Let's put him to the test.

Ricki: Isn't an understanding of metabolism too complicated for kids? Most adults don't really understand it, no matter how often they hear the word.

Robert: It just depends on how it's explained and how far you take it. Even my 3-year-old daughter, Felicity, understands the basics. Here's my Reader's Digest *version of metabolism: when you consume food, your body uses energy to break it down and then it's delivered to cells and used as fuel. What isn't used as fuel is stored or excreted. When you eat an apple, a cookie, or a hamburger, your metabolism goes to work. If you run or skip rope, your metabolism starts burning calories as fuel. It's as simple as that.*

Ricki: When you explain it that way, it certainly is, but I'm fascinated that Felicity can understand it. She must be exceptionally smart.

Robert: Well, you're talking to a very proud daddy, but what Felicity understands is not how food is broken down into fuel and expended as energy. Rather she understands that she needs to listen to her body's signals.

Ricki: Could you give me an example of that?

Robert: When Felicity gets up in the morning, she knows she needs some carbs to get her going for the day. If she's turned into the

"Grumpy Monster" by midmorning, she knows that to feel good again she needs some "fast carbs," like a piece of most fruits, for example. If she's been playing hard and is low on energy, she knows she needs something like a carb-rich yogurt, which also contains some protein. Felicity doesn't know the word "metabolism," but she does understand the connection between her mood and food. It always surprises me how many adults are so out of touch with their body that they don't understand this concept at a gut level. Pardon the pun.

Ricki: How would you explain metabolism to older children, like my boys who are 8 and 13?

Robert: I'd explain that metabolism is like a factory with lots of workers. Just as when you take your car to the repair shop, every time food comes in, the workers get busy. And here I'm talking about enzymes, cells, and the like. Your job is to keep them employed. If food isn't coming in on a regular basis, your metabolism slows and "workers" get laid off. But when you eat an apple, for example, you're burning calories to break down the food and getting the energy your muscles depend on and your brain is screaming for—and lots of workers are busy.

Ricki: What happens if you eat too much at one time?

Robert: Then there's too much for the "workers" to do. If the enzymes and cells can't get the job done, your metabolism slows down. Remember, just as businesses fail if they don't have enough work, they can also fail because they can't handle the volume of work. They also fail when they don't have a business plan. Your metabolism benefits when you form a plan and put it into action.

Ricki: I think I know the answer to this question, but let me ask it anyway. Is it OK to miss a meal as long as you eat all the foods on your meal plan over the course of the day?

Robert: A basic principle of the AllStride program is blood sugar management. Going for more than three hours without eating will lead to unstable blood sugar, extreme hunger, and overeating at the next meal.

Ricki: But the reality is that you aren't always able to eat right on schedule.

Five Ways to Max Your Metabolism

Forget about losing weight and focus instead on the goal of maximizing metabolism. The more efficient one's metabolism, the more the body becomes a fat-burning machine. The whole idea of watching weight and counting calories has led to the diet mentality that plagues most adults and puts them on the diet merry-go-round. Spare your kids that approach with these five ways to burn more fat.

1. Engage in cardiorespiratory activity. Almost everyone is aware that vigorous activity speeds up the heart rate and boosts metabolism. But you don't have to be a jock to get the benefits. Walking, using Wii Fit, shooting hoops, and many other aerobic activities do the job.

2. Eat at intervals. Every time you eat, you initiate a burst of energy—it's called the thermic effect. Assuming you don't overeat, breaking down food, turning it into energy, and the process of excretion all burn calories. Eating three moderate-size meals and two or three snacks spreads the intake of calories over the day, which burns more calories, for a real win-win effect.

3. Get a good night's sleep. Kids should settle in for at least eight or nine hours. Most adults can do with a bit less, but numerous studies show that the less sleep you get, the more likely you are to be overweight.

4. Drink plenty of water. Consume enough H_2O so that your urine is clear (but no more) and you don't go more than four hours between bathroom breaks. (Urine may be yellower first thing in the morning or after taking some vitamin/mineral supplements.) The less water you drink, the more sluggish your blood, and blood carries water and nutrients to the muscles. If your muscles are dehydrated, they can't work optimally and maximize fat burning.

5. Play and get happy. For adults and some teen-agers, exercise that builds muscle increases metabolism because the more muscle you have the more calories your body burns—even at rest. Adults and some teen-agers can benefit from resistance training. But preteens and younger children would not. Instead, playing, laughing, and having fun releases endorphins and puts their metabolism on express mode.

Robert: Right. You or your child may have days that aren't perfect examples of eating at frequent intervals. So, if your teen-age daughter isn't able to eat breakfast within 30 to 60 minutes of waking, I recommend that she eat a snack and then have a late breakfast. Or if your son knows he has to run an errand at lunchtime, he can have another snack until he can eat a meal. Just make sure they're eating a meal or snack every two to three hours until an hour before bedtime. On a day in which a kid can fit in only two meals, he'll need to rely on snacks for the rest. Snacking in place of a meal is necessary when that's the only option.

Ricki: In general, to get rid of some excess body fat, you want to burn more energy, meaning calories, with activities than you're consuming as food.

Robert: That's the most obvious way, of course, but it's not the only one. Even when you're asleep, your body's normal processes burn energy in the form of calories. (See "Five Ways to Max Your Metabolism" on page 169 for some other ways.)

Ricki: Why is it so important for a child to understand his or her own metabolism?

Robert: If they learn early enough that eating often, combining certain types of foods, being active, getting enough sleep, and practicing a few other good habits will make them a bundle of health and energy, they'll just naturally want to live that way. And as a wonderful side effect, they'll burn more fat and remain fit.

It's Not Just About Fat

Although our culture is fat obsessed, slimming down is not just a matter of eating less fat, as Robert explains. Despite the fact that there's a low-fat version of almost every product you can imagine, we're still a nation full of overweight people.

Ricki: What's the connection between eating fat and being fat?

Robert: Fatty foods per se don't pack on pounds. Dietary fat is a source of calories—as, of course, are protein and carbohydrates. And consistently consuming more calories than you metabolize can lead to being overweight, or more accurately, overfat. But here's the catch. The number of calories in a gram of fat is more than twice the number in a gram of protein or carbohydrate, 9 calories and 4 calories, respectively. So dietary fat is more calorie dense.

Ricki: So that's why you should restrict fat intake?

Robert: Yes, but the best way to stay or become leaner involves three habits. First, eat vegetables and other slow carbs or fast carbs in the right amount and in combination with protein. Second, eat enough protein to feel full—it's inherently satiating. And third, don't overdo the fat. Above all, the amount of food you eat at a sitting is key.

Ricki: I still think many people don't realize that fat isn't all bad.

Robert: Protein, carbohydrate, and fat are all essential for life. There are dozens if not hundreds of reasons we need fat to be healthy and for our bodies to function properly, including the repair and maintenance of cellular structures. Fat also adds flavor, and we need fat in our diet to absorb fat-soluble micronutrients like vitamins A, D, E, and K. However, we get plenty of fat in most protein sources so we don't need to add much more than what we already get in meat, fish, eggs, and the like. But don't overlook the healthy fats in avocado, nuts, and whole grains.

Ricki: Let's go back to protein. Why does it fill you up and keep you satisfied longer than carbohydrates and fat?

Robert: Protein takes longer to digest, so you feel full longer. And when you eat a protein source and a carbohydrate source at the same meal, the protein slows down carbohydrate metabolism, keeping your blood sugar from spiking. So eating sufficient protein helps boost fat burning.

Ricki: What are some of the other good things protein does?

Robert: Many of your hormones are made up of protein, which is also necessary for the manufacture of the red blood cells that oxygenate your body. Our skin, nails, muscles, and organs are made of protein, and eating protein maintains their health. Without protein, we'd die. Here's another cool thing: digesting protein demands more calories from your stores of energy than digesting fats or carbohydrates.

"Health" and "Energy" Drinks

Dr. John talked about the detrimental effects of drinking soda in Chapter 5, but there are several other beverages worth looking at. You've probably been hearing a lot about vitamin waters, health drinks, and energy drinks. The advertising and marketing for these relative newcomers (including a whole new look for the old Gatorade®) has been brilliant, and nearly everyone in America has tried at least one of them. While there are some significant differences in these products, the common denominator is usually a form of sugar. Let's talk to him about whether kids should be drinking any of these products.

Ricki: Dr. John, what do you think of these latest drinks?
Dr. John: Approach so-called health drinks with caution and read the labels carefully. Gatorade is full of sugar and calories. For someone who's running six or seven miles a day and uses this product for rejuvenation after a run, this may not be a problem. But for a sedentary kid who chugs Gatorade while playing video games, the calories can quickly mount up. If kids simply won't drink "plain" water, there are some alternatives with fewer calories, like Propel®.
Ricki: What about energy drinks?
Dr. John: First, even the manufacturers of Red Bull®, Rockstar®, Amp Energy®, Monster®, and Shockwave® acknowledge that they should not be used by anyone for rehydration. And kids should stay away from them altogether. The energy they provide comes from sugar, as well as caffeine and other stimulants. Research has linked energy drinks to headaches, insomnia, nervousness, and even irregular heartbeat.
Ricki: How about so-called fruit drinks?
Dr. John: Kids love these, and why wouldn't they? They're loaded with sugar. Read the list of ingredients on the label and you'll often find very little actual fruit juice. Instead, they're usually full of artificial flavors and colors and, no doubt, high-fructose corn syrup. If you want your kids to have fruit, give them fruit! Juice beverages are so sweet and bear so little resemblance to fruit itself that kids may no longer be interested in actual fruit once they've become accustomed to these hypersweet concoctions.

Too Small to Be Big

Ricki: Do you feel the same way about OJ and other real juices? I have very little juice in my fridge these days.

Dr. John: That's a good decision. Even 100-percent fruit juice has a lot more concentrated sugar than the actual fruit. So enjoy them occasionally, but don't make them an everyday staple. Or dilute them half-and-half with water. When I inquire about the eating habits of my overweight patients, many tell me that they are big fruit-juice drinkers. The other thing they drink a lot of is my next suspect for helping make kids pack on pounds—milk.

Ricki: Whoa, isn't milk a healthy drink for growing kids?

Dr. John: One of the basic tenets of AllStride is balance and moderation. Nothing is good in excess. Few of us get enough calcium and vitamin D in our diets, which may well contribute to developing osteoporosis later in life. Lack of calcium and vitamin D are also associated with impaired heart function, the inability to fight disease effectively, and even a propensity for some cancers. So a couple of glasses (or even three) a day are fine, but anything more is excessive. Nor is milk the only source of calcium and vitamin D. Numerous other food sources, including leafy greens, which have lots of other benefits, are probably a much better choice than loading up on milk.

Ricki: So you're telling me that too much milk can contribute to a child being overweight?

Dr. John: Absolutely. Americans are one of the few cultures that drink the milk of another species. I've seen too many overweight kids whose parents tell me that their youngsters drink milk constantly. This is particularly true of overweight babies and toddlers.

Ricki: But you would agree, wouldn't you, that one of the pleasures of childhood is eating chocolate-chip cookies warm from the oven with a glass of ice-cold milk?

Dr. John: Of course, and not just for kids! We don't want to take the joy out of eating, but we do want to prevent overindulgence. Kids (and adults) need to understand that treats are for special occasions, but when we indulge in certain treats every day, they lose their significance. We seem to have evolved into a culture that thinks if some is good, more is better; however, more of certain foods is definitely worse.

Nutrition Facts

Serving Size 1 cup (32g)
Servings Per Container About 13

Amount Per Serving	Cereal	with 1/2 cup skim milk
Calories	120	160
Calories from Fat	15	15
	% Daily Value**	
Total Fat 1.5g*	**2%**	**2%**
Saturated Fat 0g	**0%**	**0%**
Trans Fat 0g		
Polyunsaturated Fat 0.5g		
Monounsaturated Fat 0.5g		
Cholesterol 0mg	**0%**	**1%**
Sodium 190mg	**8%**	**10%**
Potassium 50mg	**1%**	**7%**
Total Carbohydrate 28g	**9%**	**11%**
Dietary Fiber 1g	**5%**	**5%**
Sugars 11g		
Other Carbohydrate 16g		
Protein 1g		
Vitamin A	10%	15%
Vitamin C	10%	10%
Calcium	10%	25%
Iron	25%	25%
Vitamin D	10%	25%
Thiamin	25%	30%
Riboflavin	25%	35%
Niacin	25%	25%
Vitamin B$_6$	25%	25%
Folic Acid	25%	25%
Vitamin B$_{12}$	25%	35%
Phosphorus	6%	15%
Magnesium		
Zinc		

	Calories	2,000	2,500
Total Fat	Less than	65g	80g
Sat Fat	Less than	20g	25g
Cholesterol	Less than	300mg	300mg
Sodium	Less than	2,400mg	2,400mg
Potassium		3,500mg	3,500mg
Total Carbohydrate		300g	375g
Dietary Fiber		25g	30g

Ingredients: Whole Grain Corn, Sugar, Corn Meal, Corn Syrup, Canola and/or Rice Bran Oil, Salt, Tricalcium Phosphate, Trisodium Phosphate, Red 40, Yellow 6, Blue 1 and Other Color Added, Natural and Artificial Flavor, Citric Acid, Malic Acid. BHT Added to Preserve Freshness.

Nutritional Facts panel and ingredients list from a popular breakfast cereal marketed to children.

Required Reading: Food Labels

OK, get out your reading glasses. Robert and I are going to talk about the nutrition information that the Food and Drug Administration (FDA) requires on every packaged food. If you don't regularly scan these labels, now is the time to get into the habit. For a tiny document, it packs in a huge amount of content.

Robert: The label has two parts. One is a list of ingredients, which must appear in descending order of weight. The other part is a Nutrition Facts panel, which tells you both the number of grams of an adult's daily needs of carbohydrate, fat, and certain micronutrients provided by one serving of this food, as well as the percentage of RDA (recommended daily allowance) for each.

Ricki: Should you start with the ingredients list or the Nutritional Facts panel?

Robert: Start with the list of ingredients so you won't waste time on the Nutrition Facts panel if the product is made with ingredients that you don't want your child to consume. (See "Reading Between the Lines" on page 178.) Case in point: if hydrogenated or partially hydrogenated oils (trans fats) are listed, you may not want to bring this into your home. But if the list of ingredients gets a thumbs up, you can move on to the Nutrition Facts panel.

Ricki: And the first thing there, of course, is the serving size.

Robert: Right. Let's say we're looking at a bottle of iced tea or a can of soda. Most people assume either one is a single serving, but that's often not the case. For example, a 20-ounce bottle of flavored ice tea sweetened with high-fructose corn syrup would appear to be one serving, but when you look at the serving size on its Nutrition Facts panel, you'll see that a single serving is 8 ounces.

Ricki: That's really confusing. It means that the calorie and sugar content listed is for less than half the whole bottle.

Robert: Right. If you drank the whole bottle, you'd have to multiply the calorie and sugar count and everything else by two and a half. If you're looking at this with an 8-year-old, it's a great opportunity to challenge him to use his multiplication skills—or a calculator.

Ricki: What else can we learn from the panel?

Robert: The next thing you'll find is the number of calories in the serving. Remember, the number refers to a single serving, not necessarily the whole can, bottle, or package.

Ricki: Then we get to the detail on the fat, carbohydrates, and protein.

Robert: Right. It starts with total fat content, and then saturated and trans-fat content, in grams and as a percentage of RDA. Saturated fats are those that are solid at room temperature, like butter and most other animal fats. Trans fats are manufactured hydrogenated or partially hydrogenated fats. You want to minimize the intake of both saturated and trans fats. The percentages immediately tell if a food contributes a lot (20 percent or more) or a little (5 percent or less) of the RDA (known as the daily value) of either or both these fats. The fat information is followed by cholesterol and sodium content, again in both grams and percentages of RDA.

Ricki: Can you tell fast carbs from slow carbs on the Nutrition Facts panel?

Robert: No, but the fiber is broken out, so you can get a good idea if a product is a good source of fiber. If it is, it's more likely to act as a slow carb. The sugar content is also provided. The more sugar, the more the food behaves as a fast carb. Please understand that fast carbs aren't bad. They simply become sugar in your bloodstream more quickly than slow carbs do. After the carbs come protein and finally a listing of some of the micronutrients, such as vitamins A and D, iron, and calcium.

Ricki: I notice that the protein component only lists grams of protein, if applicable, not the percent of daily value. Why is that?

Robert: It's to avoid confusion because a product may be marketed to a certain age group—toddler dinners, for example.

Ricki: That brings up the question of whether the RDAs on a food label have any relevance to kids and teens?

Robert: You've just hit upon one of several deficiencies in the Nutrition Facts panel. The RDA is designed for adults and is based on 2,000 calories a day. Once a girl is 15 and a boy is 18, she or he is regarded as an adult for this purpose. The data is theoretically based on what an average person "should" be consuming daily. But no one is average, and the needs of a petite grandmother differ significantly from those of a 6-foot, 4-inch linebacker, to say nothing of those of an 8-year-old. This is another reason why we need *education to understand labeling and realize these data are merely guidelines, not rules.*

Ricki: Which sugars are you OK with?

Robert: I prefer brown-rice syrup and evaporated cane juice, which are the sweeteners found in most higher-quality energy bars and other products. (For sugars best avoided, see "The Dirty Dozen" below.)

Ricki: Which sugar substitutes do you recommend?

Robert: I'm not a big fan of so-called non-nutritive sweeteners for children. If you are going to use them, I suggest using stevia (made from an herb) or sucralose (marketed as Splenda®). Although sodas are hardly my first choice for beverages, use those sweetened with Splenda, rather than aspartame or saccharin, whenever possible. My wife and I prefer to use natural sweeteners, such as raisins or applesauce, but not sugar, to sweeten cookies or muffins.

Ricki: It almost sounds like you need a doctorate in organic chemistry to understand a food label. Can a kid really do it?

Robert: I would say that from age 7 or 8 on, they could begin to look at them. In the next chapter, we'll talk about how to make that a fun game to play in the supermarket.

The Dirty Dozen

Robert recommends that people keep a close eye out for— and eat sparingly if at all—any of the following forms of sugar:

1. Brown sugar
2. Corn starch
3. Corn syrup
4. Dextrose (glucose)
5. High-fructose corn syrup (HFCS)
6. Malt syrup
7. Maltitol (a sugar alcohol)
8. Maltitol syrup (a sugar alcohol)
9. Maltose
10. Maple syrup
11. Modified corn starch
12. Sucrose (table sugar)

Reading Between the Lines

Ingredients must be listed on food labels in descending order, as measured by weight. Sounds straightforward, right? Well, yes and no, depending on the product. Here are the things you should be on the alert for:

- *Is it full of sugar? Here's where you'll find the names of the actual sugars used in the product. You'll probably be surprised by how much sugar is in foods like mustard and mayonnaise. If the first or second ingredient is some form of sugar, best steer clear.*

- *Do many of the ingredients sound as if they come from a chemistry lab instead of Mother Nature? You might want to think twice about eating foods full of preservatives, emulsifiers, flavor enhancers, and other often-unpronounceable ingredients.*

- *Does it contain trans fats, despite what the Nutrition Facts panel says? If you see the words "hydrogenated" or "partially hydrogenated," it does. (See "When None Means Some" on page 84.)*

- *Is the list of ingredients almost as long as your arm? If so, this is likely a highly processed food that isn't a great source of nutrition.*

Chances are, once you become an adept reader of food labels, you'll start to change your purchasing habits.

In the next chapter Dr. John, Robert, and I will look at how to implement the food component of AllStride in family life, including how to restore the family meal to its rightful place of honor, plus fun ideas for cooking with your kids, and lots more.

Jakory Now Thinks Before He Eats

Success Story

With his 12th birthday and a switch to a new school coming up, Jakory knew it was time to slim down. He and his mom, Arnette, just weren't sure how to do it. After we met, they decided to embark on the program. Eight weeks later, an older, wiser, slimmer, and happier Jakory returned for another chat. By then he'd lost 17 pounds overall and 2 inches from his waist. But first, listen in on our initial visit.

Arnette: About two years ago, I noticed that Jakory's extra pounds had started accumulating rather rapidly. He's very picky. He'll just eat certain things and at certain periods during the day.

Ricki: Give me an example.

Jakory: Mac and cheese. I eat it all the time and drown it in hot sauce.

Arnette: Other kids would make fun of him and say stuff he was really heartbroken about. And so was I.

Ricki: May I ask what they said to you, Jakory?

Jakory: They called me fat sometimes. When I was in fourth grade, I wasn't used to people calling me names, but it doesn't really hurt my feelings now.

Ricki: I can relate, but no one should ever have to get used to being called names.

Jakory: In fifth and sixth grade, I started getting attitude from other kids, and when they'd say something smart I'd just yell at them.

Ricki: So you have maybe anger issues because of this?

Jakory: Yeah.

Ricki: Arnette, you have a master's degree and you counsel kids in community colleges, right? Could you counsel your own son?

Arnette: It seems I can help others, but I feel paralyzed when it comes to Jakory. Diabetes runs in his dad's and my side of the family, so I know how serious this is for him. I just want him to have a fair chance in life. We tried multiple things, but they weren't working. When I found this program and saw the before-and-after pictures of kids, I thought, "Wow, this might be something that might work for him."

Ricki: Jakory, what would you like to change about yourself?

Jakory: My stomach and the chubbiness in my face.

Ricki: May I ask how tall you are and how much you weigh now?

Jakory: I'm 5-feet, 6-inches tall and weigh 192 pounds.

Ricki: Good luck, Jakory. I'll see you in a couple of months.

After he'd been on the program for eight weeks, I met with Jakory and Arnette again. He's now 12 years old, but that's not the only change in him.

Ricki: Jakory, you look awesome. So, how did you do? And was it easy?

Jakory: Good. I lost 17 pounds. I was hoping that I wouldn't cheat, but I did well and didn't sneak anything. The meals are really good.

Ricki: That's incredible. Do you feel like a different kid?

Jakory: I feel happier and more energetic, and I can run faster and for a longer time.

Ricki: Mom, was it challenging to jump into the program?

Arnette: The meals are easy to do, and it was just a matter of my being organized. I would make three dinners on Sunday. Then on the week-nights when Jakory gets home before I do, he just heats up dinner and makes sure he has the appropriate portion size.

Ricki: Jakory, what's it like for you at your new school?

Jakory: It's fine now. I make new friends all the time and I know two kids from my other school. They said I got skinnier from last year. I just laughed, but it made me feel like I'd accomplished something.

Ricki: Arnette, what have you learned through this program?

Arnette: Now when I go to the store, I read labels and I might look at a product and think to myself, "I'd rather buy this because it's lower in calories and has less sugar than the brand I'd usually pick up." I also realized that I was overfeeding him, so I was contributing to the problem. Now he's having seven meals a day, but he's eating different things. And he always looks forward to dessert.

Ricki: OK, so what's your favorite dessert?

Jakory: The banana split with a graham cracker and low-fat ice cream.

Ricki: What's been the hardest thing about this program?

Jakory: At school they sell chips and ice cream and slush puppies everywhere, but I just have my own lunch and I eat it.

Ricki: What do you tell yourself when you're tempted by that stuff?

Jakory: What my mom told me: "Think about it."

Ricki: And obviously you've thought about it because you've lost almost half of what you want to lose. Arnette, has the program affected the way you eat? Because I have to say you look slimmer too.

Arnette: Yeah. I'm more conscious of what I eat. I'll ask myself, "Do I really need that?" Or I'll go to a healthier choice versus what I used to have.

Jakory: I'm like her thought bubble. I'll say, "Think about it."

Chapter 13

Let's Get Real at Home

By now, you're undoubtedly convinced that AllStride can make a huge difference in your family's life. But how will you deal with the inevitable issues around soda and such? And are there really enough hours in the day to do everything you're already doing, plus the things you know will boost your kid's chances of success?

In this chapter, we'll confront some of the inevitable day-to-day challenges and explain how to overcome them. We'll also get up-close and personal about how to encourage dialogue with your kids. Once you've made some changes yourself and are communicating well with the kids, they'll start to change their own habits. And they'll be able to share some of these same techniques with their peers and teachers to help leap over roadblocks on their way to a healthy, happy future.

Too Small to Be Big

Real-Time Challenges

The first question in many parents' minds may well be how much time the AllStride program will involve. My coauthor, Dr. John, offers his advice.

Ricki: How would you advise parents to find the time for the changes in family life inherent in the AllStride program?

Dr. John: It's a matter of priorities and swapping one thing for another. The AllStride meal plans can actually save time for busy parents. Most of us waste far too much time in front of the TV. In the half hour spent watching a sitcom, you and your kid could make Jell-O®, or personalize next month's meal plans.

Ricki: Still, playing with your child, helping with journal entries, and making sure that you have all the food in the house to satisfy the meal plans does take some time.

Dr. John: Actually, you get a two-week shopping list along with the meal plans, which is a tremendous time saver. Other than the shopping, which you'd be doing anyway—and you'll be shopping in the same places you already do—playing with your kid and tracking progress do unquestionably add to the workload, but the bright side is that they're wonderful opportunities for togetherness.

Real-Life Lesson #1: Fruit Doesn't Come in a Container

Kids love the natural sweetness of most fruit. Instead of juice, which eliminates most of the fiber, encourage kids to have fruit snacks they can prepare themselves or with a little help. All provide antioxidants, fiber, and tempting taste:

- Make sugar-free gelatin with berries or fruit cubes and top with sugar-free (and trans fat-free) Cool Whip®.
- Make balls of cantaloupe, honeydew, and watermelon for a colorful mix.
- Layer parfaits with plain yogurt, fruit, and granola. Add some currants or cut-up raisins for sweetness.
- Make fruit kebabs with orange segments, apple slices, and strawberries.

Ricki: And then there's the cooking! I'm not the only mom who doesn't have much time to cook or has never really gotten comfortable enough in the kitchen to be able to get a meal on the table quickly at the end of the day.

Dr. John: Feeling you're too busy to cook, lacking confidence in the kitchen, or simply not liking to cook is nothing new. After all, Peg Bracken sold four million copies of her I Hate to Cook Book, first published in 1960. The recipes relied heavily on canned soup, processed cheese—Velveeta®, anyone?—and similar short cuts to get dinner on the table for her family after her day job.

Ricki: I wonder if my mother had that cookbook. She hated to cook, which is probably why I've always been afraid of cooking.

Dr. John: Fortunately, the meals on the meal plans are quite basic and most take no more than half an hour to get on the table. And, as Robert is so fond of saying, start where you are.

Ricki: So takeout could work?

Dr. John: Sure, although you may want to change your order slightly as you become more health conscious. Nor do you have to cook everything from scratch. The food on the meal plans is the "regular" food your kid has been eating. Plus, many convenience products, such as precooked rice in a pouch you just pop into the microwave, shortcut the process of getting a meal on the table. With rice, a salad from a salad bar, and some chicken drumsticks from the corner deli, you could have a decent meal on the table in minutes. You don't have to turn into a Rachel Ray overnight! One of the best gifts you can give your kids is some culinary confidence, which will happen naturally if you involve them in meal prep.

Ricki: How would you go about that?

Dr. John: I'm not talking about just having a teen-ager help out with dinner, although that's always welcome. Enjoying the process of preparing a meal or a snack can start in toddlerhood. Standing on a steady stepstool, a 4-year-old is perfectly capable of stirring ingredients in a bowl or sifting flour—and he'll love it! Just be prepared for a mess. Kids are fascinated by the "magic" that occurs when ingredients change their texture, shape, and color as they become food. (For more on cooking with your kids, see the five "Real-Life Lessons" starting on page 183.)

Sit Down Together, for Real

In many households, having dinner as a family has gone the way of rotary phones. However, many families—mine among them—are beginning to rediscover its value. My boys and I haven't been eating together enough. All too often, they're plunked in front of the TV or Xbox console. Along with increasing the likelihood that kids will get a healthy meal, there's no substitute for the time spent around the table, when there's no choice but to talk to one another.

You may be thinking, "Come on. How could something as basic as eating a meal with your kids help their health?" And how can eating together help combat overeating? Seems counterintuitive, doesn't it? But dining together is hardly a revolutionary concept. If you finish this book and do nothing else that we've suggested, we hope you'll schedule meals with your kids on a regular basis. Let's explore with Dr. John why eating together is so powerful, and how to actually make it happen, even when older kids may resist the idea outright.

Family Meals Boost Self-Esteem

Sitting down together as a family obviously can improve intergenerational communication. But there actually are health and weight implications to not sitting down to eat as a family. Numerous studies provide evidence that kids in families that don't eat together consume more calories, more added sugar, more fat, and less fruits and vegetables than kids who do eat with their parents. Clearly, kids are more likely to learn good nutritional habits by eating with adults. But interestingly, it turns out that family dinners also appear to promote better self-esteem in kids—at least in girls. One study based at the University of Minnesota looked at the eating habits of more than 2,500 adolescents who filled out two surveys five years apart. Teen-age girls who sat down to eat with their families at least five times a week were considerably less likely to use diuretics and self-induced vomiting to control their weight than girls who did not eat frequently with their families. This pattern didn't show up in adolescent boys.

Time-Savers for Busy Families

Lisa Daniel, a great cook and one of the creators of what is now AllStride, offers her tips on how to get meals on the table quickly:

- *First, check out the more than 150 recipes at allstride.com. Although I love to cook, I'm as time-deprived as any other working mom. Most of the recipes contain six or fewer ingredients and take no more than 30 minutes. There's also a special section for quick dishes that take no longer than 20 minutes.*

- *Never make just one of anything, whether it's a meatloaf or mac and cheese. Freeze the second one or serve it a few days later.*

- *Make big batches of chili, soup, and casseroles. Then freeze what you don't eat right away in single portions so they can be defrosted quickly in the microwave. It's as easy as getting takeout and far more economical.*

- *Freeze leftovers as soon as they cool down, and then reheat them for a quick second meal.*

- *No time to wash, spin, peel, and chop? Pick up salad fixings at a salad bar. Add salad dressing and you're good to go.*

- *When you do have a few minutes on the weekend, chop onions, peppers, and other veggies and freeze them in resealable bags. Press out as much of the air as possible to avoid freezer burn. When you need one of these ingredients, pour out what you need to shave off a few minutes of prep time.*

- *Do the same with raw veggies, fruit, and cheese cubes for snacks. Twice a week, cut up enough for the next three or four days and refrigerate in individual portions, so you can have a snack in a hungry child's hand (or a backpack) in seconds.*

- *Boned chicken or cut-up stew meat reduces prep and/or cook times.*

- *Cut down on trips to the supermarket by filling your freezer with the foods that your family eats most often.*

- *Always have certain kid-friendly staples on hand, so you can quickly get a tuna-fish casserole or spaghetti with tomato sauce on the table—fast.*

Real-Life Lesson #2: Tools Are Cool

Lurking in your kitchen drawers and cupboards are many "toys" kids can use, depending upon age and proper supervision, of course. Best of all, kids get to eat the fruits of their labor.

- **Salad spinner.** *A 4-year-old can help you pull the string or crank the spinner, and older kids can handle it themselves.*

- **Plastic-encased dicer.** *These devices allow for safe chopping of fruit or veggies at an early age.*

- **Vegetable peeler.** *Make sure to use one with a safety feature so kids can't cut themselves. Scrape the skin off carrots and cucumbers, and then pull the peeler along their length to make curls.*

- **Apple corer.** *Core apples for applesauce or baked apples.*

- **Air corn-popper.** *With no moving parts (except the popcorn), this device is safe and easy to use. The most difficult thing for kids is to contain their excitement while they wait for the popping to start. Have a big plastic or metal bowl on hand to catch the kernels. Just add some olive oil or grated cheese and enjoy.*

- **Blender.** *This appliance is a real power trip for youngsters. Little ones love to push the buttons. Older kids can whip up their own fruit smoothies and other concoctions.*

- **Food processor.** *Younger kids can help feed nuts or other ingredients into the tube. Older kids can make hummus, guacamole, and other dips.*

Ricki: I'm particularly aware of the importance of family meals. I grew up in a family that rarely sat down together, unless we were in a restaurant or celebrating a holiday with relatives.

Dr. John: Eating together isn't just about eating; it's also about communicating. Turning off the TV, cell phones, and iPods and sitting down together offers the opportunity for family interactions. My grown kids are now the ones who push for sit-down meals. The students have become the teachers!

Real-Life Lesson #3: Cooking Is an Art Form

Nursery school children and chefs both get to play with their food. Whether it's making pancakes or pizza, salad or toasted cheese, cooking offers limitless opportunities for creativity:

- *On a weekend, ask for help making pancake batter, and then show the kids how to pour it into metal cookie cutters on the griddle to form fun shapes or "draw" faces—or whatever—on the batter with blueberries.*

- *Follow the recipe for Lisa's Pizza at allstride.com, but also provide bell-pepper slices, onions, olives, and jarred artichoke hearts. Give the kids free rein to "decorate" as they wish before the pie goes in the oven.*

- *For a quicker version, do the same with pita bread or English muffin halves as the foundation for each mini-pizza. In this case, precook the peppers and onions.*

- *Make smiley faces on open-face toasted cheese sandwiches with cut-up deli ham (nose), pimento strips (mouth), and sliced olives (eyes). You can also use small pitas smeared with cream cheese or hummus as a canvas.*

- *No need to make the same salad each night. Make it fun by setting out a salad bar of unusual ingredients: nuts, sunflower seeds or pepitas, shelled edamame, baby corn, black beans, feta or other cheese, and berries and other fruit, in addition to the greens. See what your kids come up with.*

Real-Life Lesson #4: Not All Snacks Come in Packs

Older kids can create these snacks themselves:

- *Stuff celery sticks with peanut butter, cream cheese, hummus, whitefish salad, or deviled ham.*
- *Ham and cheese are natural partners for roll-ups, but any sliced meat or poultry will do.*
- *Make wraps with low-carb tortillas, lettuce, and favorite sandwich fillings.*
- *Dip carrot sticks in hummus or blue-cheese dressing.*
- *Combine softened cream cheese and grated Cheddar cheese, form into a ball or cylinder, and roll in chopped nuts. Chill for in the fridge before serving.*

Ricki: What's a reasonable number of meals to aim for in a week?
Dr. John: It's different for every family. A couple with young children and only one parent who works outside the home might have breakfast and dinner together almost daily. If both parents work and commute to their jobs and their teen-age kids participate in sports and other activities that can run into the evenings, twice-a-week dinners might be a reasonable goal.
Ricki: Now it's time to get our family coach in on the conversation. Robert, how would you get an older child to commit to family dinners twice a week or so?
Robert: It's best to get that tradition in place when kids are little. That said, if a teen-ager or a younger child isn't accustomed to sitting down to dinner with the rest of the family or has decided to rebel against this custom to test you, the key is to offer a choice so that he feels he's part of the decision. First, I'd tell him that you'd like to have dinner as a family more often because much of the rest of the time everyone is doing his own thing. You might say that you always enjoy going out together to dinner and you'd like to replicate some of that experience at home. Then I would get him involved with the decision by asking whether he prefers having family dinner, say, on weeknights or weekends. Remember, you always want to present options so the kid doesn't feel deprived of choice.

Ricki: Dr. John, how about advice on "safe" topics of conversation?

Dr. John: Let the kids take command of the conversation. You'll learn a lot more about what's important to them by not taking center stage. "What did you do at school today?" invariably leads to a one- or two-word response to appease you. Instead, you might comment on things that they're apt to know more about than you do. I might ask a teen-ager, "Why is Lady Lala so popular?" He'd get a kick out of telling poor old dad that her name is really Lady Gaga, and then he'd probably share how outrageous she is. Such conversations will give you a glimpse into what makes your kids tick. If appropriate, thank them for assisting you with the shopping and the preparation.

Ricki: If adults are lying low when it comes to conversation, what should we be doing?

Dr. John: Listening and watching. Observe the way your kids eat and which foods they concentrate on. When they were tiny, you knew every drop or spoonful they put in their mouths. Eating together puts eating habits and likes and dislikes up-close and personal in a way you might miss if everyone is eating at a different time.

Real-Life Lesson #5: Veggies Grow in the Dirt

All too many young kids don't know celery from a cucumber. When they think vegetables, ketchup and French fries come to mind. Here's a field trip with lessons that will last long after the veggies are in their tummies. Take your kids to a farm stand or greenmarket. Let them pick out radishes, carrots, string beans, sweet peas, or whatever else strikes their fancy. At home, younger kids will have fun washing off the soil, and their older siblings can handle chopping and slicing—well supervised, of course. Your brood may not learn to love spinach overnight, but getting down and dirty with veggies may at least make them more willing to try them.

Ricki: Robert, any other tips or suggestions?

Robert: Clearly you don't want kids to feel they're chained to the table for half an hour. Use your time at the table to empower and encourage them. Above all, make this time together pleasant. Keep the tone light to encourage freedom of speech and actions. Don't insist they try everything or clean their plates. If they want seconds, let it happen—and no raised eyebrows or comments or talk of starving children in third-world countries. If you comment on table manners, do it with love and grace. Agree with your partner ahead of time to avoid topics in which kids have no interest, such as office politics. And no arguments. You could even add some party atmosphere by lighting candles, putting flowers on the table, and playing some background music that everyone likes. You might also ask kids if they'd like to invite a guest to dinner. It's amazing how much you learn about your own child when he's talking with a friend.

Get Real About Vegetables

Vegetables (like fruit) are packed with antioxidants. The USDA Food Guide Pyramid for Young Children (see Resources on page 258) recommends that kids between 2 and 6 consume three servings of vegetables a day. Older kids are encouraged to have three to five servings a day. AllStride meal plans comply with these guidelines, making it easy to get the recommended number of servings. Now Robert is going to teach us how to turn your spinach-hating kid into a real-life Popeye, who not only eats his veggies but also actually likes them. Once again, on AllStride kids eat only the food they like.

Ricki: OK, Robert. Big challenge here. How do you encourage kids to eat veggies?

Robert: You probably know the first thing I am going to tell you?

Ricki: Let me guess. Mom and dad have to eat vegetables if they expect their kids to.

Robert: Bingo! If you eat vegetables, it makes it easier for your child or teen-ager to eat them. If you like them, he or she will eventually feel the same way. This said, there's a "patience curve," during which parents benefit by waiting. In time kids almost always come over to the veggie side. That may not happen in a week, a month, or even a year, but eventually they'll come around. If you're not yet a veggie lover, start experimenting yourself and get your child involved. Tell her that this is your first time eating zucchini and that you could experiment together. After you eat it, be sure to ask her what she thinks before you share your opinion.

Ricki: What do you do while waiting for kids to see the light?

Robert: Here's the second secret to getting kids to enjoy veggies, and it's a no-brainer: make them taste better. Only one problem: you must get kids to taste them, right? Tell them that you'd love it if they'd be the testers for some new veggies or new ways of cooking familiar ones. Make it clear that one taste is all you ask.

Ricki: So how can we make vegetables tastier?

Robert: Start by not overcooking them. Simply steam fresh vegetables until they're tender but not overdone, and add a splash of olive oil and a dash of salt and pepper. Or stir-fry them. Roasting brings out the natural sweetness in many vegetables, particularly root vegetables like carrots and beets. Or grill vegetables like zucchini and asparagus alongside burgers or chicken breasts. They take on a smoky flavor that many kids will find appealing. Thread bell peppers, onions, and cherry tomatoes on skewers and grill them by themselves or with lamb or beef kebabs. For some strange reason, kids will often eat veggies when they're cut up small in soup, which reminds me that tomato soup is a perennial kid favorite.

Ricki: Some of my friends hide veggies in other foods.

Robert: That too. You can add veggies to foods your child already likes, such as my camouflage approach of lacing mac and cheese with broccoli, zucchini, or cauliflower. (For other sneaky strategies, see "Hiding in Plain Sight," opposite.)

Ricki: But don't many younger children prefer their veggies raw?

Robert: Many do. The same kid who'll spit out cooked carrots may love his carrot sticks, although he may change his tune after he tries a roasted carrot. Many vegetables have a higher vitamin and mineral content raw. In fact, a great way to get some veggies into kids is to put out a plate of "appetizers" to hold off the troops while you're cooking. Carrots, string beans, bell-pepper strips, and other raw veggies with dip can be quite inviting. Most kids love bite-size cherry tomatoes. Peas right out of the shell are another favorite. And for some reason, kids don't think of salsa as a vegetable, so you could put out some mild salsa with the raw veggies.

Ricki: My boys used to come home from nursery school all excited about making "ants on a log," by spreading peanut butter on celery sticks and topping them with raisins or currants.

Robert: Yes. Fun is the third key to making veggies more appealing to kids. My 3-year-old has fun eating puréed peas in soup, although she doesn't like whole peas. She likes to see if she can keep the soup on her spoon as she transfers it from the bowl to her mouth. Then, we sip on our soup and make funny faces.

Hiding in Plain Sight

- If your kids like smoothies, they'll never notice a leaf of kale, spinach, or chard whirred into a banana or strawberry drink. Dark fruits and berries have the added advantage of further masking the veggie.

- Likewise, you can easily sneak some grated carrot, zucchini, or puréed pumpkin into quick breads, muffins, and even cookies.

- Cocoa is a great way to hide other ingredients. A chocolate-zucchini cake was an Internet sensation a few years back. You'll find recipes on numerous food sites.

- Don't stop with "sneaky snacks." You can stash chopped-up veggies in chili, meatballs, meatloaf, sloppy Joes, pasta sauce, and lasagna.

Ricki: How about serving salads to kids?

Robert: You'll probably want to expand your definition of a salad. While adults may love arugula tossed with olive oil and vinegar, young kids are more likely to enjoy coleslaw or grated carrots with some raisins.

Ricki: One of the problems with vegetables is the time it takes to prepare them, even before you get to the cooking part.

Robert: *You've just hit upon the fourth key to eating more veggies. Prepping vegetables needn't be a hassle. You can buy most salad greens prewashed and many veggies already cut up. Or use frozen vegetables. Flash-frozen fresh from the field, they're likely to be as nutritious (if not more so) than those that may have traveled cross-country to your kitchen. If frozen veggies are in a sauce, check for high-fructose corn syrup or partially hydrogenated oil. Also make sure there's no more than 350 mg of sodium per serving. If your kids like chickpeas or other legumes, canned versions are major time savers without any sacrifice in taste.*

Ricki: *Could there possibly be anything else to say about more ways to get more veggies into kids?*

Robert: *Yes, and it's a biggie: psychology. The way to get kids to eat more vegetables is not to push them. Instead, serve the vegetables your kids will eat, while you continue to eat those you'd like them to enjoy one day. Instead of focusing on your frustration or annoyance about their preferences, come up with creative new ways to serve vegetables. Accept the twin realities inherent in all child rearing: you can lead, but pushing only builds resistance.*

In the next chapter, we'll move beyond the confines of home to look at the day-to-day challenges that occur in the world of fast-food restaurants, the school cafeteria, and interactions with buddies and bullies. We'll also touch on the inevitable bumps in the road—along with more tactics to help your child achieve total wellness.

Finally, we'll have some fun with role-playing. How often has a food server tried to up-sell you a plate of fries when all you wanted was a burger? Or tried to interest you in dessert when you'd resolved to just have coffee after dinner? Well, Robert will teach you a few simple techniques for handling such situations in a good-humored fashion, while sticking to your guns. And then in turn you can role-play with your kids.

Too Small to Be Big

Chloe's Parents Helped Her Nip "It" in the Bud

Success
Story

Six pounds may not sound like much, but 7-year-old Chloe was toting around a new tummy and her face was puffing up. All too aware of the epidemic of childhood obesity, her parents, Karen and Kendall, decided to take action before things got out of control. As a side benefit, dad lost his "gut" and mom lost a few pounds, while learning how to cook differently.

Ricki: What made you decide to do something about Chloe's eating habits?

Karen: It seemed that her face was getting a lot fatter, and I also saw it in her arms. She had put on maybe 6 to 8 pounds over the summer.

Kendall: We also that noticed that her tummy had started to poke out a bit, which affected how her clothes fit. So we were concerned and we wanted to see what we could do to reverse that trend or prevent it from continuing.

Karen: I didn't want it to escalate out of control. And I didn't want her to have problems for the rest of her life. I wanted to tackle it now.

Kendall: We were also concerned because childhood obesity in this country is a major issue. We didn't want our daughter to have problems when she got to high school, being teased and taunted because she's overweight.

Ricki: What attracted you to the program?

Karen: This was the only one that I found that had actual meal planning. I was able to go online and choose what she liked and avoid what she didn't like so the meal plans were customized for her. I needed it all spelled out for me.

Ricki: How long was it before Chloe started to slim down?

Karen: We started seeing results right away, but her weight loss was gradual, which is exactly what we wanted and what we expected. I actually got a lot of comments just from people at church. People have come up to me and said, "Oh, she's really gone down."

Chloe: I lost 6 pounds.

Ricki: What attracted you to the program?

Karen: I really like the fact that it's tailored to the child. That helps a lot. It's very easy for her to do.

Ricki: Kendall, you lost quite a bit of weight yourself, didn't you?

Kendall: When Karen implemented the program in our home, it changed what we ate for our main meal and snacks as well, and I actually lost about 20 pounds. I used to have a big gut. If parents get involved, then what we're doing for the kids will actually allow us to lose weight as well.

Ricki: And how about you, Karen?

Karen: I lost about 5 pounds.

Ricki: So the program achieved your goals for Chloe?

Kendall: It did. Parents need something to counteract their kids' lack of activity.

Karen: A lot of kids are not getting the proper exercise they need at school and after school. When they come home, they're just sitting in front of the television or playing video games. They're just not as active as we were as kids, and the food choices are a lot different nowadays. When I was a child, everything was prepared, not packaged. So that's definitely a difference.

Ricki: Will the program make permanent changes in your life?

Karen: I learned how to prepare things lower in calories.

Kendall: It will definitely impact the way I eat from now on. And for Chloe, we want her to be conscious of her size and maintain her weight throughout her lifetime. Through this program, she's learned skills that will allow her to make better food choices.

Ricki: Do you feel the program was worth the cost?

Karen: It's a small investment upfront, and the skills you learn stay with you for the rest of your life.

Kendall: I think it's priceless. Not only does it impact her health—when you eat healthy, you eat right—it also impacts her quality of life and how she feels about herself. As she's growing up, she doesn't have to worry about being taunted. You can't put a price tag on that.

Chapter 14

The School Cafeteria and Other "Real-Life" Challenges

One of the reasons the AllStride program is so effective is that your child can do it anywhere, not just with familiar food at home and surrounded and supported by people who love him. Because the meal plans are driven by his or her own food preferences, they can be followed at school, camp, a friend's house, a restaurant—or wherever.

In this chapter, you'll learn how to integrate your kid's meal plans with what's available outside the home. In fact, the process of learning how to make the right choices is exactly why AllStride works—and why it lays the groundwork for a lifetime of total wellness. Family coach and nutritionist Robert Ferguson and I will also introduce some techniques you and your child can use to follow the program without—OMG—attracting unwanted attention.

AllStride Goes to School

Let's start with school, because that's where kids spend the most time outside their home. Of course, school encompasses many situations. We'll deal with several of the ones that could impact a child or teen-ager's ability to follow the AllStride program or open the door to teasing or bullying.

Ricki: The worst thing for most kids is to appear different from their peers. Does a kid have to bring lunch and snacks to school to do AllStride?

Robert: The AllStride philosophy centers on choice. A kid on the program doesn't have to brown-bag it if her meal plan includes foods readily available at school. Ditto with snacks. On the other hand, if she doesn't like the choices at school and prefers to bring her own lunch and snacks, she has that freedom. My 3-year-old goes to preschool with her food in her backpack. She knows that she can either have the meal or snack being offered or her own food.

Ricki: Should you talk to the child's teacher about her bringing snacks from home?

Robert: If a child were allergic to certain foods, would parents alert the teacher? Or if she has type 1 or type 2 diabetes and eating too many carbs at once could lead to diabetic coma, would they do so? Of course they would. Likewise, in a pleasant, respectful way, parents can share the fact that they prefer that their child eat her own snacks when she doesn't want the food being served. There's another aspect of snacking we should discuss.

Ricki: What's that?

Robert: It's crucial that a kid not skip a snack because she dislikes it or it isn't on her meal plan. It's better to keep one's metabolism revved up by eating every two or three hours than have nothing. If a kid's blood sugar level drops too low, it could affect mood, concentration, and the ability to control emotions. Even if snacks sit uneaten in a backpack, the option should still be there. Or the kid can substitute the snack for a meal if the food served in the lunchroom doesn't pass muster.

Ricki: How would you explain that to the child?

Robert: I'd tell her that eating lunch at noon is part of our tradition, but when the meal she wants isn't available, she should snack until she can eat a meal she does like. Just don't go without.

Ricki: But wouldn't bringing lunch and snacks instead of eating the cafeteria fare put a kid at risk for being teased by other kids?

Robert: Definitely. But like so many issues, to a large extent this one involves a child's age, level of self-confidence, and the culture of the school. Some schools celebrate individual differences. Many do not. If a child wants to bring her own food, the goal is to empower her to do so. Or if she's not sure, send her with lunch and snacks. And let her know that it's her choice whether or not to eat them. When a child feels that she has a choice in the matter, she has power. If she feels as though she "has to" eat this or that, she's lost that power. The hope is that at a certain point, she internalizes her meal plan and picks the best options available.

Ricki: How would you empower her?

Robert: If she's nervous about teasing or simply dealing with questions from her schoolmates, I'd suggest the parent role-play some techniques to deflect them. The response could simply be, "I don't want that" or "I don't like that." Or she could make it clear she prefers her own food by saying, "I brought one of my favorite sandwiches" or "I've been looking forward to biting into this pear all morning." There is no need to mention AllStride or a meal plan, which could draw unwanted attention. We've actually heard from many kids that the lunches they bring from home are so good other kids try to swap with them!

Ricki: If your child opts to eat the cafeteria meals, how would you help him to make the right choices?

Robert: Most school systems post the week's lunch menus online, so parents and kids could get in the habit of checking them on Sunday night and planning for the week. A kid's understanding of the basics of nutrition, meaning carbohydrate, protein, and fat sources, also comes into play. He also needs to know how to estimate portions, using the hand-and-fist method. So, for example, if he decides that he wants the spaghetti and meatballs on Tuesday, explain that he can have two fist-size portions, because one fist represents a protein source (the meatballs) and the other represents a fast carb (the pasta). Additionally, he can have a side of slow-carb veggies or salad.

Ricki: We're been assuming that kids want to stay with their meal plan. What happens if some of the lunch choices or snacks available at school are just too tempting?

Robert: First, remember that no food is totally off limits, if eaten in the right quantity and with the right amounts of other foods. So a snack of a chocolate-chip cookie and milk is fine, but four cookies and chocolate milk are not.

Ricki: But it's also a matter of ceding control, right?

Robert: You got it. The only attitude a parent can have is, "We expect the best. We accept the rest." There's no point in resisting things that are out of your control. That process begins the day a toddler starts preschool. We have to believe that children have their best interests in mind and even if they occasionally go off plan, that has to be their choice. Kids are learning life skills, as well as following a meal plan.

Ricki: I notice that you are not suggesting that a child say anything negative about the school food or snacks to other kids.

Robert: Right. If she says something like, "My snack is better than those cookies" or "My mom says that the school lunches aren't healthy," she's being judgmental. It's not a good idea to tell her friend who's eating a Snickers® bar that it's not good for her. If parents don't make judgments about food and how other families eat, their kids won't either.

Ricki: Help me out with how you would instill such behavior.

Robert: Say a kid makes a comment about a friend eating fast food almost every day. The parent might respond by saying, "I would never allow that. It's OK to eat fast food occasionally, but eating at home is much better." Wow! That comment demeans that other family, probably without knowing anything about their circumstances. Instead, one could reply, "That can be quite convenient," which is a neutral statement.

Ricki: And what if the kid then says, "So why can't we have fast food more often?"

Robert: All the parent has to say is something along the lines of, "Our choice is to eat at home most nights, but we'll continue to occasionally go out for fast food." Or simply omit the second part of the sentence. The parent could also ask her kid, "Is there something you'd like to eat at a fast-food restaurant that we can't make at home? Or is it the experience of eating at a particular place?" Keep the dialogue going. This is an opportunity to teach a kid that it's perfectly possible to make a tasty burger with all the fixings, fries, or a sundae at home.

Peer Power

We've mentioned the issue of peer pressure before, but now let's look at how it impacts a child on the AllStride program— or rather, how it needn't. Until kids are about age 7, parents are still the primary influence in their lives. From 7 to 12, their peers increasingly influence their attitudes and opinions, and by the time they're teen-agers, kids are usually part of a pack. This subject goes right to the heart of Robert's profession as a family coach.

Ricki: Obviously, it's normal for any kid to want to fit in with other kids, but how can parents help children deal with the negative aspects of peer pressure—particularly when a child may be labeled as uncool because he's heavier than other kids or not as competent in sports?

Robert: It starts with teaching kids that all people are different, which makes each of us unique and special. The key is to learn to appreciate and respect himself and others. Then, if parents later hear the child saying something negative or degrading about another person, they can communicate the need to be compassionate and nonjudgmental.

Ricki: Another aspect of peer pressure is that a kid may want to eat only certain foods or drinks because her friends or the cool kids at school eat or drink only those products. So it may be cool to drink chocolate milk at school and dorky to drink "white" milk. How's a parent to handle that?

Robert: I can only repeat that parents determine their own shopping list, but they can't control what the child does outside the home. By forbidding chocolate milk, for example, parents may be forcing him to disobey them because he's powerless to be the only kid who drinks plain milk. (In Chapter 17, we'll talk about how you might want to get together with other parents and talk to the appropriate officials about why there is anything but unflavored milk in the school lunchroom, as well as other issues.)

Ricki: *So you just have to give into it?*

Robert: *Another approach is to find out why the child feels the food is so cool and suggest a substitute. When my daughter encountered chocolate milk at school, we quickly found a brand with the ingredients that we encourage in our home. So she had the option of chocolate milk, but she chose to stay with white milk. I wholeheartedly believe that if we'd forbidden chocolate milk, it would have made her curious and she might have opted for it so as to not feel deprived of a treat.*

Ricki: *This gets into the realm of marketing food products linked to a movie or a character kids love. Say my 8-year-old son loves a certain action hero and a fast-food chain is promoting the hero's latest movie by giving away a related trinket with a particular meal. His friends are talking about this trinket, but I'm not inclined to eat at that restaurant and I'm not happy with companies marketing directly to children in this fashion. How can I handle that without making my son feel like an outsider?*

Robert: *My advice would be to ask him why he wants to go to that restaurant and get that meal. I sincerely doubt he'll say that it's because this is the best burger in the world. Instead, he'll probably say he wants the trinket. In that case, you could suggest an action figure or another branded toy linked to the film. Chances are he'll think this is a much better idea, and likely his friends would agree.*

Ricki: *Thanks. I'll remember that. Peer pressure is stressful on a child, and bullying is outright cruel. And sadly, heavy children are far more apt to be the target of bullies. How can you coach your child to handle a bully?*

Robert: *Bullies like to take advantage of another person's perceived vulnerability, often because they have their own insecurities. Help a child understand where the bully is coming from. Teach him to use diversionary tactics to get the bully's focus off him. If a bully sees another kid eating differently, he may realize that he himself might be eating something of lesser nutritional value, which fuels his insecurities. So, when the bully comments on a meal or snack choice,*

a kid needs to know how to redirect the attention to another subject.
Ricki: Give me some examples, please.
Robert: OK. The bully might say, "Why aren't you eating pizza like the rest of us? I bet you're on a diet." The first approach would be to redirect the conversation by saying something like, "What was the score in that basketball game? You guys looked great. When's the next game?" If the bully returns to the subject of food, the child could say something like, "I like that, but I'd rather eat this because it's one of my favorites." Or take the less upfront approach by saying, "I can't eat that because it upsets my stomach."
Ricki: I'm not sure I could pull that off. How can you get an overweight teen-age girl short on self-confidence to stand up to the most popular girl in her class, who enjoys bullying kids not in her orbit?
Robert: Whether or not these scenarios work, the key thing is for the kid not to feel demeaned or disempowered. That depends in large part on instilling confidence that she's a unique and wonderful person. She'll also need some practice—with the parent acting as the bully. Then switch places and have her play the bully. Chances are you'll both wind up laughing. Instead of standing up to her tormentor, she's actually avoiding confrontation by initiating a change in the conversation. When all else fails, empower a kid with the knowledge that it's OK to respond with a little white lie like, "My mom is making me eat this" in order to eliminate the unwanted attention.
Ricki: Kids are sometimes so ashamed of being bullied that they don't tell their parents. If you suspect this is happening, how can you draw your child out?
Robert: Always encourage a kid to talk about his day. You could mention some examples of bullying, along with some solutions. For instance, a parent could share an experience she had with bullying and how she dealt with it. Explain that bullying is an unfortunate fact of life, but we always have the ability to rationalize the behavior of the bully, which allows us to remain empowered. Add that a bully may embarrass you or arouse negative feelings about yourself, but it's critical not to feel guilty and blame yourself.
Ricki: Do you think it's appropriate to go to your child's teacher or the school principal if, despite your kid's best efforts, the bullying continues?

Robert: Absolutely. Ask for help and guidance. Seasoned teachers have seen bullying time and time again. If the teacher can't help, go to the principal, coach, school board, or anyone else in authority. Keep asking for assistance until there is resolution. Also take advantage of the AllStride Community for tips and tactics on how to cope with such situations.

Eating Out and Enjoying It

Let's switch gears and discuss dining out with the family. Whether you're at a fast-food place or your favorite family restaurant, eating out is usually a break in routine. The chief cook and bottle washer gets a night off. Everyone gets to order what he or she wants. And sitting at a booth or table creates a certain intimacy. How do dining out and the AllStride program come together? I'm sure that Robert is going to have some pretty interesting opinions and suggestions.

Ricki: Would you suggest some guidelines for eating out when one or more of the children (and perhaps you) are following AllStride?
Robert: The objective is to make it fun for everyone by following the same guidelines we discussed in Chapter 12 for family dinners at home. But when eating out, let kids make their own decisions about what to order. Parents should also be sure to leave any judgmental comments (and looks) at home. Better yet, send them into outer space! Again, although adults can guard the gates at home, kids should be able to make their own choices in a restaurant, just as they do at school.
Ricki: But you certainly could set a ceiling on the cost of an individual meal.
Robert: Of course, parents have every right to explain that the only way the family can continue to eat out regularly is if they stick to the budget. That might mean that the kids need to decide if a Coke is more important than ice cream after dinner. Again, choices always work better than restrictions.
Ricki: It makes sense to not "police" the kids' choices. If you nag them, you could turn a pleasant outing into a contest of wills and spoil things for everyone.

Robert: Exactly. But here's one way to exert some influence. All restaurant chains and even many local restaurants post their menus online. Some also provide nutritional information. (You'll find links to the websites of major chains at allstride.com.) This allows kids and parents to preview the menu. Deciding what to order before being seated in the restaurant increases the chances of making choices that kids will be proud of after the fact. If a kid solicits a parent's opinion, feel free to offer advice. But don't be heavy handed. Eating out is about fun, as well as sustenance.

Ricki: One of the things I often see when I take my boys out is that the server or the cashier tries to convince them to add to their order. For a kid who's following an AllStride meal plan, this could be the last thing needed. What would you advise?

Robert: Sometimes the server will even offer a larger portion for the same price, or a free beverage as an enticement. Again, this is a good reason to look at the menu ahead of time and then stick to one's guns. Always order what you plan to order, not what they're trying to sell you, even if it's free. After explaining that restaurants always want to sell you more than you plan to order, make this into another opportunity to role-play with your kid. Let's say that your 8-year-old decides he wants to get the fish fillet on a roll with coleslaw. Here's what often happens next:

Server: Hi sweetheart, do you know what you want today?

Child: Yes. I'd like the fish sandwich, please, and a diet soda.

Server: How about some fries with that?

Child: No, thank you.

Server: Actually, we're giving them away today, so I'll put them on your plate just in case you decide to have them.

Child: OK.

Ricki: How could a kid change that outcome?

Robert: First, you could play your son and he could play the server. Then swap roles. When he gets to the hard sell on fries, you (pretending to be your son) could say, "No thanks, I really don't want them" or "Not today, thank you" or "Thank you, but I hate to waste food since I'm not going to eat them." Chances are the server will back off at that point.

Visiting Other Families

As children get older, they're increasingly likely to eat at another child's house or dine out with another family. This can produce various forms of pressure, along with the realization that other families' habits and standards may be very different. Let's check in with Robert to get some tips on how to manage such situations.

Ricki: It's important for kids to experience other families' lifestyles, but how can they avoid awkward situations?

Robert: First and foremost, accept the reality that a kid has to make her own decisions. Don't interrogate her when she comes home to find out what she ate. However, it could help if the parent and kid role-played some situations ahead of time. For example, she might feel pressured by her friend's parents to eat or drink something she doesn't want.

Ricki: How would a kid handle that?

Robert: Teach a child that a closed-ended response, like "No," will probably make the other parent or friend want to know why. This usually causes kids to give in or feel guilty. To achieve the outcome she wants, she could say, "No thank you. I ate before I left home and I'm not hungry" or "Thanks for offering. Do you have diet soda or iced tea?" If she gets pushed on this issue, the go-to move would be, "I don't like the taste of regular soda and prefer iced tea."

Ricki: How about the "grandparents' syndrome?" In order to win their affection, they often shower kids with treats and ignore your wishes about what to feed them. They may even joke with your kids about conspiring to do things mom and dad won't let them do. What's a parent to do?

Robert: There's no question that food can be a loaded topic between generations. Parents or in-laws may regard different attitudes about food as an implicit judgment on the way you or your partner was raised. That said, the younger the child the easier this is to handle. With grace and love, simply explain to grandparents that you'd like them to serve the foods that you've prepared. Don't forbid them to take your kids to fast-food restaurants, even if you don't patronize them yourself. Instead, give recommendations about what to order. Just as you would with your kids, show some latitude. Otherwise, they may go behind your back. With older children, it's best to simply leave the choices to them, as we've discussed before.

Ricki: Would you tell grandparents that the kid is following the AllStride program or let him or her bring it up?

Robert: With a teen-ager, it's best to let him tell his grandparents, if he so chooses. With a child of 8 or under, the parent can talk to the grandparents, explaining that AllStride isn't a typical weight-loss diet but an all-encompassing lifestyle. I recommend that parents encourage grandparents to show interest and get the child excited about walking them through allstride.com. This can be an empowering experience.

Ricki: What about the opposite problem—when grandparents are too focused on a child's size? I've seen grandmothers nagging their granddaughters about their weight, which is scary.

Robert: Gently explain that it's not in the grandchild's best interest to pay much attention to weight. It's also important that they not make any sarcastic comments about weight, or talk about how active kids used to be or how everyone ate in the "good old days." Such comments plant more seeds of damage than you realize.

Ricki: Let's move to divorced or separated parents with different attitudes toward food. How do you keep your kid from getting caught in the middle when he spends time in two households?

Robert: The issues here often go far deeper than food. Even if the parents are not speaking positively about each other, the children want the love of both. They will likely eat what's served when they are with him (or her) to avoid raising issues. Or sometimes, just to annoy one parent, they'll eat the way the other parent eats. Once more, one should avoid referring to one dietary approach as healthier or better.

Ricki: How would you broach the subject?

Robert: Obviously, one's ex is not going to be receptive to pressure about anything, but stroking his (or her) ego may produce results. If I were in such a situation, I might say I'm learning more about nutrition and found this really cool book that's becoming part of my lifestyle and wanted to share it. I might ask, "May I give you a copy because you pick up things so well? And I'd love your feedback

on some ways to implement this in our kids' lives." Of course, each individual would have to tailor this to fit the ex's talents or attitudes.
Ricki: *What if the ex is resistant to the idea of your child doing AllStride?*
Robert: *First, a parent must have done her homework so she can answer reasonable concerns about putting a child on a "diet"—which, of course, AllStride is not. She might say something like this: "Lanie has told me she's being teased about her weight at school. I did some research and discovered AllStride, which integrates nutrition and activity to help kids feel better about themselves. It also enables them to have online buddies who are part of the All-Stride Community. I know you're busy, but would you look at the website with me so you can learn more?"*
Ricki: *Or a kid could have such a conversation with the other parent.*
Robert: *Right. An older child might find that spending time with the other parent gives him an opportunity to either visit* allstride.com *or simply put into practice his new skills in keeping his body on the fat-burning track.*

In the next chapter we'll discuss how to motivate and encourage without coming on too strong. The last thing you want to do is remove control from the only person who has the power to transform himself into a shining example of total wellness: your child. You can help in numerous ways, including gently passing on your knowledge of nutrition as reflected in your own lifestyle choices. But you can't do AllStride for him.

Grace Got the Ball Rolling, and Levi Joined In

Success Story

Tamra and Caleb were always careful about what their kids ate. Eleven-year-old Grace and 10-year-old Levi were also very active, preferring to be outside jumping on the trampoline or riding their bikes rather than watching TV or sitting at the computer. They even walk to school, where Grace plays soccer and Levi plays basketball. Nonetheless, year after year, the kids got larger—and we're not just talking about height. Let's hear how Grace lost 32 pounds, including whittling 3½ inches from her waist and 4½ inches from her hips, and how Levi lost 17 pounds.

Ricki: Grace, I understand you heard about the program first.

Grace: I was going to ask my mom if we could do something to help my weight, but then a friend told me about the program. She said she got to eat three snacks and three meals a day and how it's fun having online friends. When I got home, I talked to my mom about it.

Ricki: Tamra, did you have concerns about putting the kids on a weight-loss program?

Tamra: My gut reaction was, "I don't want you on a diet. I don't think it's the healthiest thing for you."

Ricki: What changed your mind?

Tamra: After I went online, I saw that one of the founders of this program is a nutritionist who had the same concerns I did, which is why it isn't a "diet." After we signed up, I was amazed at how well it worked.

Grace: My mother said we could only do the program if my brother and I promised to stay committed to the meal plan.

Ricki: So you were really motivated, weren't you?

Grace: I weighed about 127 pounds and I was only 11 years old. And people were making rude remarks at school.

Ricki: What kind of things?

Grace: Once I walked into the bathroom to change and there were other girls there. One of them said, "I hate how fat girls wear clothes that only thin girls should wear."

Tamra: Grace is going into middle school this year, and I knew this kind of name-calling was going to get a whole lot worse. As a parent, you want to protect your children, to do the best for them, and have them feel good about themselves.

Ricki: Did you talk to Grace and Levi about these self-esteem issues?

Tamra: I would remind them that even though they might struggle with their weight, being healthy on the inside is the most important thing. And I would tell them they are beautiful, incredible, and intelligent, and they should feel good about themselves, no matter what.

Ricki: It sounds as though you were as motivated as Grace was to find a solution.

Tamra: I was very frustrated after years of trying to do everything I could. I'd hear Grace talk about how she'd seen a cute outfit, and then she'd put it on and feel worse about herself because it didn't look the way she thought it should.

Ricki: Why do you think the program worked so well for the kids?

Tamra: If you're teaching your children a lifestyle, it needs to be for everyone. It didn't single out the children in any way. Once we began the program, we lived by it faithfully. Now it's just our way of life.

Ricki: Grace, in addition to losing 32 pounds, which is fabulous, what other changes have you experienced?

Grace: I can run faster and swim faster and jump higher on the trampoline. I feel really good about myself, and not only because I'm now a better athlete. Before I did the program, I wasn't so confident about how I looked. It feels good to know that my weight is right where it should be.

Ricki: I bet you're enjoying clothes shopping more these days.

Grace: It's really fun. I'm into trying on different things just to see how they look on me.

Ricki: Levi, you lost 17 pounds. You must feel great about that.

Levi: I feel good. Now that I've lost weight, I'm not embarrassed to take my shirt off in the summer.

Tamra: It's not just about weight. My greatest concern was their health. They're also very confident now and social. The biggest impact is how they're treated in school. They're well liked, and there are no more mean comments.

Ricki: What have they learned?

Tamra: They now know how to make the right choices about what they're putting in their bodies and how it will affect them. They love having dessert every night. That's something they never got to do, except on special occasions, in the past. But now we know how to do it.

Ricki: Grace, you must be really proud of yourself.

Grace: When I look in the mirror, I feel happy and grateful that I found this program and that I helped my family.

Too Small to Be Big

Chapter 15

How to Help Your Child Succeed

There's a thin line between doing everything you can to help your child improve his appearance, health, energy, and self-esteem on AllStride and being an overbearing parent whose efforts backfire. Nutritionist and family coach Robert Ferguson brings a unique perspective to this challenge of motivating without pressuring, of teaching without lecturing, and ultimately, of understanding that even a young child has to be in control of his body. Finally, you want to give your child the tools not just to get trim and active, but also to embark on a healthy, happy future.

Great Expectations, Not

Let's chat with Robert about how to help your kid achieve these ambitious goals—without turning him or her off.

Ricki: Is there a secret to success on AllStride you can share with us?

Robert: There's no magic wand a parent can wave over a child, but there are three components essential to success. First, she needs to want to do the program. Second, she has to understand in her heart that she'd rather make changes than remain where she is. Finally, she must like the program—meaning the activities and, of course, the food. And most importantly, she needs to know that there's no connection between her appearance and her parents' love for her.

Ricki: What should a parent expect when her kid starts AllStride? And what can the kid expect?

Robert: The only thing the parent can expect is a great opportunity to bond over this experience. That said, the larger answer to both questions is the same: nothing. Have no set expectations. Even if one can't erase them from one's mind, certainly don't convey them to the child. The length of time it will take him to reach a healthy weight depends upon how "overfat" he is and how faithful he is to the program. Finally, hard as it may be to accept, a parent's expectations are irrelevant. To prove it, consider signing a contract, promising to remain hands off, unless the kid asks for help. (See "Put It on Paper," opposite.)

Ricki: This raises the question of whether you or your child should set a goal weight.

Robert: Dr. John and I agree that the answer is unequivocally no. Everyone has a unique metabolism, so setting a specific number is problematic—regardless of what the BMI charts show—particularly for a growing child. Establishing a goal weight could also play into a child's desire to achieve an unrealistic body image. That's not to say that the pediatrician might not suggest a target range.

Ricki: But goals are motivational. So what kinds of goals could a kid aim for?

Robert: It's reasonable to look for her clothes to fit better, to go down a clothing size or two, to be able to run faster and longer, and to feel good about herself.

Ricki: What if a kid asks how long it will take?

Robert: Just admit that you don't know. Showing your own vulnerability can help encourage communication at a time when your child feels vulnerable. If mom is also starting on a self-improvement program, she can honestly say, "I wish I knew how long it will take me to fit into my favorite jeans again, but I don't know that either. We'll both see as some time passes." Obviously, the closer the child sticks to his personalized meal plans and the fitness program, the sooner the desired outcome will be achieved.

Put It on Paper

Relinquishing control to your child isn't easy for most parents, particularly if that's not been the pattern in the past. But once you accept that you can never truly control another person, whether it's your spouse, your child, or an employee, it's a tremendously liberating experience. Here's an idea that might work with a skeptical child. Offer to draft a contract and sign it. The key thing is that your kid isn't promising anything. It's all on your shoulders. Then he gets to call you on it if you don't follow the agreement. You can write your own contract or follow this model:

- I promise to support you on AllStride in any way you ask me to.
- I promise to not nag you about your goals and progress.
- I will offer help only if you ask for it.
- I will be sure to always have the foods on your meal plans in the house.
- I promise to make or provide the meals on your meal plan.
- I will join you in your favorite activities at least twice a week.
- I will help you track your food intake, if you want me to.
- I will help you measure yourself, if you want me to.

Then add some sort of consequence for not fulfilling your end of the bargain! Now sign it and abide by it.

Ricki: *So the first lesson for parents is to project no expectations on their child.*
Robert: *Exactly, except for the fact that kids can expect parents to be in the game with them—all the way. We want to stay away from any hint of a win-lose mentality and the idea that there's only one way to succeed. I may sound like a broken record, but the child*

has to set the goals. Whatever the motivation is, that's what will provide the fuel to get started. At first, it might be as simple as: "I want to feel good about myself" or "I want boys to like me" or "I don't want to be teased anymore" or "I want to join the basketball team" or "I want to wear cool clothes."

Ricki: I'm curious about why you used the term "at first."

Robert: We always have to meet a person where she is. Of course, a parent is after much larger goals, like improved health, but it's essential to not mention those. Once the child begins to see results, the momentum will become contagious. She'll probably then discover other ways she wants to change, such as cutting back on sugar or eating more vegetables or being more physically active. I can advise, but what you discover yourself is a thousand times more powerful. In fact, human nature is such that if I tell you to do something, you may do just the opposite!

Ricki: If goal weight is out, how can a kid feel he is making progress?

Robert: Remember, weight is only one of many parameters. We've all seen a kid shoot up 2 or 3 inches over summer break. In this case, a kid's weight could remain the same, but he's gotten taller and narrower—and that's a good thing. That's one reason why Dr. John and I recommend using a tape measure, as well as a scale, to track results. Inches are actually more important than pounds, because as he slims down, a child will be eliminating fat and building lean muscle.

Ricki: Does muscle weigh more than fat?

Robert: That's a common misconception. But muscle is denser than fat. Believe it or not, a pound of fat takes up six times as much space in your body as a pound of muscle. So weight may not change, even as inches trend downward—remember muscle takes up less space. One reason we recommend tracking measurements on both arms and legs is that it naturally yields a higher number of inches, which is a big motivator. (See "Measuring Up," opposite.) Eventually the pounds will follow suit because the more muscle a child has, the faster she'll burn fat. We recommend measuring once a week and taking a new photo each week. Again, weight loss is not the objective of the AllStride program; it's a side effect.

Ricki: I can see another problem with setting a goal weight. If there's a big span between existing weight and goal weight, it could be overwhelming.

Robert: Exactly. If all a kid sees is how distant the finish line is, he could get terribly discouraged. By setting some intermediate goals, he can enjoy a string of successes. It's part of the glass-half-full mindset. Even if Jimmy has 30 pounds to lose, when the first 5 peel off, it's cause for celebration. I also strongly advise that other objectives be factored into the equation: having more energy, sleeping better, being more active, and even fitting into a new pair of jeans.

Measuring Up

Before a kid starts AllStride, Robert recommends that she enter her baseline data in her journal, against which she'll chart her results. Depending upon her age, she may want your help or she may not be comfortable having you do this. Perhaps, she'd prefer working with a sibling or a friend. If so, make sure that person is old enough to do this properly. Or maybe she can do it herself. In addition to weight and height, she'll want to record the following measurements, using a cloth measuring tape:

- Widest part of the neck
- Widest part of the chest
- Both upper arms at widest point
- Both forearms at the widest part
- Both wrists
- Waist (1 inch below the navel for boy; 1 inch above the navel for girls)
- Hips at the widest point
- Both thighs at the widest part
- Both calves at the widest part

A few full-length photographs—one a front view and one a side view—can also be a powerful motivator. Use a plain background like a wall or a sheet hung in the doorframe and have her wear clothing in a contrasting color. Your child may be able to do this herself with a timed-delay feature if she's uncomfortable with having you do it.

Changing Habits

If your child is in agreement with the AllStride program from day one, you have a leg up—but no parent should ever pressure a kid if he isn't ready. This doesn't mean that he has to love it every day, but it does mean that he agrees it's worth doing. For most children this isn't a problem, since many of them have been dealing with self-esteem issues for some time. Let's talk to Robert about the role parents can play in lovingly motivating a child when resolve falters, boredom sets in, or he momentarily loses sight of his goals.

Ricki: How do you keep a child on the straight and narrow?

Robert: Parents love their kids and want to do everything for them. But part of loving them is letting them make mistakes, so they can learn from them. Give a child an opportunity for self-motivation and the realization that actions have consequences. This is much more impactful than simply demanding or even gently prodding her to do something. Clearly, if a child veers off the meal plans on a regular basis, she won't see the results she desires. That connection between actions and results will likely provide the necessary motivation. But that's not to say that parents can't always be there for support, gentle reminders, or whatever. And of course, they also need to offer praise and appropriate rewards. Nonetheless, the child gets to take the lead, even if she's only 4 years old.

Ricki: So no nagging and no withholding other food.

Robert: Never insist on anything. Instead, parents can ask her what she'd rather have and later record (or have her record) the food she did eat in her online journal. It may be a struggle to remove judgments from the situation, but believe me, they'll get parents nowhere. And worse, they could take her to a bad place emotionally.

Ricki: We'll come back to praise and judgment, but we all know how hard it is to change ingrained habits. I'd love your insights.

Robert: There are five steps to developing good habits. (See "Five Steps to New and Improved Habits" on page 221.) Regardless of age, it's never too late to change habits. And that includes eating habits (See "The Five-Star Opportunity to Give Your Kids the Edge," opposite.)

The Five-Star Opportunity to Give Your Kids the Edge

Anyone reading this book is clearly interested in feeding her children well. But even if you're new to the subject of nutrition, don't be distressed if you feel you no longer have a five-star opportunity. Robert's philosophy is that you always start from where you are at the moment, so here are the five opportunities that any parent has to give kids a metabolic edge:

***** Before birth. Before and during the mother's pregnancy, her nutrition can affect the infant.
**** From infancy to age 2. The child gets a grounding in nutrition. Breast-feeding is ideal, if possible.
*** From age 2 to age 6. The child will have developed certain eating habits, but they are not yet fully ingrained.
** From age 7 to age 12. Habits have been formed and peer pressure is powerful.
* From age 13 on. Habits are strong and peer pressure has supplanted parental influence.

Practice Your Poker Face

Isaiah calls it a game face; Robert refers to it as a poker face. Both suggest that you learn how to avoid signaling disappointment, whether it's over bungling a catch at second base or eating junk food. We already talked about not being judgmental about how other families eat. Let's delve deeper into the reasons for this with Robert.

Ricki: Most parents feel that part of their job is to teach their children the difference between right and wrong, but you say we should also teach them not to make judgments. Can you clarify that?
Robert: There are really two issues here. Of course, we want to help our children develop a moral compass. But we don't do that by laying down the law and then trying to catch our kids when they break the rules. And, I assure you, they will. Instead, I believe the way to raise children is to build an atmosphere of trust and com-

passion. *Being judgmental destroys trust because a child intuitively wants to please his parents and therefore has to hide anything they won't approve of. I call it the "candy-wrappers-under-the-bed" syndrome.*

Ricki: *I know all about that!*

Robert: *Being judgmental about certain foods can lead to conceal-ment and "cheating" because the kid will try to reconcile his own actions with his desire to please his parents. The last thing parents want is for a kid to feel he's a failure because he can never live up to expectations. And another thing, parents: learn how to wipe that look off your face when your son walks into your vegetarian kitchen with a Big Mac in his hand. Even if you say nothing, a kid can read your body language like a book. Yes, it's hard not to react with either words or actions. But it gets easier with practice.*

Ricki: *Obviously we all have opinions about a food or behavior, but you're saying it's better not to judge other people, including your own kids.*

Robert: *I think most people do the best they can, but we all fall short at times. Expecting perfection at all times is unreasonable. Most parents try to serve their kids the best food they can, based on their knowledge and their pocketbook. By setting up a system of "goods" and "bads" you can put kids in a difficult situation.*

Ricki: *You've touched on this when kids are guests in other people's houses.*

Robert: *Right. Say the family next door eats differently than you do. If parents negatively label other people's eating patterns, they put kids in an untenable position. Their children can either hold true to their family's food "rules" or be polite guests who eat what's offered to them, despite the fact that mom and dad would disap-prove. The same applies when visiting relatives.*

Ricki: *What would you advise instead?*

Robert: *It goes back to the control issue. Parents have every right to purchase, cook, and serve only the foods they want their kids to eat. But when visiting other people, leave judgments at home. Appreciate the hospitality and enjoy the foods that best serve you. My wife and I want our daughters to grow up knowing that it's perfectly all right to have their own food preferences, without imposing them on others.*

Ricki: *Your daughters are still young. How does this work when your kids are pre-teens or teen-agers?*

Five Steps to New and Improved Habits

If parents can help kids change their habits, they'll have given them a gift that keeps on giving. Here is Robert's method for helping kids bust the old and develop the new:

1. Identify the habit. For example, Lucy is eating too much candy.

2. Ask yourself why this is a bad habit. In this case, it might be that it's making her blood sugar unstable, so she's crabby and tired in the afternoon and ravenous by dinner. Plus, you're worried about her getting more cavities.

3. Ask yourself what is the benefit of the habit to your child. Perhaps eating candy bars gives Lucy pleasure and/or they're convenient to toss in her backpack. Also ask yourself what the benefit is for you. In this case, it might be the price and the fact that you don't have time to bake after-school snacks.

4. Come up with a replacement strategy. Before taking action, find products made with different ingredients but that taste similar to Lucy's favorites and are equally affordable and convenient. So, if she has a Snickers® bar every day after school, find an energy bar with a similar flavor and texture. Never try to change a habit until you have an alternative in place.

5. Observe the reaction to the replacement. If she eats the energy bar with no comment, you're home free. If she proclaims it yucky, go back to the store and find some other candidates. With a young child, you might be able to swap out one product for another. But with teens you'll probably have to engage them in the process. The best way is to ask which of two new products you've provided they like better. Whenever you offer choices, you'll get a better response.

Now here's the clincher. Don't under any circumstances refer to the replacement food as healthier, better, or more nutritious. That kind of language is the kiss of death. Also resist any impulse to draw attention to the replacement. Just put it wherever the Snickers bars used to live. Being healthier is not something most kids care about. In fact, it can be a major turnoff. If you're asked why you switched brands, just say it was on special or a friend told you they were yummy—something unrelated to the calorie, fat, or sugar content. And this is important: it's helpful for your child to see you eating the substitute as well. Again, do as I do, not as I say!

Detecting and Inspecting

If by 8 or 9 years of age, your kids are proficient readers and have some basic math skills under their belts, you could make a game out of reading food labels. After you show them how to read both the Nutrition Facts panel and the list of ingredients, ask them to help decide what to buy by finding the answers to these questions:

- Which of these three breakfast cereals has the most fiber?
- Which of these two granola bars has more fat?
- Are there any trans fats in this product?
- Is this food primarily a source of protein, carbohydrate, or fat?
- Does this serving size seem realistic?
- Can you find the spaghetti sauce with the highest protein content?
- Can you find any mustard without any added sugar? How about mayonnaise?

Robert: Obviously, the younger children are, the more parents control the food that comes into the house. But once a child is out of the house for part of the day, she confronts decisions her parents cannot make for her. Yes, they can pack alternative snacks, but whether or not the kid eats them is out of their hands. If a child is following the AllStride program, it's his responsibility to follow his meal plan—or not—and experience the consequences.

Ricki: Are you saying that "cheating" is OK when a child is not at home?

Robert: Not at all. Instead, I want to remove the whole concept of "cheating" from the conversation. On AllStride nothing is forbidden and balance is all. What counts is how much a child eats, what she eats, when she eats, and what foods she combines with other foods. She has her meal plan and she decides at every meal and snack whether to follow it to the letter, to make reasonable substitutions, or to veer off her norm. If she sticks with it, she'll make timely progress. If she's less compliant, her results will show it. This may be hard to watch, but she'll come to understand that the only person she is "cheating" is herself. That's assuming her parents can maintain their poker faces and refrain from judgmental remarks.

A Rewards Program

In an ideal world, eating great food, doing fun things, meeting new people, feeling and looking better, having more energy, and being able to fit into smaller sizes may be motivation enough to stay with AllStride. But in the real world, adding a little more incentive can help. Let's talk to Robert about this issue.

Ricki: How do you feel about incentivizing kids to reach certain milestones?

Robert: The best incentive is always a parent's praise. This is the time to get rid of your poker face! Say how proud you are and how happy you are that he's lost 5 pounds—or whatever.

Ricki: What if he didn't reach a stated goal by a certain point?

Robert: Put on that poker face again! Never express upset or disappointment that he didn't make a goal he set himself, or even fell back a bit. This could make a kid want to call it quits. Imagine that your son is running a race around the track four times. Each time he passes, there's an opportunity to encourage him. You'd never say, "Hey, you're in last place. I'm so disappointed in you!" The same holds true with a child's journey on AllStride. If he were in a race, you might say, "Hang in there for just three more laps. Don't worry about your time. Just concentrate on your goal!" Some intermediate goals will be easier to reach than others, just as some laps will be run faster than others. Remember, the last lap is usually the hardest. Most importantly, parents need to project positive energy and excitement and see the glass as half full. As I always say, a fall is not a failure. Keep on keeping on.

Ricki: Should intermediate goals be tied to time frames or dates?

Robert: The objective is to give a child as many opportunities to win as possible and few to lose. By rewarding a kid when she's lost so many inches, for example, instead of so many inches in two weeks, she's almost certainly going to win.

Ricki: That could slow things down, though, couldn't it?

Robert: It could, but she's not in a race. Her real objective is to maximize her metabolism and feel better about herself for good, not lose 7 inches by May 15 and then fall back into her old ways. If possible, don't tie rewards to weight alone, which just reinforces

Troubleshoot for Success

If your child is stalled in his progress, he should ask himself the following questions:

- **Are you eating often enough?** If you're not having a meal or snack every two to three hours, you may be encouraging your metabolism to slow down. Remember, we want to maximize your metabolism so you burn more body fat.

- **Are you active enough?** If you're not following your activity program or have backed off it, you may have lost some lean body mass, which slows your metabolism. Muscle burns calories more quickly than fat does.

- **Are you eating before and after activity?** Make a point of having a snack before and a meal or snack within an hour after active play.

- **Are you eating enough protein?** If you've been getting enough protein at mealtimes, take a look at your snacks. If most of your snacks are fruit and other primarily carb foods, try swapping one for an energy bar with at least 10 grams of protein. Some people just need more protein—particularly if they're very active.

- **Are you drinking enough water?** Adequate water keeps your muscles hydrated so that they burn more fat. It may seem odd, but the the more water you drink, the less your body holds on to.

- **Are you getting enough sleep?** Adults who sleep less than seven hours a night are more apt to be overweight. Kids should get at least eight or nine hours a night. So go to bed a little earlier and see what happens.

a diet mentality and an obsession with the scale. As we know, weight loss slows down after the initial weeks. It also almost always happens in fits and starts. It's unrealistic to expect a regular loss of a pound or even half a pound a week. Lost inches are a much more dramatic and reliable indicator of progress. It's a great way to demonstrate to kids that they're getting smaller, regardless of what the scale says. When a teen-ager says, "I'm not losing weight fast *enough," I would ask, "Would you like to see the number on the scale go down, or would you prefer to have your weight remain the same but fit into a smaller size?" They always answer the latter.*

Ricki: How often should the child or the parent check on progress?

Robert: I recommend taking measurements every week or at least once a month. Each time the measurements will demonstrate progress.

Ricki: How would you establish intermediate goals?

Robert: It depends on the size of the kid, but I would let him make suggestions and then the parent can decide whether they're reasonable. He may be overly optimistic about certain goals, and he shouldn't set himself up for disappointment. A loss of a half-inch at every part of the body is an attainable goal.

Ricki: How about rewards?

Robert: Again, I'd let the child take the lead, reining him in if the rewards are unreasonable. Or if he's at a loss, the parent can suggest a reward, tailoring it to the kid's interests. Rewards certainly don't have to be expensive. Nor need they be things. The pleasure of a family trip to the skating rink or going to that 3-D movie or hockey game with dad may last longer than the momentary pleasure of a silver dollar or a new T-shirt. On the other hand, for a child who hasn't been able to wear the kind of clothes her friends have been wearing, new clothes could be very motivating. A pedicure with mom is a great way to spend quality time together. There are only two no-no's: don't make food a reward, and never substitute a reward for praise.

Help Your Kid See Results

It's human nature to get all fired up over a new project and then find your commitment slacking off as everyday life intervenes. After starting AllStride, the excitement of watching inches practically fall off his body will motivate your child. But the pace of change will naturally slow, which can be disconcerting. If discouragement leads to lapses in following the activity program and the meal plans, your kid's progress will slow even more. Let's talk to Robert about how to gently challenge a child or teen-ager to hang in there for the long haul.

Ricki: How can you help a kid troubleshoot if he meets a bump in the road?

Robert: First of all, parents want to wait for him to take the lead. If they say, "James, you're not losing weight fast enough, so you must be doing something wrong," it's guaranteed to induce guilt and resistance—to say nothing of making him feel like a failure. Dear reader, if such a thought even crosses your mind, please go back and reread the last chapter!

Ricki: So you wait for him to express frustration or confusion?

Robert: Exactly. If James says, "Mom, I thought I was doing everything right, but it's taking so long and I'm discouraged," it gives his mother an opening. She might respond, "You're doing a great job and I'm really proud of you, but sometimes your body just has its own agenda. Why don't we take a look at some of the things that could be slowing your progress?" (See "Troubleshoot for Success" on page 224.) With a child younger than 8, the parent may want to ask these questions herself, but be careful to do so without making it feel like an inquisition.

Keep Enthusiasm Alive

Let's talk to Robert about how to gently influence a child to stay the course if his interest in AllStride begins to flag.

Robert: The key here is what my mother used to call "reverse psychology." The more the parents push their child to do AllStride, the less responsive she'll be.

Ricki: So give me an example of the kind of conversation that could actually push a kid away from the program.

Robert: OK. I'll be the parent and you play the child. "Ricki, I notice you're not following your AllStride meal plans and you're not getting outside to play enough. Don't you want to look prettier?"

Ricki: "Leave me alone. All you care about is how I look, not who I am." Then I'd retreat to my room and slam the door!

Robert: Very good. Of course, you are an actress! That's exactly the kind of response such a direct attack provokes. Now let's take the reverse psychology approach. The goal is to get the child to initiate a conversation that will position her to choose to return to the program. This involves the parent knowing when new recipes, activity videos, or anything else new appears on the site. Then when All-Stride comes up in conversation, mom or dad can comment on it. Or the parent can act as if the kid is paying attention to AllStride, but just isn't visiting the site when she's around. Mom could create a conversation by saying something like, "I love the new recipes on allstride.com. Shall we choose one for dinner tomorrow night?" Then she needs to wait for a response, which could either be something like, "I'm bored with AllStride" or "I haven't seen the new recipes, but I like the others, so let's do it."

Ricki: How would you follow up?

Robert: The first response is obviously is a negative one. The second suggests the kid may have not been that involved but is still open to the program. In either case, the parent shouldn't push the conversation. Instead, be patient and wait for the kid's next comment. If it's related to AllStride, that means she wants to talk. If it's not, she clearly doesn't want to pursue the topic—at least for now.

Ricki: So you'd have to leave it at that because until she's ready to return to the program, it's fruitless to push her.

Robert: Yes. Just be sure to leave the door open to discuss the program and her feelings when she's ready.

Ricki: Wow! This could try the patience of a saint.

Robert: There's a poem entitled "Don't Quit" by an unknown author. The last few lines are:

"And you never can tell how close you are,
It may be near when it seems so far,
So stick to the fight when you're hardest hit—
It's when things seem worst that you must not quit."

AllStride parents must keep the faith. When they least expect it, their kids are likely to experience a breakthrough.

In the next chapter, Isaiah Truyman returns to talk to us about the challenge of finding the time for your children to be active. He'll also suggest ways to help them to motivate themselves to have fun—and burn fat while they're at it.

Brianne Now Loves Clothes— and Veggies!

Success Story

Who would have thought that we'd have two girls with the same unusual name (although they do spell it differently) in our roster of success stories? This 11-year-old, who used to hide in baggy gym shorts, loves to clothes shop now that she's lost 17 pounds. And the kid who once often didn't have the energy for swim team now looks forward to dance and kickboxing classes. Perhaps most amazing of all, the girl who didn't like vegetables is now into making healthy food choices. Listen in while I talk to her and her mom, Kate.

Ricki: Kate, when did you notice Brianne was getting bigger?
Kate: It started in second grade, a few pounds here, a few pounds

there, but it got to the point where it was looking unhealthy. I didn't want her to go through the kind of self-esteem and self-confidence issues that I've had in the past. I wanted her to feel great about herself, whatever she decided to do.

Ricki: What made you choose this program?

Kate: It's geared toward children. And not only are there healthy meal plans, but there's also an exercise program.

Ricki: Brianne, how about you? How do you feel about the program?

Brianne: I like that you're not starving yourself. You have breakfast and then a snack, then lunch, and then a snack, then dinner, and then dessert. I could actually pick what I wanted to eat, and not be forced to eat stuff I don't like—string beans and broccoli or hot dogs and seafood.

Kate: We were able to pick and choose the types of food that she likes. One of the reasons that we love this program is that it's teaching her to make healthy choices now and 10 years from now.

Ricki: Brianne, did it hurt your feelings when your mom suggested you go on this program?

Brianne: My first reaction was that my parents cared that I was overweight and they would spend money on me to make sure that I got to a healthy weight.

Ricki: How long was it before you saw results?

Brianne: I lost 17 pounds over 12 weeks.

Ricki: What other changes did you see?

Brianne: All my friends every day, they're like, "Wow, you look way skinnier than you did at first." It just feels great. I didn't like the way that my stomach looked, so I used to wear my phys-ed shorts and baggy shirts every day. But now I like wearing form-fitting things, and I feel just way better about myself.

Ricki: So you've become more clothes conscious?

Brianne: When I started seventh grade, I noticed people wearing more fashionable stuff than they did in earlier grades. It feels really great to be able to wear what everybody else wears and not feel like, "Wow, I really don't fit in with these clothes and these people."

Ricki: Kate, have you seen other changes in Brianne?

Kate: This program has definitely helped Brie to come out of her shell. Before, she lacked the motivation to exercise and sometimes she had no energy.

Brianne: It was a little bit harder for me to do swim team and PE than it was for everybody else. Now I'm dancing twice a week, and I'm at the gym doing kickboxing or conditioning another two times a week.

Ricki: Kate, let's switch back to the food. Was it easy for you to get the meals on the table?

Kate: Yes. Essentially it's all laid out there for you. You look at the meal plan, you make your grocery list, and you go to the grocery store.

Ricki: Brianne, do you have any favorite foods on your meal plan?

Brianne: I enjoy cooking and eating the chicken taco salad the most.

Ricki: Have you learned about nutrition as a result of doing AllStride?

Brianne: Knowing about sodium and carbohydrates and proteins and fats helps me make choices that are better for my body. Before, I would have picked a bag of chips over some carrots or an apple. But now I would rather have fruit and vegetables than fattening chips full of salt.

Too Small to Be Big

Chapter 16

Coach Your Child to Fun-Filled Fitness

If many of us are not very knowledgeable about nutrition, it pales in comparison to our lack of understanding of the body's physiology. That's why we have Isaiah Truyman on board. He doesn't just know how our muscles and tendons work; he also understands how our minds and emotions are entwined with our physicality.

Time to Get Physical

So let's hear from our "fun" expert about how to mentor your child in the activity portion of the AllStride program. Later, Dr. John will chime in.

Ricki: Isaiah, how does a parent take off her "parent" cap and put on her "mentor" cap to help a child improve his physical prowess?
Isaiah: I'm glad you brought up physical prowess. From the time of the gladiators on, it has been one of the most coveted and tangible attributes of human beings. Look at the adulation we give athletes

today. Kings can't buy physical prowess. So I like to have kids see the goal of active play as physical prowess more than as losing weight. What kid doesn't want to shine in this arena?

Ricki: So help me out on how I would do this with one of my sons, for example.

Isaiah: I'd start out by saying, "We're going to work on this together." Then find the smallest, most insignificant success and capitalize on it. Everyone has at least one strength. It might be good aim, the ability to catch, speed on his feet, or flexibility. To build self-esteem, identify this skill and play games that highlight it. It's like starting a fire with a few tiny sparks, until you have a roaring blaze. Don't ask for too much too soon or expect your kid to immediately love the activity. First he has to get satisfaction from the simple process of learning one skill and then moving on to the next. Most people don't sit down at a piano and fall in love with it. First it's "ting, tong, ting," and then it's "dada, da, daah, dah." Then they're playing a song. That's when love blossoms.

Ricki: This is so totally the opposite of what happens in most phys-ed programs. Everyone is standing around seeing how many pull-ups you can do. I'll never forget what a nightmare it was when I was a little girl.

Isaiah: It's a nightmare for everyone, except the one kid who can do the most pull-ups. And it's the polar opposite of empowerment. Everyone has a memory of that one teacher or coach or big brother who spoke some powerful words of encouragement that echo ever after. Perhaps your third-grade gym teacher told you that you were the best jump-roper she'd ever met, and from that moment on you decided you wanted to star in the Cirque de Soleil. Or perhaps your dad told you that you really stink at football. From that day forward, you never really wanted to play it again. Tell a kid she's smart and she's smart. Tell a kid she's dumb and she's dumb.

Ricki: That totally resonates for me. When I was 3 years old, my grandmother Sylvia told me that I would be a star. She instilled a confidence in me that enabled me to handle it when my department head told me at 18 that I would never make it as a performer.

Isaiah: One little thing that parents could adapt is something that my staff and I do at the gym. We send out motivational messages to clients on their cell phones. Rule Number 1 is positive feedback. You could do the same with notes under a child's pillow, in the pocket of the jacket he wears to school, or in his backpack. Of course, notes or phone messages are never a substitute for saying the words to his face. They're a little added booster. (For more tips, see "Ten Secrets from a Coach" on page 236.)

Ricki: Mentoring sounds really important, but it also sounds like it takes a lot of time. If both parents are working or you're a single parent, it could be difficult to find the time to mentor your kid this way. Any suggestions?

Isaiah: Just as you might hire someone to tutor your child in math, you can ask someone else to take on the role of activity mentor. In fact, sometimes a younger child will be more willing to listen to a teen-ager he looks up to. Parents want so much and care so much that they can be heavy-handed. Someone closer to the kid's own age is often better. Or the surrogate could be a sitter or a grandparent or even a volunteer in a "big brother" or "big sister" program. Obviously, it's still the parents' job to oversee the program and make sure it's on track.

Ricki: It's good for kids to see their parents be physically active. Fortunately, I love exercise and make a real point of doing physical things with Milo and Owen, like swimming, biking, hiking, and white-water rafting. Most of our recent vacations have been sports oriented. How much time should a kid spend on physical activities?

Isaiah: I recommend a minimum of an hour a day of sustained activity to maintain a healthy weight. An hour should be the goal, and half an hour the minimum. The International Health, Racquet and Sportsclub Association (IHRSA), of which I'm a member, recommends a minimum of half an hour of phys ed for elementary school children and 45 minutes for middle-school and high-school students. This is in line with the recommendations of Let's Move! (Michelle Obama's program), the NFL program, and many others. However, "minimum" is the operative word, particularly if the child is not currently at a healthy weight.

Ricki: Let's get Dr. John in on this conversation because I know this subject is dear to his heart.

Dr. John: It used to be easy or at least possible to get in two hours of activity each day. This would include gym classes three times a week and daily recess, plus an hour or more playing outside after school. But today it's difficult—with gym classes being cut and recess shortened. What kids should get and what they actually do get are miles apart. More is always better. At the moment, only one in five teen-agers gets even one hour of activity a day, and only one-third attend physical education classes daily.

Ricki: What about all the after-school sports activities that many kids participate in?

Dr. John: By filling their schedules with organized activities, we've actually limited, and in some cases eliminated, time for simple, active, imaginative play. Even preschoolers participate in structured activities. For older kids, ballet lessons, tennis lessons, team sports, and meetings of such organizations as Boy Scouts and Girl Scouts occupy time that might have otherwise been spent just playing. And remember, just because you're on a team doesn't mean you're actually active. You may be warming the bench. I spent many an evening in Little League standing in right field, hoping that for once a ball would come in my direction. None of these activities is bad in themselves. Nor are they new. What has changed is the need for these activities.

Ricki: You're talking about how nowadays a kid is considered to not be living up to his potential or isn't well rounded if he isn't involved in all sorts of activities, right?

Dr. John: Yes. It's the kind of pressure high-school kids thinking about college might have experienced years ago. But now many parents expect grade-school kids to shine in several areas, as though they are building their resumes. Ironically, this tightly scheduled lifestyle leaves little time for so-called purposeless high-energy output. Kids are actually less active than they were before, and organized activities can interfere with family mealtime, putting it even lower on the list of priorities.

Ricki: Why is this unstructured play so important, even if a kid is physically active, perhaps playing lacrosse or soccer?

Dr. John: When kids invent their own games, they're beginning the process of taking responsibility for themselves and learning how to interact in an informal situation. It also stimulates their imaginations.

Too Small to Be Big

Ricki: I guess you could compare it to filling in the lines in a coloring book or drawing from scratch. The second is obviously more creative, although today kids often also create art on a computer, as my boys do.

Dr. John: I was walking in my neighborhood one evening recently when I saw a gathering of boys and girls. They were throwing a ball around, kicking a soccer ball, messing with a skateboard, and one was even attempting to climb a tree. Meanwhile, they were bantering back and forth, jumping from one topic to another, freely expressing their thoughts. You rarely see this kind of thing anymore. It gave me hope that the intrinsic nature of childhood is alive and well and that our recent cultural evolution hasn't erased it.

Ricki: Surely the issue of safety is a factor in how much time kids spend outdoors doing kid things, right?

Dr. John: It's indisputable that many neighborhoods, and certainly inner cities, are much less safe than when I was a child. It's no surprise that urban groups, particularly African-Americans and Latinos, also have higher obesity rates than suburban white populations. There are simply fewer outlets for activity. Even most suburban parents don't feel comfortable letting their kids play outdoors without supervision.

Making Activity a Way of Life

Now let's move on to motivation. Let's get Isaiah to talk to us about how to keep kids motivated to stay with the fun-activity part of AllStride after the first blush of excitement wears off.

Ricki: Isaiah, what advice do you have for getting kids to choose to incorporate fitness into their lifestyle?

Isaiah: Parents have to earn their child's trust and encourage him to exert control over his own life. They need to understand where a kid is, to walk in his shoes, so to speak. For example, if a child is fascinated by fire, forbidding him to play with fire will only increase his fascination. Instead, I would say to him, "I think fire is really neat too, and I love to watch it." Then teach him how to handle fire safely. It's the same thing with fitness. You want to help a child experience it from the inside out.

Ten Secrets from a Coach

Here are more of Isaiah's suggestions for motivating your child:

1. The first thing I say when I'm coaching a team is, "It's not about winning or losing; it's about how you play the game." Just because that's an old cliché doesn't invalidate it.

2. Then I tell them to practice sportsmanship, be part of the team, and try their best. You won't win every game this season, and when you do lose you shouldn't feel bad. Those same messages have value with kids who are not as athletic as other kids.

3. Positive feedback, positive feedback, positive feedback! If you can't say anything nice, don't say anything at all.

4. Lead by example. Engage in active play with your children. Keep it fun and safe.

5. Consistency is key! Remember Aesop's fable about the tortoise and the hare: slow and steady wins the race.

6. To create drama, challenge, dare, and bet against your kids. But keep the tone light. "Bet you can't do 10 jumping jacks."

7. Create a positive environment for progress by ensuring that expectations are within reason. You can still occasionally challenge kids to do something just beyond their abilities. You may be surprised. But if you try too much too soon, the child will have a negative experience with fitness.

8. Define success with performance results, such as speed or number of reps.

9. Celebrate progress, award improvements, and make achievements public.

10. Narrate a kid's performance as she's doing it, with praise like "Unbelievable! Keep up the great work!"

Ricki: *It's human nature to be excited about new activities in the beginning and then to slack off. How do you keep a kid energized about the program without inducing guilt?*
Isaiah: *Instead of pushing him, a parent might use a parable. For example, talk to him about driving across the country. If he turned*

Too Small to Be Big

around the first time he got lost, he'd never get from New England to California. We all start out with an idea of how something will be, but what happens when we get lost or it turns out to be different from what we expected? Do you go back? No, you recalculate— just like your GPS! It's the same with AllStride. Each day is a new day, and a person simply has to focus on where he is and where he wants to be. Then figure out how to get there. As the old saying goes, "Success is a long, long road." These are major life lessons. Keep the tone light and help him with encouraging words like the ones my mom used to whisper in my ear, "Hey, just maintain a positive attitude and keep that smile on your face." Her faith in me got me through some difficult times when I was a kid.

I'd like to turn the end of this chapter over to Isaiah, who has inspired me with his own story of being a "different" kid who went on to success and has empowered others to do the same.

"One of the most empowering things I've ever learned is that we already have everything we need now to achieve what we want. The puzzle is on the table with all the pieces, but it's up to you to pick them up and put them together. Or you can sit there and tell a sob story about why you couldn't. It's your choice. The very fact that you're reading this book is evidence that you're committed to helping motivate your child to make changes. But ultimately she has to come to terms with where she is and make changes herself. Then your job is to act as her cheering section.

"I grew up in a broken family without much money and a lot of adversity. It made me feel like an outsider, but my mother gave me a whole lot of love and support. When I left for school, she would whisper in my ear things like, "It's OK to be different" or "If you argue for your limitations, then they define you." She made me realize that it was better to try my best and see what happened than not to try at all. I had learning disabilities and was placed in special ed. So I struggled and had to develop a coping mechanism. For me, it was deciding to see life as a glass half full. My father wasn't around, but in my mind I made him a great man because that's what I wanted him to be.

"It's all about having a specific goal. I call it the point on the horizon you can look to. 'I want a perfect body' isn't an attainable goal, but 'I want to feel good and feel good about myself' is. Your child can then find enjoyable activities to tie into the one point on the horizon. Likewise, deciding whether to have that humongous frappe instead of an apple and a slice of cheese for a snack connects to the same point on the horizon.

"This book and the whole AllStride program are one huge call to action. It's about what you can do right now. It's about the art of parenting. Parents are often afraid or embarrassed to ask for help because they think they're supposed to automatically know how to deal with their children. But none of us have any training, except for the role models our parents provided. That's why AllStride has brought together a pediatrician, a family coach, a nutritionist, and a fitness coach (that's me) to collectively offer our experience, advice, and support."

Thank you, Isaiah. In Part IV, we'll turn our focus to the various community groups that can partner with families to support healthier, happier children. We'll start with schools because after home, that's where kids spend most of their waking hours. You'll also hear about some inspiring efforts by individuals and groups that have made a difference in fighting the war against childhood obesity. Perhaps their efforts will inspire you to reach out beyond your own family to join the crusade to make a world where every child can be healthy and happy.

Part 4

Become Part of the Solution

By Ricki Lake

Chapter 17

Make a Difference in Your Child's School

There's always great debate as to where the responsibility for the health and welfare of children lies. No one will argue that what happens at home is the ultimate influence on kids, but they also spend much of their lives in school, and the school's role cannot be discounted. After all, from kindergarten through 12th grade, the average child attends school for roughly 2,000 days.

How does a school system impact our kids' physical and emotional health? The obvious factors include the lunch program, the content of vending machines, the presence of physical-education programs, and the amount of time devoted to outside play. Other more subtle yet powerful influences are also at work. Peer pressure, unintentional comments from teachers, and competition in and outside of the classroom can have profound effects on how children view themselves. All of these influences, in turn, can affect eating habits and contribute to children being overweight. How can parents impact the policies in the schools their kids attend?

Bye-Bye Bag Lunches

Not only are most kids eating more junk food at home and eating more meals away from home, parents also have less control over what their kids eat at school. Once upon a time, bag lunches were the norm. Today, kids can often order double cheeseburgers from a McDonald's franchise and lattes and frappaccinos from an in situ Starbucks, where a Double Chocolaty Chip Frappaccino® Blended Beverage weighs in at 500 calories. Add whipped cream and the number jumps to 640. (And by the way, when did kids start drinking coffee?)

Even though there are usually quite a few choices, kids almost always veer toward high-fat, high-carb, high-sugar offerings. And if they don't find anything to their liking in the lunchroom, they can often turn to vending machines for snacks in lieu of lunch. Older students can head off to the nearest fast-food restaurant. What's a parent to do?

A few schools—and fortunately an increasing number of them—have taken on this problem in a thoughtful and comprehensive way, with demonstrated results. To play an important role in improving children's health and to combat the obesity epidemic, schools must tackle every aspect they have control over. It starts with nutrition, obviously, but extends to the amount of time kids spend moving and the quality of exercise programs. Also important is creating a culture of health and wellness, so that kids become aware early on of the effects of food on their bodies. As the last objective—and perhaps the biggest challenge of all—schools have to make it "cool" to eat healthy. In some schools, children are actually part of initiating changes that will achieve those goals. This further empowers kids.

The issue of healthy food doesn't just exist in the cafeteria. Learning about nutrition and how to eat in a healthy fashion should also be part of every kid's education. Whether this means reinstituting home-economics classes or incorporating nutrition into science or social studies programs, it's essential that kids learn about nutrition from a source other than advertising.

Ever See a Chocolate Cow?

How about a strawberry one? Of course not, but 70 percent of the milk kids drink in school is flavored. And did you know that chocolate milk has 50 percent more calories than "white" milk? If your child has a cup of chocolate milk every school day for a year, that alone could prompt a weight gain of up to 3½ pounds. And where do the extra calories come from in "brown" and "pink" milk? Sugar, of course. MilkPEP, the milk lobby, has been successful in getting flavored milk into schools, as it tries to beat back the competition from other beverages. Flavored milk should be treated as an occasional treat at home, but it has no place in schools.

The School Lunch Program

Before we look at some examples of what can be done to improve school lunch programs, let's talk to Dr. John to get a good understanding of how the National School Lunch Program currently works.

Ricki: One of the bones of contention many parents have with their school is the quality of the lunches served. How did the National School Lunch Program begin?
Dr. John: The program began in 1946 to ensure that kids who were coming to school hungry received basic nutrition. Today, all kids can get the same lunch, although those with a family income below a certain level get free or reduced-cost lunches.
Ricki: Are only public schools eligible?
Dr. John: Public and nonprofit private schools can participate, which means that they receive funding from the U.S. Department

of Agriculture (USDA), along with foods from surplus agricultural stocks. In return, schools must serve lunches that comply with USDA requirements.

Ricki: The quality of the lunches served has been under fire for being high in fat and lacking many fresh foods, among other things.

Dr. John: The school lunch program is far from ideal. However, as this book was about to go to print, Congress passed a child nutrition bill that expands the school lunch program and raises standards. The bill gives the secretary of agriculture the authority to control nutritional standards for all foods available in schools, including vending machines. Moreover, schools must now serve more fresh vegetables and fruits, whole grains, and low-fat dairy products. Until now, the foods the USDA supplied tended to be refined grain products and other processed foods that keep well. Meals have been heavy on chicken nuggets, flash-frozen French fries, and potato flakes, for example, but not fresh chicken parts and potatoes. Of course, the school nutritionist decides how to use these foods, and a school can purchase others.

Ricki: But this new legislation is not a panacea, is it?

Dr. John: Of course not. With reduced budgets, many schools will continue to rely primarily on foods available from the USDA, but at least the bar has been raised. And much depends on how each school system plans meals. If want to see further improvement in your school system, you may have to get involved on a local level. After all, we do elect our school-board officials. AllStride recommends that the first thing to do is send your child to school with a healthy homemade lunch. If enough of us do that, it will send a pretty clear message to school administrations, because the funding and amount of food each receives depend upon how many lunches are served.

Ricki: What else could you do that's more direct?

Dr. John: Start by dropping by for lunch at your child's school. Volunteer as a server or cashier in the cafeteria to get the lay of the land. (For more ideas, see "Get Involved in the Cafeteria" on page 244.) The fact that some schools have vastly improved their menus is proof that concerned parents can make a difference.

Get Involved in the Cafeteria

To effect change in the school cafeteria, you'll need to do your homework and connect with other parents and school staff. Here are some ideas for doing that:

- Attend PTA meetings.
- As a concerned parent and taxpayer, you have every right to meet with the appropriate personnel in the school system to ask questions about the lunch program.
- Make it clear that vending machines full of junk food have no place in a school. A number of municipalities have already made this change, so it isn't a far-out idea.
- Run for the school board.
- Ask the school administration to send out lunch menus and/or post them online.
- Suggest that parents agree collectively not to send kids to school with candy, soda, and chips.
- Give the teacher or principal a copy of this book and get together with other concerned parents to see how you can make over the current snack or meal menu.

School for Inspiration

In 2008, *Health* magazine and its associated website published an article entitled, "America's Healthiest Schools." Several of these schools have made some wonderful discoveries and instituted innovative practices, from which many other institutions could learn. Let's take a look at three that deserve gold stars for their efforts. Some schools have even involved students in the process of improvement.

West Babylon High School in West Babylon, New York. If nothing has been done to resolve a child's battle with weight by high school, this is the last time in childhood to have a meaningful impact. West Babylon High School has done just that. For starters, the administration removed all soda machines and replaced them with ones that dispensed water and fruit drinks. According to several studies, this substitution alone hasn't had a huge impact (probably because fruit drinks are as high in sugar and calories as soda). But West Babylon has also re-vamped the entire menu to include healthy choices like wraps and salads and has eliminated fried and other high-calorie foods. This sort of dramatic action can have a profound effect on kids. They might even take some of the ideas home from school.

West Babylon has also completely changed its physical-education program to emphasize overall wellness, paying increased attention to social skills and lifetime and adventure activities. The other important factor is that student input played a large role in developing the programs. Do they work? Indeed they do. West Babylon noted a 2-percent drop in student obesity in just one year.

Rawhide Elementary School in Gillette, Wyoming. Unlike many elementary schools across the country, this one has made sure that kids get lots of exercise every day. It has not only retained its physical-education program, but also requires kids to go outside for recess. In addition, 20 minutes a day is devoted to "wellness time." The program begins in kindergarten, when kids are most impressionable, and when there's the greatest likelihood that they'll form healthy lifetime habits.

Miami Springs Middle School in Miami Springs, Florida. The administration of this school has completely revamped its food program. Fried food, sugary cereals, and dessert are no longer on the menu, and have been replaced by fresh fruits and vegetables. The school has also introduced nutritional training into its science curriculum so that kids understand how different foods interact with their bodies and impact their health. At a time when obesity and good eating seem to be taboo subjects in many schools, here they're discussed frankly and scientifically.

Signs of Change

Schools like these three stand out from the crowd. Often change comes from outside the system. The efforts of British chef Jamie Oliver to change the eating habits of Huntington,

West Virginia, were the subject of a riveting reality TV show, "Jamie Oliver's Food Revolution." (See "Kudos to Jamie Oliver," opposite.) He's not the only chef disturbed by America's growing obesity crisis and its relationship to school lunches. Chef Ann Cooper, who calls herself "the renegade lunch lady," has two websites, one for parents and another for school nutrition professionals. (See Resources on page 256.)

The Farm to School Program

This new federal initiative could remove a lot of junk food from the USDA school lunch program. How so? The objective is to pair up schools and local farms to improve cafeteria meals with locally grown fruit and vegetables. The program will also provide nutritional education to kids, while supporting local farmers. AmeriCorps and the W.K. Kellogg Foundation have supplied planning grants. For more information, go to farmtoschool.org, where you can also sign up for a monthly e-newsletter.

Reactivate Physical Education

As Dr. John and I have said repeatedly, inactivity is as much a cause of being overweight as is poor eating. Any parent of school-age kids is aware of how gym class has been whittled down or removed from many school programs, and "recess" in many schools has morphed into kids milling around the cafeteria. School administrators feel increasing pressure to improve and expand their academic curriculum. Now, with standardized testing regarded as the gold standard for success, any so-called free time (once filled with schoolyard games of kickball or freeze tag) is seen as unproductive. The result is students spend more time sitting on their butts—despite many studies demonstrating that fewer breaks for physical activity decrease clear thinking and problem-solving skills. When it comes to addressing the matters of whether your child's school is devoting sufficient time for physical education and recess, many of Dr. John's tactics for influencing school lunches are equally applicable. Before you start demanding change, volunteer, spend time at your child's school, and attend PTA meetings so you'll be up to date on the issues.

Most people agree that school lunches should be healthier, that food companies have a responsibility to not market junk food directly to children, and that schools need to address developing bodies as well as developing minds. Only by working together on all fronts can we give each child the opportunity to be healthy, fit, and happy. In the next chapter, we'll take a look at more community initiatives and inspiring role models.

Kudos to Jamie Oliver

This provocative chef is no stranger to shaking up things in schools, as he did in his native Great Britain, before landing on our shores with his television show "Jamie Oliver's Food Revolution." The "revolutionary" message is only good sense: that we feed our kids healthy whole foods, at home and in school. Oliver went head-to-head with the school board of Huntington, West Virginia, as well as the cafeteria employees, in classic reality-show style. (Huntington has the unenviable distinction of being one of the "fattest" cities in the nation.) He eventually won over his critics and achieved some significant changes, presaging some of the changes reflected in the new school lunch program legislation. The show also highlighted the dilemma of tight budgets forcing schools to rely heavily on surplus food stores supplied by the USDA. Whether the changes he was able to institute will remain once the school and city are no longer in the national spotlight remains to be seen.

If you want to be part of the revolution, visit jamieoliver.com, where you can also to sign a petition to improve school lunches and save cooking skills. Oliver plans to present the petition to the president and first lady. Hundreds of thousands of people have already signed it. Oliver's approach is to involve all interested parties in his ambitious goal, including students, parents, and school boards. Among his other efforts, he has set up a cooking school to teach young people how to have fun cooking delicious meals that just happen to be good for them. You can catch episodes at abc. go.com/watch/jamie-olivers-food-revolution/SH5517964.

Chapter 18

The Power of Community

Public opinion is a powerful force. In the 1960s and '70s, when almost everyone smoked, a number of groups came together to declare war on the habit. The government never banned smoking outright, but when conclusive studies revealed the obvious health risks, they were supported by a massive and aggressive public relations campaign. Although there will always be people who smoke—and unfortunately, one in five adolescents still does—today there's almost universal agreement that it's unhealthy— even among smokers. As result, we're all a little healthier. A similar shift in mindset about the use of seatbelts took place in the 1980s, again following well-publicized studies and a public relations campaign. In this case, most states passed laws requiring the use of the safety devices.

These two examples of the power of public opinion should spur us on to combat the epidemic of obesity in America. We can learn some lessons from such paradigm shifts. Unfortunately, as yet, far fewer people think childhood obesity is a problem of similar import as smoking. And although a number of organizations, such as the Robert Wood Johnson Foundation (see Resources on page 256), have looked into the causes of the epidemic, precious few specific solutions have emerged. If there's no apparent solution to a problem, there's an impulse to sweep it under the rug. We can't allow that to happen with this crisis!

Change on the Horizon

Fortunately, there are some real solutions brewing, including AllStride, and things are beginning to change even if major change is still far in the future. As Dr. John explained in Part I, there are now obesity clinics associated with almost every children's hospital and pediatric training program in the country. Gyms and playgrounds are springing up in places where they never existed before. Major food companies like McDonald's and Coca-Cola now at least acknowledge that unhealthy eating habits have played a role in the epidemic of childhood obesity.

The Role of Communities

In an effort to come up with workable solutions, many communities have set up task forces and work groups to examine the issue of overweight children. Educators, health-care experts, representatives from the food industry, local media, and advertising executives now put their heads together. Ultimately this will go a long way toward finding answers. Nonetheless, the seeds of prevention are planted in the education of families and implementation of healthy practices at individual dinner tables—and at computers.

To date, there have been two basic approaches. One is to attack one aspect of the problem, say nutrition and/or exercise, and try to reach as many kids as possible. Michelle Obama's Let's Move! initiative is a great example of this approach. (See "Let's

Get Behind Let's Move!" below.) Others have focused on a very small portion of the public, like that of a university-based pediatric obesity clinic, with an all-encompassing approach. But obviously, such programs can handle only so many kids, while there's no limit to the number of lives that AllStride can touch. All these programs are beneficial, but we need to combine our efforts to reach critical mass.

Let's Get Behind Let's Move!

Despite its name, Let's Move!, the program initiated by First Lady Michelle Obama to focus on child health and particularly child obesity, also deals with nutrition (letsmove.gov). The organization has a strong online presence, providing helpful information for parents and kids on food and fitness. But Let's Move! also has its feet planted firmly in communities across the nation. Almost 300 cities have established "Let's Move MeetUps," where parents, teachers, chefs, and elected officials get together to share ideas and effect change. Parents can sign an online pledge to support the health of kids and join the "Partnership for a Healthier America," which offers an e-newsletter full of articles, recipes, tips on growing vegetables, and lots more, to further educate and empower parents and kids.

Use Your Power as a Consumer

In addition to becoming more involved in their community to change school policy, parents need to communicate their opinions to food manufacturers in the only way they will understand: if we stop buying, they will stop making. But before that, we all need to become better educated about nutrition. Sadly, today people obtain most of their nutrition information from advertising—and much of it is wrong! The endless stream of food advertisements on television (and now also online) introduce such troubling misinformation as the claim that eating little circles made from refined oats will lower your cholesterol or that Lunchables® are the nutritional equivalent of a healthy lunch.

Fortunately, the paradigm is shifting and these assertions are finally being questioned. The passage of the school nutrition bill is a major step. Nonetheless, government efforts to restrict what can be advertised to children as healthy have recently been stalled by the food industry; and even the regulators who are supposed to protect children can't seem to agree on a policy.

A group of individuals who question assertions by the food and advertising industries, like those cited above, have produced a documentary, entitled "All Jacked Up." This film explores how food manufacturers (like the tobacco industry, which for years did research on making its product more addictive) get people to buy their products, regardless of their health effects. Anyone involved with children and especially teens should view "All Jacked Up." It could stimulate a healthy dialogue at school or at other community gatherings. (In the spirit of full disclosure, Dr. John served on the film's advisory board and wrote some of the questions, but he has no financial interest in it.) For more information, go to *alljackedupmovie.com*.

Now let's look at some other community efforts to combat the crisis. And Dr. John will introduce you to yet another inspiring individual who has helped overweight kids shed pounds, become more active, and regain their health and self-confidence. Like the others cited in earlier chapters, he reminds us that one person can make a huge difference.

Playgrounds for All

What could be more symbolic of a true community than a place where its kids can play safely and creatively? Before our children led such scheduled, programmed lives, they found their own forms of entertainment, often in the schoolyard or a public playground. But many communities, particularly in inner cities, are without such play spaces. KaBOOM! is an innovative organization that offers a model for what communities, businesses, and government can do when they join forces. (For more on KaBOOM!, see "Kudos to Darell Hammond" opposite. To find out more about KaBOOM!, including the closest playground to your home, go to *kaboom.org*.)

Groups that build playgrounds often regard the effort as a new-fangled "barn-raising," in which individuals come together to build something that will make their community better, stronger, and more cohesive. Many playgrounds, including some built in the New Orleans area after Hurricane Katrina, include walking paths for adults. These play areas become community centers: havens for not just children but also for interested adults.

It Takes a Community

As we've seen in the last few chapters, many schools have begun to look seriously at how to incorporate nutrition and physical fitness into their educational goals. Now there are also medical resources for kids and families struggling with obesity. These resources didn't exist just a few years ago. What else can we parents do in our own homes and communities to achieve critical mass?

Dr. John and I propose a three-step process, including several particulars we've already mentioned:

- **Take charge—which includes educating yourself.**
- **Speak out.**
- **Forge partnerships.**

If families, local groups, and other organizations take ownership, larger institutions, including the medical profession, the food industry, and even the government, will be forced to respond.

Kudos to Darell Hammond of KaBOOM!

In 1995, community organizer Darell Hammond was moved to action by a news report that two Washington, D.C., children had suffocated in an old car because they had no other place to play. He realized that if these children had had access to a safe playground, they might still be alive. Although he was only 24, Hammond already had experience building playgrounds.

His vision—to make playgrounds available within walking distance of every American child—led to the birth of KaBOOM!. Many volunteers and companies contributed their efforts, and The Home Depot and Kimberly-Clark became corporate sponsors. By 1997 the program had caught the eye of then-Vice President Gore, as well as General Colin Powell. In 2007, Gore and Powell's "Let Us Play" campaign was united with Hammond's program and renamed KaBOOM! National Campaign for Play. After he left office, President Clinton started the Clinton Foundation, which identified childhood obesity as one of the problems it hoped to attack. The foundation has endorsed and supported KaBOOM!.

Once a volunteer organization decides to build a playground, KaBOOM! can help make it happen, with building directions and advice on fundraising. In some cases, KaBOOM! is able to match a proposed playground with a corporation willing to supply the materials—the local organization provides manpower. To date, KaBOOM! has been involved in building or refurbishing more than 1,400 play spaces nationwide. Eventually the visionary leaders of KaBOOM! realized that older kids also needed safe places to play and decided to add skate parks and BMX biking locations to the program. Imagine that the organization achieves its long-term goal of building play areas within walking distance of every child in the nation. Not only would kids be healthier and slimmer, but so would adults. And neighborhoods would be able to foster a stronger sense of community and cohesion. Let's use this program as a standard of the kind of activity we need to promote.

Partner with Your Community

People listen when teachers, school-board members, and visionary individuals like Darell Hammond, or high-profile figures like Michelle Obama speak out. As you become more aware of what your children are eating in school or at fast-food restaurants, you may want to share your findings with your friends and neighbors. We've already discussed how you can influence policy by getting involved in the PTA. But how about also putting your findings and opinions on your Facebook page or letting people know via Twitter? Or perhaps your style is just to lead by doing, replacing candy bars with stickers and inexpensive toys at birthday parties, or bringing a healthful snack to a school event. Whatever approach you decide on, remember that your own efforts can have far-reaching results.

It All Starts with Education

If you've never had any grounding in nutrition, or forgotten what you learned decades ago, it's time to get up to speed, for your sake and that of your kids. In addition to the information in this book, you may want to check out *Nutrition for Dummies* by Carol Ann Rinzler. Nutrition websites also abound, or you can take an online course or a local adult education class. But you don't have to read a book or take a course to start looking carefully at the labels of food products. (Review "Required Reading: Food Labels" on page 175.) Much of this information is now posted in a number of restaurants and is available on the websites of most restaurant chains. Go to *allstride.com* for links to many of these sites. For more on nutrition and fitness, see Resources on page 256.

One Child at a Time

Before we end the final chapter of *Too Small to Be Big*, my coauthor has a few words to say about the genesis of this book and about the reason we're both so committed to AllStride. Dr. John, over to you.

"Several years ago I began work on the manuscript that eventually became part of this book. At the time I was extremely frustrated because after more than a dozen years of seeing the growing epidemic of overweight kids and the related health problems, no clear solution was in sight. The book originally was to be a call to arms to parents and other people who cared about children, with advice on how to find help. When Ricki approached me about becoming part of AllStride, I quickly discovered that this was a group of people who had actually come up with a solution.

"This book has turned out to be very different from the book I originally envisioned. It is still a call to arms, but it is also a guidebook to solving the problem. From my work with AllStride, I now know that together we can turn this around, family by family, child by child, and in doing so, give children the healthy, happy future they all deserve. I now believe that the lives of our children can be very different from what I feared. Join us and help us achieve this paradigm shift by making your family an AllStride family."

Resources

In addition to the resources cited in this book, you may be interested visiting the following websites. *(All URLs were live when this book went to press, but we cannot guarantee that they are still correct.)*

Research and Consumer Advocacy Groups

Yale Rudd Center for Food Policy and Obesity (*yaleruddcenter.org*) is a research and public policy organization whose objective is to improve the world's diet, prevent obesity, and reduce the stigma against overweight individuals. Among the group's interests is the impact of fast food on kids and teens. A dedicated site (*fastfoodmarketing.org/consumers.aspx*) offers consumer tools. To download a recent study on the impact of fast-food marketing to youths, go to *fastfoodmarketing.org/media/FastFoodFACTS_Report.pdf.*

The Center for Science in the Public Interest (*cspinet.org*) addresses health, nutrition, and physical fitness. Among the issues the group champions are improved school lunches, increased vegetable and fruit intake, and the reduction in marketing of fast food and junk food to kids. The CSPI also publishes *Nutrition Action Healthletter,* the largest-circulation health newsletter in the nation.

The Robert Wood Johnson Foundation Center to Prevent Childhood Obesity (*rwjf.org/childhoodobesity*) aims to reverse the childhood obesity epidemic by 2015. To that end, the foundation funds research; publishes journals and videos on health, nutrition, and physical activity; and partners with other organizations (see below).

The Alliance for a Healthier Generation (*healthiergeneration.org*), founded by the Robert Wood Johnson Foundation, takes a multidisciplinary approach to fighting childhood obesity. The website includes sections devoted to the home, schools, the medical community, the larger community, and businesses that market to children. This program supports thousands of schools across the nation in an effort to create an environment in which healthy eating and physical activity are encouraged, including recommendations to change the beverages available. Join the program to find tools and learn strategies to promote child health in school and elsewhere.

The Children's Nutrition Research Center (*bcm.edu/cnrc*) is a partnership between the USDA, Baylor College of Medicine, and Texas Children's Hospital. The organization conducts research into the effects of maternal, infant, and child nutrition on health, development, and growth. In addition to a host of articles on nutrition, the website offers an interactive nutrition calculator (*bcm.edu/cnrc/healthyeatingcalculator/eatingCal.html*).

Penn State Center for Childhood Obesity Research (*hhdev.psu.edu/ccor*) conducts multidisciplinary research on ways to stem and prevent the epidemic and promote healthy growth and development. The website includes links to a number of resources for children and parents.

Government Agencies

The Childhood Overweight and Obesity Prevention Initiative of the Office of the Surgeon General (*surgeongeneral.gov/obesityprevention*) offers guidelines to help determine if a child is overweight or obese. It also offers recommendations for nutrition and exercise. Online publications include "The Surgeon General's Vision for a Healthy and Fit Nation." You can also a download and sign the Surgeon General's Pledge, declaring your commitment to raise healthy children. Other downloads include checklists for parents and caregivers, schools and teachers, and communities.

The Centers for Disease Control (*cdc.gov/healthyyouth*) also offers guidelines for kids' physical activity and nutrition and supports research on children's health, including such topics as the role of schools in addressing juvenile obesity.

The U.S. Department of Health & Human Services issues physical activity guidelines, including one for active children and adolescents (*health.gov/paguidelines/guidelines/chapter3.aspx*).

The Fair Trade Commission, a consumer watchdog organization, has come up with a great idea to help kids become smarter consumers—or "ad-ucated." A fun online game called Admongo (*admongo.gov*), complete with cool graphics and audio and the ability to create your own avatar, helps kids understand where advertising is coming from, what it's actually saying, and what it expects them to do in response.

The U.S. Department of Agriculture (USDA) produces the Food Pyramid (*mypyramid.gov*) that serves as a nutrition guideline. Online tools designed for kids aged 6 to 11 include a colorful poster of the kids' food pyramid, coloring pages, and an interactive MyPyramid Blast Off game (*mypyramid.gov/kids/index.html*) that helps kids learn how to best get the fuel that will fill their "tanks" so they can take off.

Sites Dedicated to Improving Lunch and Other School Programs

Chef Ann, an author and educator, has two websites, both dedicated to improving the quality of school lunches. One is for parents (*chefann.com*), which offers advice on how to make a difference in schools and includes some recipes from her book *Lunch Lessons: Changing the Way We Feed Our Children.* Her other site (*thelunchbox.org*) is designed for school and nutrition professionals.

School Nutrition (*schoolnutrition.org*) provides lots of information on the National School Lunch Program and relevant legislation and publishes *School Nutrition,* a magazine for school nutritionists, and *The Journal of Child Nutrition & Management,* which publishes current research on child nutrition and school food service management.

Planet Health (*planet-health.org*) is a complete curriculum, designed for middle-school teachers, principals, and health educators, which focuses on nutrition and physical activity. A parent section offers plenty of helpful information.

Acknowledgments

Thank you, Jack Kirby, for your vision and passion for the cause. Thank you, Howard Borris, for always believing in me and loving me unconditionally. Thanks to John Volturo and George Sylva for your tireless efforts to make this book and program possible. A big shout-out to Dr. John, Isaiah Truyman, Robert Ferguson, and Olivia Bell Buehl, for keeping the faith and getting on board. Thank you also to my agent, Nancy Josephson. Thanks to my dear friends and loved ones: Jennifer M., Josh, Simon, Julie, Mandy, Frances, Belinda, Molly, Rebecca, Abby, Camryn, Darcy, Geoff, Rob, Gamila, Christian, Emma, and many others for unending laughs, love, and support.

Thank you to my amazing home team, Caroline and Iris, for working so hard to make my life run smoothly. A big thank you to my sister, Jennifer, for helping me get through some tough times and for her belief in AllStride. To my precious Marie, thank you for continuing to inspire me to be better and do more for others. Lastly, thank you to my children, Milo and Owen—this book and program are for you and your generation. Being your mom is a gift that offers me daily joy and provides me with drive and true fulfillment.—*Ricki Lake*

I wish to thank my family and my colleagues for your patience and understanding while the preparation of this book occupied large chunks of my time. Special thanks to George Sylva, Jack Kirby, and Liz Reynolds for recognizing our shared passion and taking a big risk on the book and on me, and for adopting me as one of your own. The endorsement of Ricki Lake and Howard Borris was the icing on the cake. I also have to thank my longtime personal editor and agent Barbara Casey, who has been my stalwart supporter. As for Olivia Bell Buehl, you literally saved our lives by brilliantly pulling this mountain of material together. My appreciation would not be complete without mentioning the late, great Judy Mazel, who was one of the first to join me in sounding the alarm bell about childhood obesity. To my new friends, Robert Ferguson and Isaiah Truyman, whose contributions were invaluable in making this a complete work—I feel honored to be working with you guys. Thanks also to John Volturo and Brent Hartman, whose organizational skills came into play when they were needed most. Lastly, I must thank all my childhood acquaintances who laughed at my chubbiness and picked me last for basketball. It turns out you were my inspiration!—*John Monaco, M.D.*

Glossary

Aerobic exercise: Sustained rhythmic exercise that increases oxygen intake and heart rate; also referred to as cardio.

Amino acids: The building blocks of protein.

Anaerobic exercise: *See Resistance exercise.*

Antioxidants: Substances that neutralize harmful free radicals in the body.

Asthma: A respiratory condition characterized by overactive, "twitchy," or contracting muscles in the airways, contributing to narrowing of the airways, known as bronchospasm.

Atherosclerosis: Clogging, narrowing, and hardening of the blood vessels by plaque deposits.

Beta cells: Specialized cells in the pancreas that produce insulin.

Blood lipids: The total cholesterol (including HDL and LDL cholesterol) and triglycerides in the blood; also called lipids.

Blood pressure: The pressure that blood exerts against artery walls during a heartbeat.

Blood sugar: The amount of glucose (blood sugar) in the bloodstream; also called blood glucose.

BMI: *See Body-mass index.*

Body-mass index (BMI): A comparison of weight to height to ascertain whether someone is underweight, normal weight or overweight for age and gender.

Calorie: A measure of energy intake as well as heat, or a measure of energy expended.

Carbohydrate: A macronutrient from plants and some other foods, which are broken down by the process of digestion into simple sugars such as glucose, to provide a source of energy.

Cholesterol: A lipid; a waxy substance essential for many of the body's functions, including the manufacture of hormones and cell membranes.

Diabesity: The parallel and related epidemics of obesity and type 2 diabetes.

Diabetes: *See Type 1 diabetes and Type 2 diabetes.*

Endocrinology: The study and medical practice associated with glands, including the pancreas, and the hormones they secrete.

Essential fatty acids (EFAs): Two classes of essential dietary fats that your body cannot make on its own and must be obtained from food or supplements.

Fast carbs: Carbohydrate foods that are metabolized quickly and therefore elevate blood sugar quickly. Examples include bread, baked potatoes, and watermelon.

Fat: One of the three macronutrients; an organic compound that dissolves in other oils, but not in water; a source of energy and building blocks of cells.

Fatty acids: The scientific term for fats, which are part of a group of substances called lipids. *(Also see Cholesterol.)*

Fiber: Parts of plant foods that are indigestible or very slowly digested; sometimes called roughage.

Gastroesophageal reflux: Also known as GERD. The condition in which stomach contents revert back into the esophagus during or after eating, producing painful symptoms sometimes referred to as "heartburn."

Genetics: The study of heredity utilizing an understanding of chromosomes, DNA, and their relationship to human form and function.

Glucose: A simple sugar. *(Also see Blood sugar.)*

Glycemic: A term that refers to the relative ability of a food to raise blood sugar levels.

Glycogen: The storage form of carbohydrate in the body.

HDL cholesterol: High-density lipoprotein; the "good" cholesterol.

High-fructose corn syrup (HFCS): A sweetener manufactured from corn syrup that increases the fructose content and therefore the sweetness.

Hydrogenated oils: Vegetable oils processed to solidify them and improve their shelf life. *(Also see Trans fats.)*

Hypertension: High blood pressure.

Inflammation: Part of the body's delicately balanced natural defense system against infection, injury, and potentially damaging substances; however, excessive inflammation is associated with a number of health problems.

Insulin: A hormone produced by the pancreas that sends a signal to cells to remove glucose and amino acids from the bloodstream and stop the release of fat from fat cells.

LDL cholesterol: Low-density lipoprotein. Commonly referred to as "bad" cholesterol; but not all LDL cholesterol is "bad."

Lean body mass: Body mass minus fat tissue; includes muscle, bone, organs, and connective tissue.

Legumes: Most members of the bean and pea families, including lentils, chickpeas, soybeans, peas, and many others.

Lipids: Fats, including triglycerides, and cholesterol.

Macronutrients: Fat, protein, and carbohydrate, the dietary sources of calories and nutrients.

Metabolic syndrome: A group of conditions, including hypertension, high triglycerides, low HDL cholesterol, higher-than-normal blood sugar and insulin levels, and weight carried in the middle of the body. Also known as syndrome X or insulin-resistance syndrome, it predisposes people to heart disease and type 2 diabetes.

Metabolism: The complex chemical processes that convert food into energy or the body's building blocks, which in turn become part of organs, tissues, and cells.

Monounsaturated fat: Dietary fat typically found in such foods as olive oil, canola oil, nuts, and avocados.

Nutrition Facts panel: Mandated by the Food and Drug Administration (FDA), information that appears on the labels of manufactured food products, including a list of ingredients, the percentage of macronutrients in a typical portion, serving size, and number of servings.

Obesity: In the case of children, a body-mass index (BMI) within the 95th percentile and higher compared to peers of the same age and gender. (This means that 95 percent of those peers have less body fat.)

Omega-3 fatty acids: A group of essential polyunsaturated fats found in green algae, cold-water fish, fish oil, flaxseed oil, and some other nut and vegetable oils.

Omega-6 fatty acids: A group of essential polyunsaturated fats found in many vegetable oils and also in meat from animals that have been fed corn, soybeans, and certain other vegetable products.

Overweight: In the case of children, a body-mass index (BMI) between the 85th and 95th percentile, compared to peers of the same age and gender.

Overfat: An excessive amount of fat on the frame, as determined by a body composition analysis.

Partially hydrogenated oils: *(Also see Trans fats.)*

Polyunsaturated fats: Fats that remain liquid at any temperature. Oils from corn, soybean, sunflower, safflower, cottonseed, grapeseed, flaxseed, sesame seed, some nuts, and fatty fish are typically high in polyunsaturated fat.

Prediabetes: Blood sugar levels that are higher than normal but fall short of full-blown diabetes.

Protein: One of the three macronutrients found in food, and the building blocks of cells; also an energy source after carbohydrate and fat have been metabolized.

Resistance exercise: Any exercise that builds muscle strength; also called weight-bearing or anaerobic exercise.

Respiratory distress: A condition in which increased effort is required to maintain healthy oxygen and carbon-dioxide levels, manifested by fast, deep, and labored breathing.

Saturated fats: Fats that are solid at room temperature. The majority of fat in butter, lard, suet, palm, and coconut oil.

Sleep apnea: Obstruction or collapse of flaccid tissues in the throat during sleep, blocking air exchange and diminishing oxygen intake.

Slow carbs: Carbohydrate foods that are higher in fiber and protein and therefore metabolize more slowly. Examples include string beans, carrots, and grapefruit.

Statin drugs: Pharmaceuticals used to lower total and LDL cholesterol.

Sucrose: Table sugar, composed of glucose and fructose.

Sugar alcohols: Non-nutritive sweeteners such as manitol and xylitol that have little or no impact on most people's blood sugar level, although they may cause gastric distress.

Sugar substitutes: Noncaloric, non-nutritive sweeteners with little or no impact on blood sugars.

Trans fats: Fats found in partially hydrogenated or hydrogenated vegetable oil; typically used in fried foods, baked goods, and other products.

Triglycerides: The major form of fat that circulates in the bloodstream and is stored as body fat.

Type 1 diabetes: A condition in which the pancreas makes so little insulin (or it is so ineffective) that the body can't use blood glucose as energy, producing chronically high blood sugar levels.

Type 2 diabetes: The more common form of diabetes; high blood sugar levels caused by insulin resistance, the inability to use insulin properly.

Unsaturated fat: Monounsaturated and polyunsaturated fats.

About the Authors

Ricki Lake grew up in a suburb of New York City. At 14, she began singing professionally in cabarets and clubs. She attended local schools, until transferring to the Professional Children's School in New York City for her junior and senior years. At the end of her freshman year at Ithaca College, Lake received a call from her agent to audition for the lead in a John Waters film. She landed the role of Tracy Turnblad in "Hairspray," which was released in 1988, marking her film debut. She later appeared in other films directed by Waters, including "Cecil B. Demented," "Cry-Baby," and "Serial Mom." She went on to act in 10 other films. In 1988, Lake joined the cast of the Vietnam War drama series "China Beach" for one season. She also had a recurring role in the 1998–2007 television series "King of Queens."

At 21, after being overweight for years, Lake decided to take charge of her life and lost more than 125 pounds. In 1993, she was chosen from 100 aspirants to host her own daytime talk show. After only three years, "The Ricki Lake Show" was rated second in viewership in its time slot. The show ran for 11 years. After 9/11, Lake decided to end her talk show at the height of its popularity, relocate to Los Angeles from New York, and focus on her children.

In 2009, Lake coauthored with Abby Epstein *Your Best Birth: Know All Your Options, Discover the Natural Choices and Take Back the Birth Experience,* based on "The Business of Being Born," a documentary she and Epstein produced. Released in 2008, the film was inspired by Lake's experience in giving birth to her second son at home.

In 2010, Lake founded AllStride, the acclaimed health and fitness program with customized meal plans, online coaching, instruction, and support for kids, teens, and families.

Lake and her two sons, Milo and Owen, reside in Los Angeles.

John Monaco, M.D., has been a pediatrician for 30 years and is board-certified in both general pediatrics and pediatric critical-care medicine. After graduating from Union College in Schenectady, New York, Dr. Monaco received his medical degree at State University of New York at Buffalo in 1981. He did his residency and chief residency in general pediatrics at the Orlando Regional Medical Center and the University of Florida. This was followed by a fellowship in pediatric critical-care medicine at the University of Florida. He then moved to Louisville, Kentucky, where he established and directed the Pediatric Intensive Care Unit at Audubon Hospital, the first community hospital-based pediatric intensive-care unit in Kentucky. He returned to Florida in 1992, where he and two partners run the inpatient pediatric unit at Brandon Regional Hospital outside Tampa. There, he served as chairman of the department of pediatrics from 1998–2000 and 2008–2010.

In 1999, Dr. Monaco coauthored *Slim and Fit Kids: Raising Healthy Children in a Fast-Food World,* published by Health Communications, Inc. He continues to lecture and consult on childhood obesity and other pediatric issues. Dr. Monaco is also a longtime monthly contributor to *Pediatrics for Parents.* In 2005, he authored *Moondance to Eternity,* published by DeVorss and Co., in which he recounts his experiences caring for critically ill children. He has been named one of the best doctors in America multiple times by Castle Connolly, publisher of *America's Top Doctors.* He has also been named one of Tampa Bay's best doctors for the last two years.

Dr. Monaco and his wife live in Gainesville, Florida, with their children, Alexandra and John, Jr., who are both studying at the University of Florida.

About the Consultants

Isaiah Truyman served as fitness consultant for this book. Truyman is a cofounder and developer of EZIA Human Performance, a personalized program that enables individuals to live every day to the fullest and achieve their personal and professional best. A respected athlete, accredited coach and trainer, and consummate surfer, he can also be found weightlifting, running, biking, and generally moving very fast through time and space! Truyman holds certifications from USA Weightlifting, the National Strength and Conditioning Association, the National Academy of Sports Medicine, Kettle Bell Concepts, and the American Aerobic and Fitness Association. He has also developed a pilot video-fitness program for use in the New York City schools. At an early age, Truyman learned the importance of strength and self-reliance through sports. He has cultivated a desire to help others by giving individuals the tools to help themselves. Truyman is especially attuned to the needs of children, and he fosters health and fitness as family values.

Robert Ferguson, M.S., C.N., is a nationally recognized nutritionist, weight-loss expert, motivational speaker, and physical conditioning specialist. A doctoral candidate in sports psychology, he holds certifications in personal training and performance nutrition. He has been the top fat-loss, nutritionist, and conditioning coach for professional boxers on Showtime, HBO, ESPN, and "The Contender." Ferguson's approach to total wellness has been featured on radio and in such magazines as *First for Women, Ebony, Star, Esquire,* and *Woman's World.* He has also appeared on "Access Hollywood," "The 700 Club," "The Mo'Nique Show," "CNN Headline News," "Good Morning America," as well as FOX Network and BBC Worldwide. He is the author of *Diet-Free for Life,* published in 2011. He is also the creator of the 6-Day Detox Drop, plus the Diet-Free for Parents program, as well as the co-developer and public face of the Food Lovers Fat Loss System®, a home weight-loss program.

Ferguson is a consultant to spas, church ministries, parent organizations, wellness companies, and Gold's Gym, the world's largest coed health company. He is the founder and CEO of Diet-Free Life, LLC, and the Diet-Free for Life Challenge, which enables weight loss and the replacement of unwanted habits with productive ones.

Too Small to Be Big